G R E A T
LEGO®
SETS
A VISUAL HISTORY

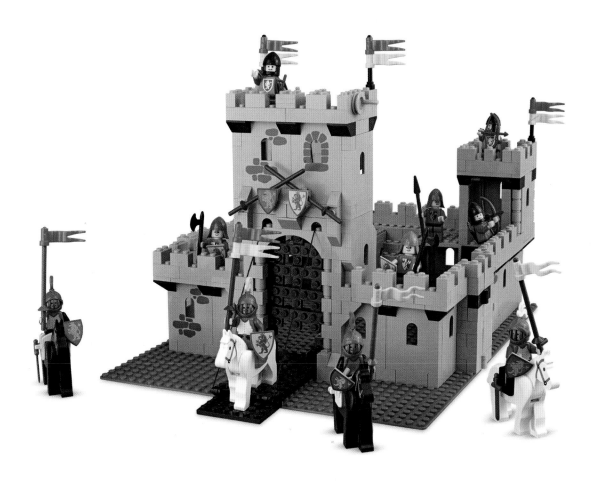

Senior Editor Helen Murray
Senior Designer Nathan Martin
Editorial Assistants Rosie Peet and Toby Mann
Additional Designers Mik Gates and Jade Wheaton
Senior Pre-production Producer Siu Chan
Senior Producer Lloyd Robertson
Managing Editor Simon Hugo
Managing Art Editor Guy Harvey
Publisher Julie Ferris
Art Director Lisa Lanzarini
Publishing Director Simon Beecroft

Additional photography Gary Ombler and Thomas Baunsgaard Pedersen

First American Edition, 2015
Published in the United States by DK Publishing
345 Hudson Street, New York, New York 10014
A Penguin Random House Company

15 16 17 18 19 10 9 8 7 6 5 4 3 2 1
001–259435–Oct/2015

GREAT
LEGO®
SETS
A VISUAL HISTORY

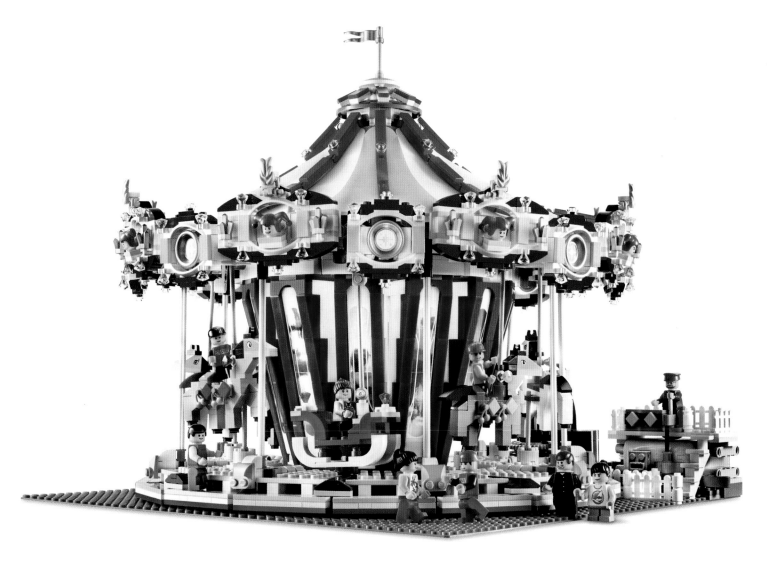

Written by
Daniel Lipkowitz with Kathryn Hill, Helen Murray, and Rosie Peet

Contents

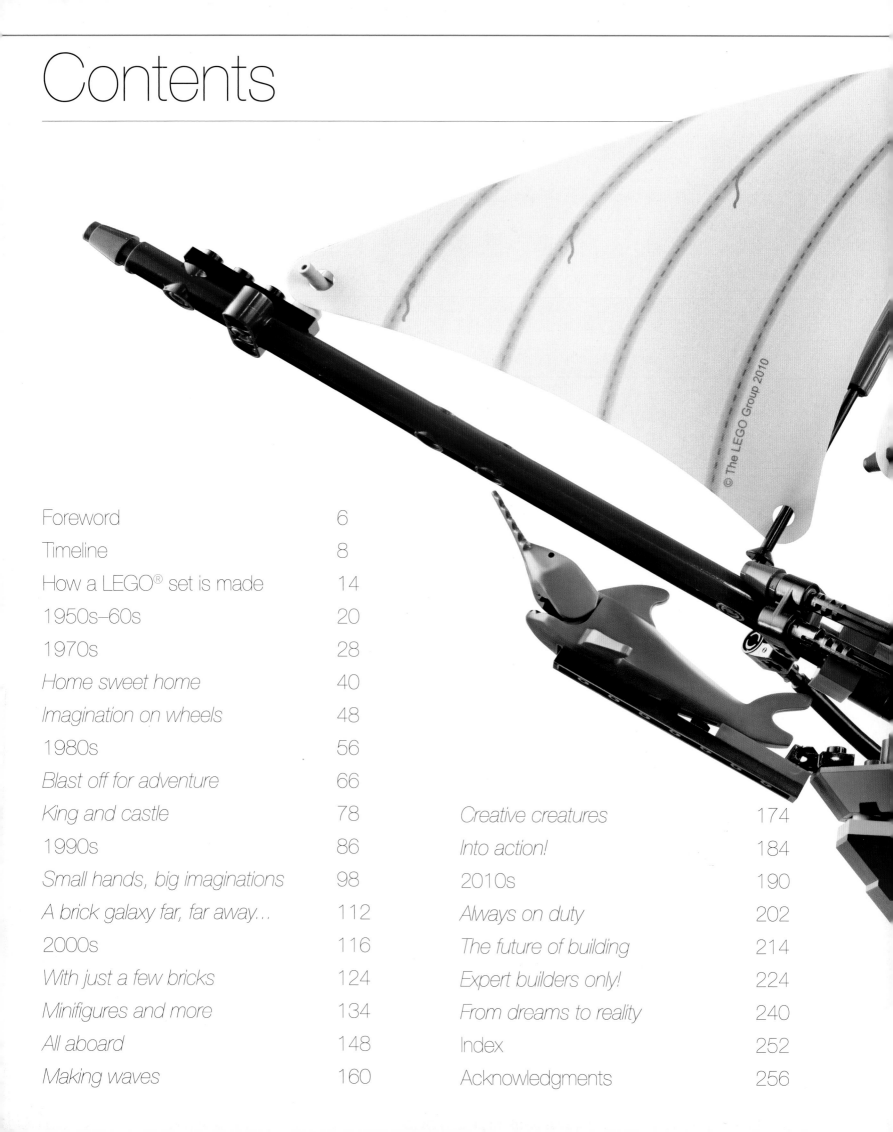

© The LEGO Group 2010

Ole Kirk's House (the LEGO Idea House)
• 2009 • LEGO Inside Tour gift in 2009 and LEGO employee Christmas gift in 2012 • #4000007

Foreword

Dear Reader,

Over the past six decades, the LEGO® brick has become a familiar and cherished toy, inspiring play and learning all over the world. I'm sure you can recall happy childhood memories playing with LEGO bricks. You may even remember the sets you received as gifts and who you got them from—or the sets you really, really wanted but never received!

Great LEGO *Sets: A Visual History* will take you and your family on a journey down memory lane. There simply weren't enough pages to show the numerous LEGO sets we have designed and launched since 1955, but this book is a celebration of a selection of the most interesting and loved LEGO sets ever produced. We hope that reading about these sets and poring over the pictures will unlock your store of memories, whether you are aged six or sixty-six.

We also hope that the book provides inspiration for building new models with the LEGO bricks you already have at home. The possibilities are endless, and each day—together with your family and friends—you can build something new. If you're a grown-up, perhaps your LEGO bricks are still somewhere in your parents' house? Be inspired, go and dig them out! LEGO elements are a timeless material—you'll find that they are fully compatible with the bricks we make today.

The intention behind the LEGO System of Play was to "create a toy that prepares the child for life, appeals to the imagination, and develops the creative urge and joy of creation that are the driving forces in every human being."

That idea is still our guiding principle, and it is just as exciting as ever to open a box and start building—or to bring out your LEGO brick collection, spread it across the floor, and give your imagination and creativity free rein to build your own unique model.

Enjoy!

Jette Orduna
Head of LEGO Idea House in Billund, Denmark

Timeline

From the earliest collections of basic bricks to today's wide variety of pieces and endless building possibilities, LEGO® sets have been developing imaginations for more than 65 years. This timeline features key developments in LEGO set history, including the first windows and wheels, the birth of the LEGO play themes, and the revolutionary rise of digital and robotics technology. Build on!

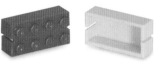

1949

- In Billund, Denmark, the LEGO Group workshop produces its first plastic, interlocking "Automatic Binding Bricks" and the first LEGO base plates.

1953

- The Automatic Binding Brick is renamed the LEGO Brick ("LEGO Mursten" in Danish).
- The first 1x2 and 2x3 bricks are produced.
- LEGO sets go on sale in Norway, the first time LEGO products have been sold outside Denmark.

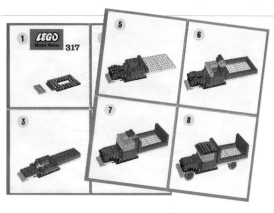

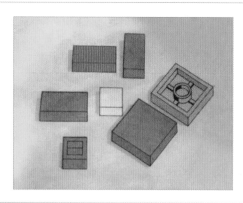

1964

- For the first time, boxes of LEGO bricks come with elaborate step-by-step instructions to help builders make specific models out of the pieces.

1965

- Tiles (flat pieces without studs) are first introduced. • A set with a motor for use with gears is first produced by the Samsonite Corp. luggage company—Samsonite had a license agreement with the LEGO Group at the time for selling LEGO sets in the US and Canada.

1966

- The first battery-powered LEGO trains can roll on their own, thanks to a 4.5-volt motor.

1973

- The first floating LEGO ship set is released.

1974

- The first LEGO building figures are introduced in the best-selling LEGO Family (200). The LEGO building figures are brick-built, with round heads and posable arms.

1975

- The first LEGO figure from the LEGOLAND range, has an unpainted face and non-moving arms and legs.
- LEGO Hobby Sets (also known as LEGO Expert in some countries) let builders construct detailed replicas of real-life vehicles.

1954

• Godtfred Kirk Christiansen, the son of Ole Kirk Christiansen, the founder of the LEGO Group, comes up with the idea of creating an entire System of Play based around the LEGO brick.
• New door and window elements, compatible with the stud and tube principle, are launched.

1955

• The LEGO System of Play launches with the Town Plan series of construction sets. • Sets feature LEGO trees for the first time.

1962

• LEGO wheels are produced, making rolling LEGO brick vehicles possible. • Other new elements include the first LEGO plates and the first black bricks.

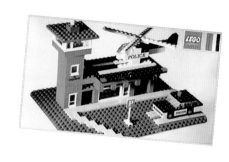

1967

• Over 18 million LEGO sets are sold in this year across more than 40 countries around the world.
• New hinge pieces add movement to models.
• There are now 218 different element shapes.

1968

• The first LEGOLAND® park opens in Billund, with 625,000 visitors in its first year.

1969

• LEGO® DUPLO® sets, with large bricks designed especially for children under five years old, are launched internationally. • LEGO trains get a boost with a new 12-volt motor. • The LEGOLAND range begins.

1972

• New specialized parts are produced for LEGO aerial vehicle models, including triangular wing plates and spinning rotors.

1977

• Technical Set models (known as Expert Builder in the US) use gears, beams, and connector pins to create realistic working functions. (These were renamed LEGO® Technic in 1984.)

1978

• The original three LEGOLAND themes are launched: Town, Space, and Castle. • LEGO minifigures, newly designed by Jens Nygård Knudsen, have printed smiling faces and jointed arms, hands, and legs.

1979

• LEGO® FABULAND™ sets offer a world of anthropomorphic animals for younger builders. • LEGO® SCALA™ sets let fashionable children create their own custom jewelry.

1984

• The LEGOLAND Castle play theme gets new medieval elements including horses and wagon wheels. The Crusaders and the Black Falcons form the first knightly factions.

1985

• Jet-setting minifigures can explore new horizons when the first airport arrives in LEGOLAND Town. • LEGO sets go electronic with Light & Sound System parts, first used as sirens in the Mobile Police Truck (6450) and the Hook and Ladder Truck (6480) sets.

1986

• The LEGO Technic figure is introduced. These are larger and more posable than standard minifigures, with bendable elbow and knee joints. • Detailed, large-scale builds of real-world vehicles are released under the LEGO Model Team theme.

1990

• The LEGOLAND brand comes to an end. The LEGOLAND logo on set boxes is removed and boxes now just feature the LEGO logo. • M:Tron sets bring magnet power to the LEGO Space play theme.

1991

• The space villains of Blacktron return in Blacktron Future Generation. • LEGO trains move to a 9-volt battery system.

1992

• Set boxes now feature the LEGO System brand. • The Wolfpack renegades infiltrate LEGO Castle. • A second series of Space Police is launched. • LEGO Paradisa offers a colorful and tropical minifigure vacation destination.

1996

• Builders go back in time with the LEGO Time Cruisers play theme. • The LEGO Western play theme is launched. • The Dark Forest subtheme of LEGO Castle picks up where the Forestmen left off. • The Exploriens comb the LEGO Space universe for alien fossils.

1997

• Things get a little spooky for LEGO Castle with the Fright Knights faction. • Robots and flying saucers appear in the Roboforce and UFO subthemes of LEGO Space. • The LEGO Aqua Raiders begin their search for crystals in the Aquazone play theme.

1998

• The LEGO Adventurers start their globe-trotting journey in Egypt. • LEGO® MINDSTORMS® sets feature buildable, programmable robots. • The short-lived LEGO Znap line creates models out of snap-together 3D frame pieces. • The Insectoids swarm through LEGO Space. • LEGO Castle takes a detour to the East with the Ninja subtheme. • In LEGO Aquazone, the Hydronauts and the Stingrays battle beneath the sea.

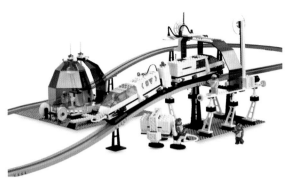  

1987

• LEGOLAND Space adds the Blacktron and Futuron subthemes, along with a motorized Monorail Transport System. • The Forestmen take up residence in the woods of LEGOLAND Castle. • A new LEGO Brick Separator makes it easy to take models apart.

1988

• The Black Knights are the newest group to join the LEGOLAND Castle theme.

1989

• LEGOLAND Pirates becomes the next LEGOLAND play theme. The pirate minifigures are the first to have different facial features, such as beards and eye patches. They also introduce new body parts, such as hook-hands and peg-legs. • The Space Police arrive to clean up the galaxy of LEGOLAND Space.

1993

• LEGO Space blasts off for the frozen planet Krysto in Ice Planet 2002. • Fantasy and wizardry abound with the Dragon Masters of LEGO Castle.

1994

• LEGO® BELVILLE™ introduces dollhouse-style building sets and BELVILLE figures. • The Unitron and Spyrius subthemes of LEGO Space begin.

1995

• The new LEGO Aquazone play theme dives into the underwater world of the Aquanauts and Aquasharks. • The Royal Knights provide LEGO Castle with its first King minifigure.

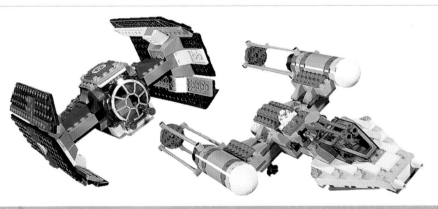 

1999

• The first LEGO® *Star Wars*® sets are released to galactic success. • The LEGO Rock Raiders dig for crystals on Planet U. • The LEGO Adventurers travel deep into the Amazon with the Jungle subtheme. • LEGO Throwbots, also known as Slizers, use LEGO® Technic parts to make disc-slinging robot warriors. • LEGO Town becomes LEGO® City—until 2003.

2000

• The LEGO System brand on set packaging is shortened to the basic LEGO logo. • LEGO Studios sets let fans make their own stop-motion films with LEGO bricks. • The LEGO Sports theme kicks off with soccer sets. • LEGO Castle introduces the first LEGO® KNIGHTS' KINGDOM™ subtheme. • LEGO Mosaic sets let builders reproduce photographs in tiny black, white, and gray LEGO pieces. • Things get chilly with LEGO Arctic sets. • The LEGO Adventurers journey to the mysterious Dino Island. • Wheeled LEGO RoboRiders use LEGO Technic parts. • A line of advanced models for expert builders begins with a Statue of Liberty set.

2001

• Epic action begins with the buildable BIONICLE® Toa heroes. • The first LEGO® Harry Potter™ movie sets cast their spell. This theme introduces the first double-faced minifigure, Professor Quirrell. • The members of LEGO Alpha Team start their mission to save the world from the evil Ogel.

2002

• LEGO® Spider-Man™ sets swing onto the scene, including a LEGO Studios set. • Sets based on the *Galidor: Defenders of the Outer Dimension* TV series materialize. • LEGO Island Xtreme Stunts sets are launched, based on the successful LEGO Island and LEGO Island II video games.

2003

• LEGO Sports signs up NBA Basketball, Hockey, and Gravity Games™. • The Adventurers wrap up their adventures with an Orient Expedition. • The company teams up with the Discovery Channel to produce the LEGO® Discovery™ space sets. • LEGO City becomes LEGO World City. • LEGO® CLIKITS™ kits offer a new way to build jewelry and decorations. • LEGO Designer Sets, which come with an ideas booklet, open up more freestyle building possibilities. • Licensed minifigures start to be produced with realistic skin colors, starting with the LEGO Sports NBA Challenge basketball players.

2007

• Some classic play themes make a triumphant return with LEGO Space Mars Mission, LEGO Castle, and LEGO Aqua Raiders. • The LEGO Modular Buildings series of connectible builds is introduced (they are now part of the LEGO Creator Expert line). • Electronic LEGO Power Functions, with features such as motors, lights, and remote controls, appear in LEGO Creator sets.

2008

• New licensed themes include LEGO® *Indiana Jones*™ and LEGO Speed Racer. • Fans of iconic architecture get into building with micro-scaled LEGO® Architecture models, designed by Chicago architect Adam Reed Tucker. • The LEGO Agents use hi-tech spy gear and vehicles to battle Dr. Inferno and his cybernetic henchmen.

2009

• The LEGO Power Miners battle rock monsters beneath the Earth. • The LEGO Pirates and LEGO Space Police return with new sets. • LEGO Games enter the world of buildable board games. • LEGO City expands into the countryside with farm sets. • LEGO Factory becomes LEGO Design byME.

2012

• Two major super-powered universes are brought to life with the release of LEGO® Marvel Super Heroes and LEGO® DC Comics™ Super Heroes sets. • Movie-based LEGO® *The Lord of the Rings*™ and LEGO® *The Hobbit*™ sets are released. • LEGO® Friends introduces the creative mini-dolls of Heartlake City. • Dinosaurs and dino hunters clash in the LEGO Dino theme. • The LEGO Monster Fighters face vampires, werewolves, and other classic monsters. • The first LEGO® MINECRAFT™ set results from a vote on the LEGO CUUSOO website. • LEGO® *Disney Princess*™ sets start as a LEGO® DUPLO® line before adding mini-dolls and classic brick construction in 2014.

2013

• LEGO® Legends of Chima™ presents a world of CHI-powered animal tribes. • A new LEGO Castle theme pits Lion Knights against Dragon Knights. • The Galaxy Squad battles alien bugs in outer space. • LEGO® Teenage Mutant Ninja Turtles™ sets arrive, based on the Nickelodeon computer-animated TV series. • LEGO CUUSOO releases a fan-created DeLorean Time Machine set from the Back to the Future™ films. • Western models return with licensed LEGO® & Disney *The Lone Ranger*™ movie sets. • LEGO set boxes get smaller to be more environmentally friendly. • Sets released from this year now have 5-digit identification numbers, instead of the classic 4-digit numbers.

2004

• Several classic LEGO brick colors, including the original dark gray and violet, are retired, and new ones are introduced, such as light purple and cool yellow. • The second LEGO KNIGHTS' KINGDOM line features the heroes and villains of the kingdom of Morcia. • The LEGO Factory website lets fans create model designs online and then mail-order the pieces to build them at home.

2005

• The 50th anniversary of the LEGO System of Play. • LEGO World City becomes LEGO City. • A new theme is released as Dino Attack in some countries and Dino 2010 in others, with vehicle models that have either dinosaur-fighting weapons or capture gear. • The LEGO Vikings battle monsters of myth and legend. • Tiny Turbos sets shrink LEGO Racers down to palm-size.

2006

• LEGO® Batman™ sets let super hero fans make their own brick Gotham City. • The LEGO® EXO-FORCE™ theme features mecha action and light-up weapons. • The next generation of robotics activates with LEGO MINDSTORMS NXT. • A partnership with Nickelodeon produces LEGO® SpongeBob SquarePants™ and LEGO® Avatar™: The Last Airbender™ sets. • LEGO trains go remote-controlled.

2010

• Disney renews its partnership with the LEGO Group, leading to LEGO® Toy Story™ and LEGO® Prince of Persia™ sets, plus LEGO® DUPLO® Cars™ sets for younger fans. • LEGO Atlantis and LEGO Kingdoms keep the underwater and Castle themes going strong. • The collectible LEGO® Minifigures line launches with its first series of 16 tradable characters. • The LEGO® World Racers go on a cross-continent race. • LEGO Hero Factory "constraction" sets feature snap-together robot heroes. • LEGO® Ben 10 Alien Force™ sets are produced with Cartoon Network.

2011

• Space sets come home when LEGO Alien Conquest invades the Earth. • The wildly popular LEGO® NINJAGO™ theme spins into action. • Captain Jack Sparrow and his friends and foes sail the high seas with LEGO® Pirates of the Caribbean™ sets. • LEGO City and NASA team up to create space shuttle and spaceport sets. • LEGO Master Builder Academy features sets and handbooks that teach official LEGO building techniques. • The Shinkai 6500 submarine is the first fan-created set to be released based on a popular vote on the LEGO CUUSOO website. • Bricks and apps combine with LEGO® Life of George.

2014

• The blockbuster THE LEGO® MOVIE™ arrives in theaters, accompanied by a line of movie-based sets. • The mischievous LEGO® Mixels™ offer mixed-up building fun. • Super-spy action strikes again with the LEGO® Ultra Agents. • A special-edition LEGO® The Simpsons™ Family House set and a line of special Springfield-inspired minifigures celebrate the 25th anniversary of The Simpsons. • New LEGO Teenage Mutant Ninja Turtles sets rebuild the live-action film. • In the US, LEGO® Fusion sets allow LEGO models to interact with smart devices using an app. • LEGO CUUSOO becomes LEGO® Ideas and releases a fan-designed Ghostbusters™ Ecto-1 set, among other LEGO Ideas sets.

2015

• The LEGO Pirates set sail again for plunder and adventure. • LEGO® BIONICLE® returns. • A girl named Emily discovers the secret world of the LEGO® Elves. • LEGO® Scooby-Doo™ sets feature the whole Mystery Incorporated gang and a host of "ghouls" and "ghosts" for them to foil. • The expanded minifigure-scale LEGO MINECRAFT line becomes an instant smash hit.

How a LEGO® set is made

Making a new LEGO® set involves a lot more than just putting bricks into a box. It takes many months of brainstorming, designing, and testing to produce a set, not to mention building, and rebuilding... and building again! A LEGO model needs to be strong and sturdy, but not too difficult to put together, and to be taken apart again. It has to be cool and fun to play with, but also interesting to take apart and turn into other things. And above all, it has to inspire endless creativity!

CREATING A PLAY THEME

"We create a universe or a story that triggers children's imaginations. We'll show them our ideas, and if they can start telling stories with those ideas, then we know we're onto something."

Mark John Stafford, LEGO Senior Designer

A new LEGO set starts with a play theme. The LEGO creative team thinks about what kind of world the story should take place in, what people and creatures live there, and what the overall feeling should be—is it funny, action-packed, spooky, realistic, or something else?

These ideas are turned into storyboards that summarize each concept in just a few pictures. The storyboards are shown to children, and they pick their favorites. The LEGO team pays

close attention to which ideas are the most popular. If the children like part of one story and part of another, then they may take those pieces and combine them into a third idea made from the best parts of the other two. The end result is a brand-new LEGO play theme!

INSPIRATION AND BRAINSTORMING

"Every time we have a brainstorming session, they say, 'What do you want to do?' and I say, 'I want to do a carnival,' Simon says, 'I want to do helicopters,' and then everybody has their things that they want to throw out there. And we're like, 'OK, now we've got those out of the way, what do we really want to do?'"

Jamie Berard, LEGO Design Manager Specialist

Now it's time to come up with the sets. The LEGO designers look at what today's children find exciting, and they also remember what they liked building when they were young. They explore older sets to see what made them great, and they take trips or do research to get extra inspiration. They read books, watch movies, and play video games. By the time they're done, the designers have ideas for dozens of new LEGO sets. But how do they decide which ones to make?

"For Legends of Chima, we spent a night in the local zoo. Seeing the lions at feeding time changed the way we thought about them and the way we built models for them."

Mark John Stafford, LEGO Senior Designer

The answer: brainstorming sessions! These are meetings where all the designers for a play theme meet to share ideas and put their heads together to choose the models for the theme. LEGO designers come from many different countries and backgrounds. They studied different subjects at school, and they all have different hobbies and interests. Some of them have been designing models for many years, while others are new to professional building. Because of this, each designer has his or her own unique perspective on what would make the best sets. After lots of discussion, and under the supervision of a creative lead, they agree on the models they will design.

Getting all their bricks in a row: Before they start building sets, the LEGO designers brainstorm ideas for models, minifigures, color schemes, and other important details.

MODEL DESIGN AND DEVELOPMENT

Some LEGO designers begin a new model as a pencil drawing, while others just start putting bricks together to make a quick rough-draft version called a sketch model. By making a simpler sketch model first, the designer can prove that the set's design and special features will work well. Many sketch models are built out of pieces that are all the same color so that the designer can refine and improve its

shape and functions without having to worry about the color scheme yet. Sometimes a designer will have already come up with some model designs for fun that can be incorporated into the new set.

"I have a little parking lot on my desk. There are so many little things, like trees. I have all these different explorations of trees, and all these different explorations of lamps and window treatments— bow windows, detailed windows, big windows, small windows. They're just all lined up. And when I decide to make one of the Modular Buildings… we can go to this parking lot as it's already an inspiration bank. I can pick and choose; I just go shopping."

Jamie Berard, Design Manager Specialist

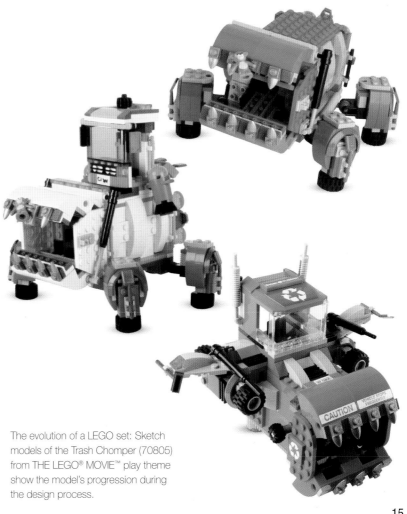

The evolution of a LEGO set: Sketch models of the Trash Chomper (70805) from THE LEGO® MOVIE™ play theme show the model's progression during the design process.

> "I use white pieces at the beginning to make a rough sketch. Then if the style and shape looks right, I work on the colors."

Fenella Blaize Charity, LEGO Design Manager

Each team of designers has cabinets full of drawers that hold all the current LEGO elements in all of their colors. They go from basic bricks, to plates and slopes, to specialized pieces, such as wheels and plants and walls and doors. With so many parts to work with, the only limit to what they can build is their imagination.

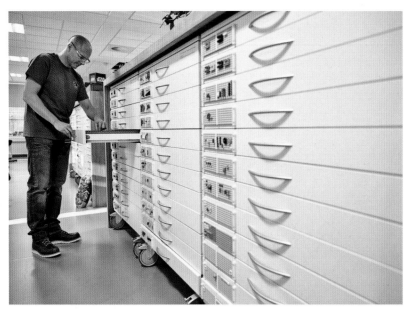

Building drawers: Each LEGO design team has more than 80 drawers stocked with elements of a particular size, shape, or building function—in all the many colors.

A treasure trove: Inside the drawers, individual containers keep all the LEGO pieces sorted and organized.

One of the most important questions in designing a LEGO set is what elements it will use. To give builders something new, a set will often include existing pieces in new colors, or with special new printing, or even used in a surprising new way. But sometimes, it is decided that a set will include a brand-new LEGO element.

There are only a certain number of LEGO element molds that can be kept at a time, so a new piece may replace an old one that isn't used any longer. The best new pieces are ones that can be used in multiple ways across multiple themes and models. If a car's wheel hub can also be a jet plane's engine, or an underwater helmet can work as a globe, then it is much more likely that the new part will be made.

> "We have a wall of all the elements that we have molds for. Every year, we're given a list of elements that haven't been used in the past five or 10 years, and we're asked if we really need them. Sometimes we'll say, 'Well, we're holding on to the pirate stuff, because we know we're going to do LEGO® Pirates again,' and they let it stay for another year. It's a good thing to get rid of elements that we really don't use, because it makes room for new pieces, but it's also that chance to say, 'No, this is a classic LEGO element that we should keep. Let's use it.'"

Jamie Berard, LEGO Design Manager Specialist

In the early years of LEGO set design, new pieces were sculpted by hand and re-scaled by a machine called a pantograph, which recreated the element at a smaller size. Nowadays, computers make the process much easier.

Sculpted pieces are scanned into a computer and adjusted by a part designer, while more geometric elements like bricks can be constructed completely within 3D software. Every LEGO piece needs to be precisely measured so that its shape and connection points work with all the other LEGO pieces that have been produced throughout the company's history.

> "It's fun to sculpt a hair piece, but to make the shape of the hair is only 20 percent of the work. It's refining it that takes the time. For an animal, I have only a few surfaces. But with hair, I have so many surfaces to consider."
>
> Gitte Thorsen, LEGO Design Master

Sculpted elements: New minifigure parts, such as hair pieces, and animal molds are hand-sculpted at a large scale before being reproduced in their smaller, final size.

Cow creation: LEGO Design Master and element sculptor Gitte Thorsen designed and sculpted the cow element with a head that can move up and down.

Along with bricks, a new LEGO set may need printed decorations or stickers to add extra visual flavor to its models, such as control panels, racing stripes, or numbered license plates. The set designer works with a graphic designer to come up with just the right patterns—detailed enough for their purpose to be clear, but simple enough to fit in with the blocky style of a LEGO set.

Look closely: As the graphics progress from doodles to final designs, the graphic designers sometimes sneak in special in-jokes and references.

Of course, there's one more key ingredient to most LEGO sets: the minifigures! It's especially vital to get these famous and friendly little characters just right. Minifigures have their own design team, where element and graphic designers work together to give each new character its own unique look and personality.

"Designing minifigures requires a certain amount of pulling faces in front of the mirror and watching other people's expressions."

Chris Bonven Johansen, LEGO Design Master

"Separate people design the minifigures and the sets. It's a very collaborative process. It needs to be coherent, and the models need to look like they go together."

Mark John Stafford, LEGO Senior Designer

TESTING AND APPROVAL

"We do testing to see what makes the children happy. It might be little things, like a slide for figures, or we look at what stories they play out so we can create elements to fit those stories."

Elisabeth Kahl-Backes, LEGO Design Manager

Throughout the development process, the sets are shown to children to get their opinions on the designs and functions, and to see whether the models hold up to serious play. The designers look at all of their feedback and make any necessary changes to the models that will create a better building experience.

Product safety assessments are also carried out during a set or element's design. Potential issues, such as protruding parts and shooting functions, are tested carefully by the product safety team to ensure that they will not cause anyone any harm, and a set or element's design will be altered to make it safe if necessary.

All models don't become finished sets. Some might not quite work right, or don't test well enough with children—the ultimate judges of a set's success. Other challenges include making sure that the building process isn't overly hard for the age of its builders, that there aren't too many or too few pieces to meet the price point, and that the set is built according to the company's careful rules for how LEGO elements can be connected together. Sometimes the story or direction of the theme changes, and the designers have to start all over again. As many as nine out of ten models may be scrapped during this phase of development!

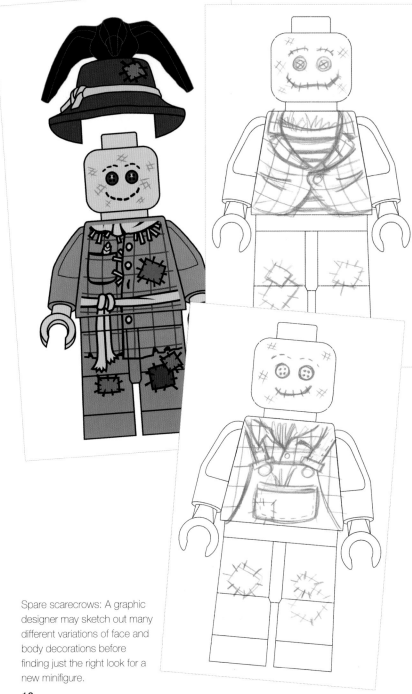

Spare scarecrows: A graphic designer may sketch out many different variations of face and body decorations before finding just the right look for a new minifigure.

For those sets that get all the way through, there is still one more test. A Model Committee of experts—builders, engineers, part designers, and instructions developers—thoroughly reviews the model and looks for any flaws. If the committee finds an issue, then the designer has to fix it before the set is at last approved.

INSTRUCTIONS AND MANUFACTURING

"The biggest challenge is usually the building instructions. Working together with the building instruction people and working out how we can show how to build the set takes a long time. It's very important for us to have the right steps."

Markus Kossmann, LEGO Senior Designer

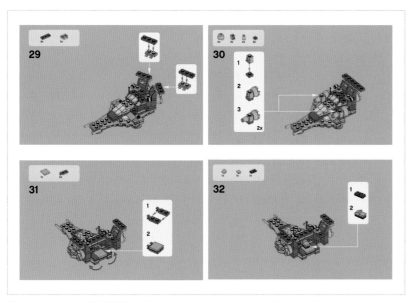

Clear instructions: All LEGO models get precise step-by-step directions that show what new pieces to add and where they go at each stage of building.

The approved model is disassembled piece by piece by the instructions team, who use a 3D computer program to make the pictures for the booklet of building steps (instructions were hand-drawn in the early years). The team ensures that each step of the construction is clear and easy to follow, yet challenging. At the same time, art designers work on creating the packaging, with graphics that will look appealing on a store shelf while communicating all of the set's main features and functions.

Ready for sale: As the last part of the manufacturing process, newly packaged LEGO sets are automatically packed into cardboard shipping cases.

On their way: Robotic arms stack up piles of full shipping boxes for transport to distribution centers and creative customers all around the world.

Finally, the set is complete and ready for production. At the factory, tiny plastic granules are melted down inside molding machines and pressed into the shapes of bricks—in 2014, more than 6 billion bricks were produced by the LEGO Group! Robots pick out the needed bricks and elements for the set at the warehouse, and they are transported to be assembled or decorated if needed, and then sorted and sealed into plastic bags. Together with the instruction booklets, the bags are dropped down chutes into waiting boxes, which are sealed, packed, and sent off to your local toy store!

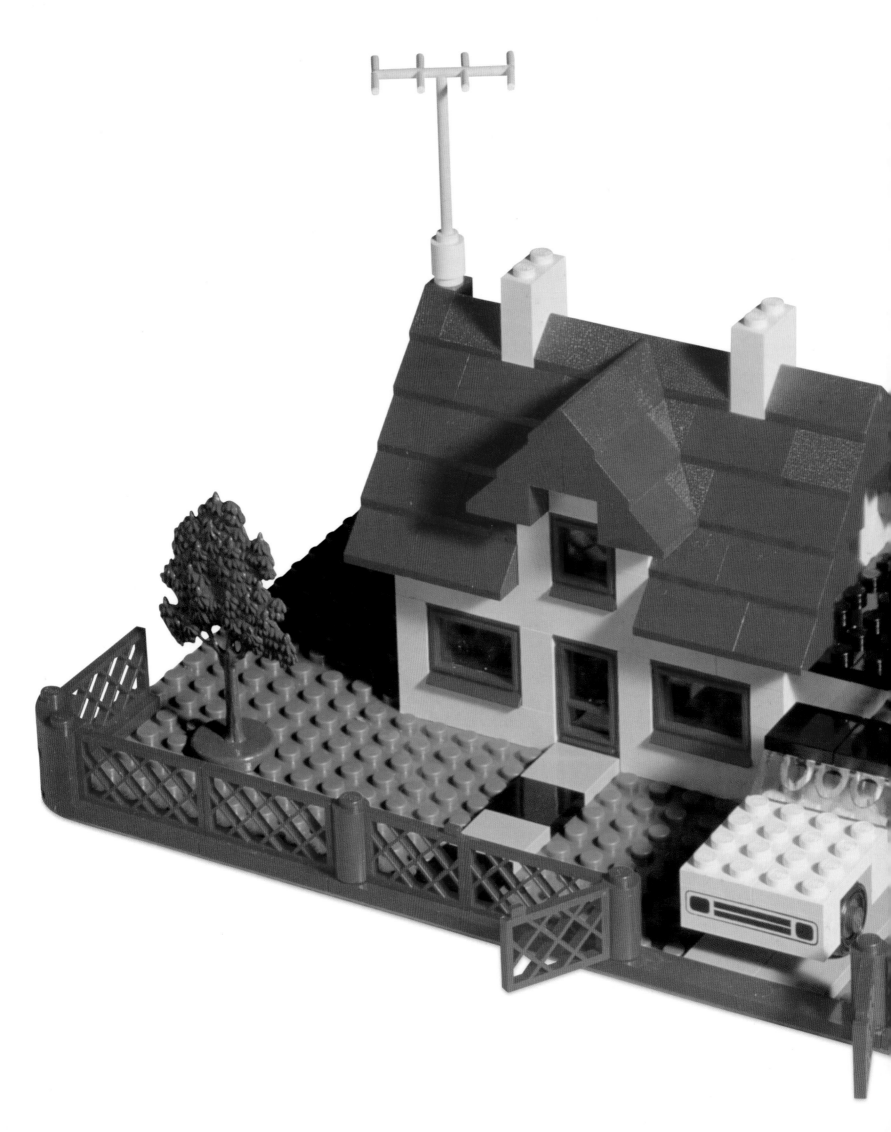

1950s–60s

Introduced to the toy market in 1949, the LEGO Group's "Automatic Binding Bricks" became a phenomenon in the 1950s. Renamed "LEGO® Bricks" in 1953, they gave rise to an entire building system that was improved in 1958 with a newly patented stud-and-tube connection method. Now simple interlocking bricks could be combined with specialized pieces such as doors and windows to let builders assemble houses, spaceships, and anything else they could imagine. The following decade expanded the potential of LEGO models even further by adding rolling wheels, electric motors, and, in 1964, the first sets to include separately printed building instructions.

Town Plan 1200

1955 • LEGO® System of Play • #1200

Here's where it all started! When they first appeared, connectable plastic bricks were just one of many different kinds of toys produced at the LEGO Group factory in Denmark. But in 1955, they became the core of the new LEGO System of Play, a structured range of products that could all work together for an ever-expanding play experience. It all kicked off with the famous Town Plan series of sets and accessories.

Among the early items in the line was set number 1200, a vinyl play mat for builders to use to create their own town displays. The first of its kind produced by the company, the large plastic mat measures 47x29in (120x73cm), and is printed with an overhead town layout so that builders can use their separately-sold LEGO bricks to add buildings to the island-like city blocks.

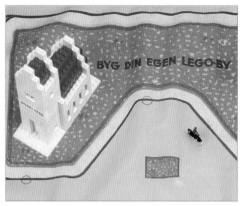

∧ **INSPIRATION TO BUILD** The text printed on the mat reads "Byg Din Egen LEGO-By," or "Build your own LEGO town."

• No stickers come with the set. All the detailed elements, such as the "Hotel" sign, gas pumps, and road signs, are printed.

• The road signs were produced in collaboration with the Danish Road Safety Council to help children learn about traffic safety.

• Simple instructions are included in the set as well as images of extra building ideas, such as a windmill, ship, and lighthouse.

• In 2008, a new special-edition 1950s-style Town Plan (10184) was released to celebrate the 50th anniversary of the patenting of the modern LEGO brick.

Trees add greenery to the Town Plan

Painted crossing guard guides the traffic

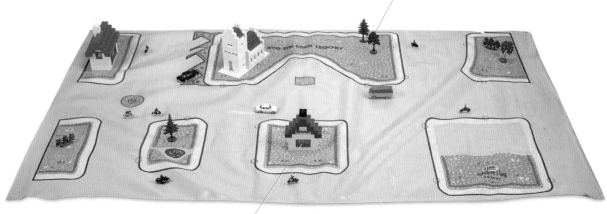

Buildings built with separately sold bricks can be used to populate the mat

• As well as brick buildings, pre-painted and assembled miniature cars, bicycles, and road signs can be placed on the streets to simulate busy town traffic. These were all made by the company, too.

• The LEGO bricks of 1955 had hollow undersides with no tubes, so they only connected loosely to bricks under them. In 1958, the stud-and-tube interlocking system was introduced, increasing building possibilities and improving model stability.

• The soft plastic street mat, which was on sale from 1955–59, was supplemented by Town Plan sets made from wooden fiberboard in 1956.

• Godtfred Kirk Christiansen, the son of the founder of the LEGO Group and the Managing Director at the time, wrote of the new LEGO System of Play: "Our idea is to create a toy that prepares the child for life, appeals to the imagination, and develops the creative urge and joy of creation that are the driving force in every human being."

Town Plan 810

1961 • LEGO® System of Play • #810

One of a number of Town Plan sets produced between 1955 and 1966, set 810 was available with two different box designs depending on where it was released. Some sets included a street board designed for left-side-driving vehicles, and some a board for right-side traffic, matching the rules of the country where the set was purchased.

As with many Town Plan building sets, this set includes a selection of red and white bricks and other useful elements for making houses and civic buildings. It comes with a decorated street board and a variety of miniature vehicles, trees, and signs—everything the children of the 1960s could need to build their own town centers. The Town Plan sets were designed to be combined with other sets produced at the time. Here, set 810 has been displayed alongside other Town Plan sets from the late 1950s and '60s to create an even larger Town Plan.

Guided Tour

KEY

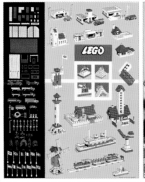

> **A TOUCH OF GREENERY** Various types of trees were included in the Town Plan sets. They are single pieces of flat, textured, painted plastic that stand on a rounded base.

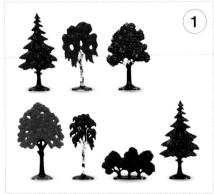

> **SET 810** The box design shows the set's buildings, street board, signs, trees, flags, realistic 1950s cars and trucks, and extra build ideas, too.

Roof is made with blue sloped bricks

Trans-clear elements form the gas station's curved window

Motorized Train Set

1966 • **#113** • Pieces: 344

The very first self-propelled LEGO® train used a battery-powered 4.5-volt motor to help its blocky blue locomotive pull its mail and passenger cars along a set of rails. The tracks could be laid over stacks of bricks to make sloping, elevated railways that the mighty little motor would tackle with ease.

The set was adapted for different markets. For continental Europe, it featured bricks printed with the locations Hamburg, Basel, and Genova. For sets released in Britain, Ireland, and Australia, the train was bound for London, Manchester, and Glasgow, and the "Post" signs on the mail car were replaced with "Royal Mail."

- The bricks printed with the two sets of city names are unique to the two different versions of the model.

- The 4.5-volt motor was also made in black. Both motors appeared in LEGO sets from 1966–1969, including 1968's Deluxe Motorized Train set, in black.

- This set comes with 40 pieces of blue track.

- The instructions contain ideas for how the track can be laid out.

- Although the passenger car didn't actually carry passengers, the carriage contained several sets of windows, made up of 32 clear bricks, offering a great view.

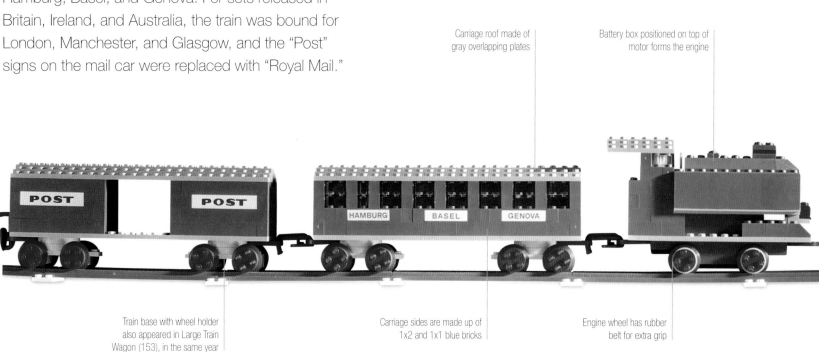

Carriage roof made of gray overlapping plates

Battery box positioned on top of motor forms the engine

Train base with wheel holder also appeared in Large Train Wagon (153), in the same year

Carriage sides are made up of 1x2 and 1x1 blue bricks

Engine wheel has rubber belt for extra grip

Guided Tour

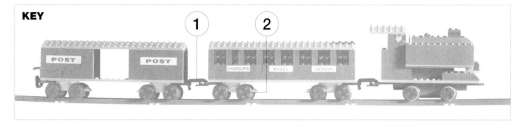

KEY

> **COUPLED UP** The parts of the train can be linked using the bright red coupling mechanism, consisting of two special plates: one with a hook and one with a hole.

∧ **TRAIN WHEELS** The red wheels of both carriages have traction teeth for gripping the rails. They are attached to an old-style 4x4 turntable assembly in white.

Building Set with Train

1967 • **#080** • Pieces: 710 • Figures: 1 (brick-built)

1967's Basic Building Set with Train enabled builders to make a push-along train. Like other sets of the era, its base plates were thin and fragile, with specific patterns of studs that showed where to place the bottom layer of bricks in each building. It was also released by American distributor Samsonite as 080 Ambassador Set, an FAO Schwarz store exclusive.

- Like some other sets of its time, this set did not come with instructions—the builder would follow the images on the box.

- The set includes builds for two trucks and a traffic cop figure.

- The green base plates for the houses and train station are exclusive to this set, and to each building.

- A piece of blue straight train track is used for the signal light.

- The build for the narrow, push-along train is unique to this set. Unusually, it is four studs wide—most LEGO trains were six studs wide.

- Two birch trees, two pine trees, and two groups of bushes come with the set.

The set's circle of tracks is built from classic blue LEGO rail pieces connected by white plates, with ridges that match those on the train's special red wheels. The train goes around the four colorful buildings.

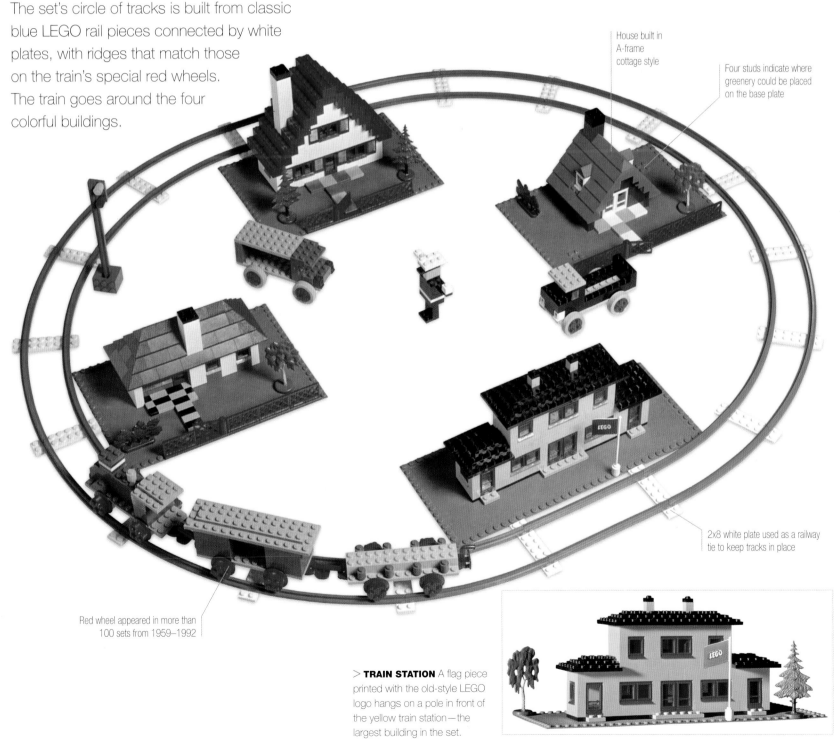

House built in A-frame cottage style

Four studs indicate where greenery could be placed on the base plate

2x8 white plate used as a railway tie to keep tracks in place

Red wheel appeared in more than 100 sets from 1959–1992

> **TRAIN STATION** A flag piece printed with the old-style LEGO logo hangs on a pole in front of the yellow train station—the largest building in the set.

Car

1968 • LEGO® Model Maker • #330 • Pieces: 65

By the late 1960s, LEGO models were getting bigger, providing more room for features and details. Some vehicle sets included special parts that made them extra fun to play with once they were put together, such as steerable wheels or working winches, and even simpler ones like 1968's Car could roll around with realistic rubber tires on free-spinning wheels. This set is particularly special as it was designed by Kjeld Kirk Kristiansen, the grandson of the founder of the LEGO Group and the company's current vice-chairman.

The Car includes a new style of small spoked wheel that the classic LEGO rubber tire can be fitted around. A metal pin lets the wheel plug into the short or long sides of a specialized 2x4 brick. The set comes with six of the new red wheel parts—four for the rolling wheels, one for the spare tire at the back, and one to act as the vehicle's steering wheel.

Jette Orduna | Head of LEGO Idea House

Jette is Head of the LEGO Idea House at the LEGO Group's headquarters in Billund, Denmark. She is in charge of the LEGO Group archive and LEGO heritage, and is responsible for trademark protection. Jette knows everything there is to know about the company's history. She takes great joy in showing employees around the private museum and archive, telling them stories, such as the unusual origin of the Car (330). The archive is a vault that contains almost every LEGO set ever produced, and is a place for employees to learn about the company's history and products, to help ensure the LEGO values are kept alive.

BRICK BY BRICK

- Kjeld Kirk Kristiansen built and tested many concept models as a child, and appeared on model packaging images. He became president and CEO of the LEGO Group in 1979, and stepped down in 2004.

- LEGO sales first began in the US and Canada in 1961, through a license agreement with the Samsonite Corp. luggage company. This Car set was distributed by Samsonite in North America as part of the "Model Maker" line.

- The wheels have small central pins, enabling them to spin, and move the vehicle.

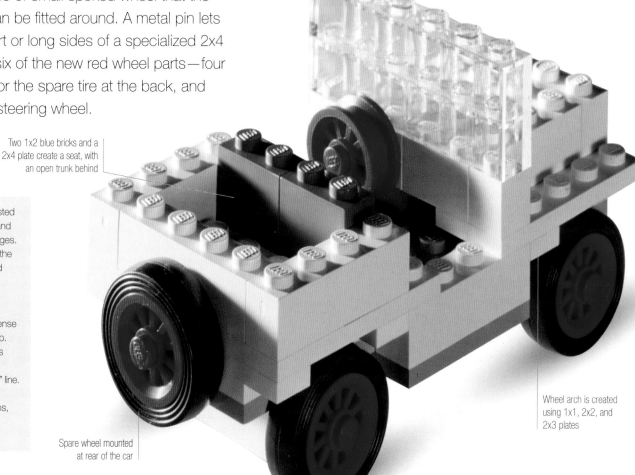

Two 1x2 blue bricks and a 2x4 plate create a seat, with an open trunk behind

Wheel arch is created using 1x1, 2x2, and 2x3 plates

Spare wheel mounted at rear of the car

> **FRONT OF CAR** Two 1x6 trans-clear bricks form the windshield. The front grille is made of a 1x2 blue brick sandwiched between two 1x2 blue plates.

"After school, Kjeld, the grandson of the LEGO Group founder, would go to the design department and play. He knew what he was doing. His design, the Car, was a bestseller..."

Jette Orduna, Head of LEGO Idea House

House with Car

1969 • Large supplementary set • #346

This charming suburban house model has a unique round-cornered, grass-colored base plate, which is fully studded, with dots of white paint to guide brick placement during assembly. The following year, the set would become part of the company's new LEGOLAND® brand, a series of houses and small vehicles that let children build their own modern worlds out of LEGO bricks.

The set comes with painted trees, an opening gate, and a smooth tile driveway so the little white car can roll up under the small attached garage. The television antenna element on the roof is quite delicate, and few are still found with all of their prongs attached today.

• The house comes with eight windows; five on the first floor, and three on the second floor.

• A single 6x8 black plate forms the roof of the garage. It is supported by two pillars made with three black 1x1 round bricks resting on two 1x1 black plates.

• This set later formed part of the LEGOLAND Village Set (380) in 1971. Three other sets were included in the collection: Bungalow (344), Fire Station with Mini Cars (347), and Vintage Car (603).

• The car in this set is indentical to the car in 1969's LEGO House with Car (345).

> **LITTLE CAR** The car's windshield—a trans-clear sloped brick—is positioned directly over the black and red wheels, giving it a sporty look.

Roof is made from 45 red bricks

Old-style flat tree is hand-painted, with hollow base

Curved "macaroni" brick forms corner of fence

Car hood is formed of two 2x4 white plates

1970s

The 1970s were a time of progress for the growing business of the LEGO Group. It had a worldwide hit with its brick construction sets, and the new LEGOLAND® range (named after the recently-opened theme park in the company's hometown of Billund, Denmark) was quickly making "LEGO" a household name. But something was still missing—something that could tie its many different building sets together. The answer came in the form of a four-brick-tall character with a yellow head. With the arrival of the LEGO® minifigure and three themes—LEGOLAND Town, Space, and Castle—the golden age of LEGO building had truly begun!

Fire Truck

1970 • LEGOLAND • #602 • Pieces: 30

The new LEGOLAND® range that was launched at the beginning of the decade included models from all kinds of categories, many of which can still be found in the LEGO® construction aisle of toy stores today. A staple of LEGO building for more than 40 years, firefighting sets—like this red, six-wheeled fire truck—let children put themselves into the seats of real-world heroes.

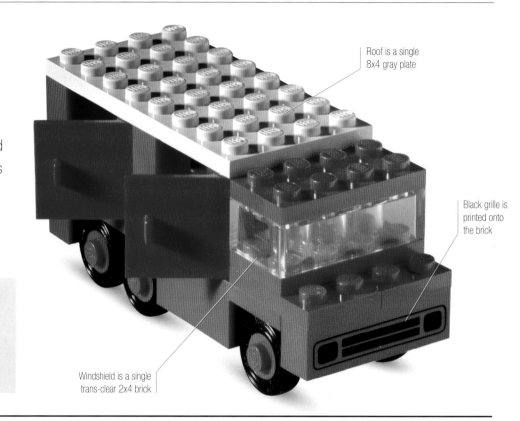

Roof is a single 8x4 gray plate

Black grille is printed onto the brick

Windshield is a single trans-clear 2x4 brick

BRICK BY BRICK

• This set was released in North America in 1971. It was called LEGO Mini-Wheel Model Maker Delivery Van (362) and it was distributed by Samsonite, the LEGO Group's North American licensing partner at the time.

• The truck has two left-opening, and two right-opening side doors.

• The truck's black tires have featured in more than 300 sets since they made their debut in 1969.

Taxi

1971 • LEGOLAND • #605 • Pieces: 18

Scenes and vehicles from everyday life were a big part of the LEGOLAND concept. With a basic, boxy design and windows built from clear rectangular and slope bricks, this taxi cab could be distinguished from other auto models of the time by its two exclusive printed "TAXI" bricks and its iconic roof light. The light is made from a yellow LEGO tile stuck upright on its edge between the studs of the roof plate—a building technique that the company no longer uses today!

Yellow taxi light is a 1x2 tile slotted between studs across two plates

Printed grille piece was also available in blue, red, white, and yellow

Sign printed on 2x3 black brick

BRICK BY BRICK

• The clear sloped brick used for the windshield was introduced in 1969. It can also be seen in 1969's House with Car (346).

• There are just four steps to the instructions in this set.

• Building methods that use bricks in ways for which they were not intended (such as the taxi light), which could damage or break the elements, or cause the models to be unstable, are known as "illegal builds."

Italian Villa

1973 • LEGOLAND • #356 • Pieces: 150

By the early-to-mid 1970s, LEGO® model design was becoming more refined. Released in the USA as "Swiss Villa" and in Denmark as "Villa Mallorca," the Italian Villa set is an elegantly elevated two-story house. It is built from a then-substantial 150 pieces, with plenty of curved arches, latticed fence pieces, and triangular roof bricks to provide the finished model with its very pleasing shape and form.

The villa's welcoming features include yellow window shutters, a front door with steps, a fruit tree outside, and a balcony for enjoying the view.

Antenna piece connects to the chimney

Five white fence pieces are included in the set

Granulated fruit tree is one piece that connects to the base plate

Tiled pathway leads through the arch beneath the building

• The fruit tree is unique to sets of the 1970s. Its leaves are actually glued-on plastic granules of the same type used to make LEGO bricks.

• There are two sets of steps made from assorted black plates. The first set leads to the front door, and the second leads out onto the upper-story terrace.

• The latticed fence piece was introduced in 1967—and it is still in use today!

• Like others at the time, the base plate is marked with white dots (not seen) for positioning the bricks.

• The windows and doors in the house cannot be opened.

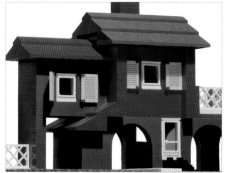

< SUMMER LIVING
There is a second bedroom in the red-roofed extension. The two sets of shutters can be opened and closed, making them perfect for keeping out the summer sun.

Family

1974 • LEGO® Figures • #200 • Pieces: 78 • Figures: 5

Until 1974, people in LEGO sets had only blocky approximations of hands and faces. But all of that changed with the arrival of the LEGO Family, a set of characters with brick-built bodies and all-new face and arm parts that gave them movement and expressions for the first time.

Since they are mostly made of standard bricks, LEGO Family members can be assembled in all kinds of ways—tall, short, standing, sitting, and wearing different colors and clothing styles. Some of the hair pieces can even be turned around to create alternate looks.

Hand piece can turn and flex at the wrist

Child's legs made with fewer bricks than adults' legs

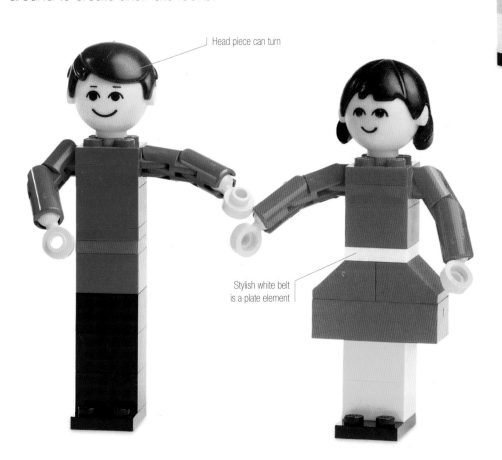

Head piece can turn

Stylish white belt is a plate element

Sloped brick forms skirt shape

• The set includes pieces for a blue and white bench for the grandma. Her skirt bricks can be rearranged to give the impression that she is sitting down.

• The hair pieces (apart from the grandma's) can be reversed for a different hairstyle—the male figures pictured are modelling the two sides (or styles) of the same hair piece.

• Unlike the children's shorter arms, the adult figures have a joint at the elbow to make them even more posable.

• Each pair of feet is made from a single 2x3 black plate.

• Eyebrows, freckles, and glasses are among the details printed onto some of the family members' faces.

Living Room

1974 • LEGO® Homemaker • #264 • Pieces: 242 • Figures: 2

The LEGO Family members were much too big to fit into a regular LEGOLAND house. Luckily for them, they were designed to be just the right size for LEGO Homemaker, the dollhouse-like line of models that featured larger-scale, buildable rooms and furnishings. The range had everything from tables and pianos to an entire living room playset.

In the colorful Living Room set, a red base plate stands in for a carpet. Tiles cover studded surfaces to create smooth and stylish furniture, including a table with sofa and chairs, a color television, and a desk with a telephone and sliding drawers.

BRICK BY BRICK

• A sticker is used for the front of the television set. It features buttons and a screen showing a smiling snowman with two children.

• The sticker sheet comes with five stickers, including two telephone dials.

• The lower parts of the two figures can be rearranged so they can sit on the chairs or sofa.

• The books on the set of shelves are colored tile pieces.

• Other LEGO Homemaker sets with figures were released in the same year, including Kitchen (263), Bathroom (265), and Children's Bedroom (266).

• Though not their official name, these larger figures from the Homemaker range are often referred to as "maxifigures."

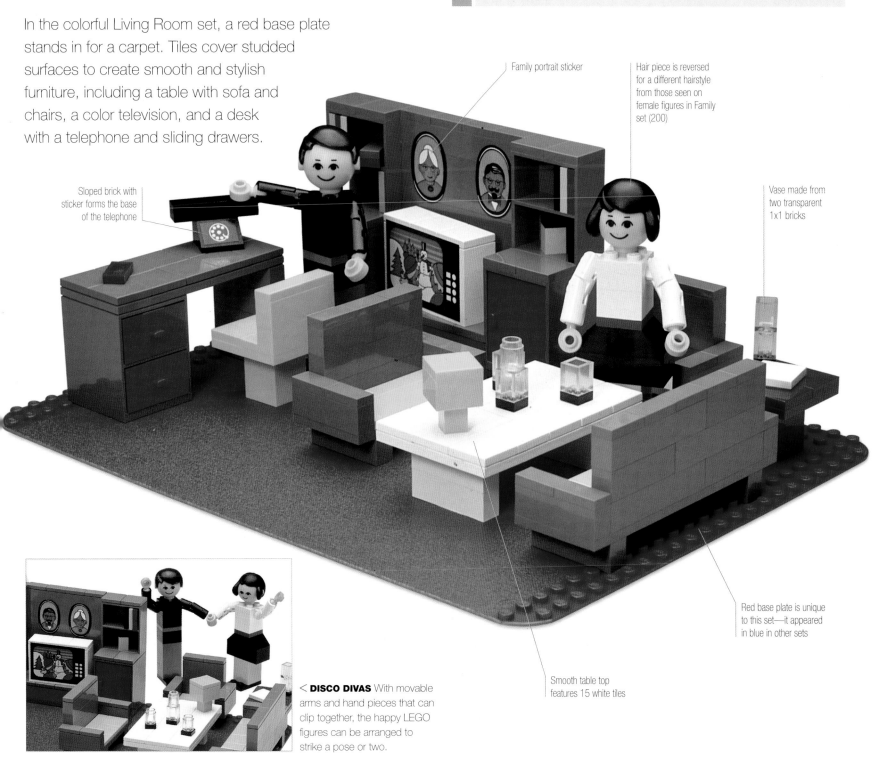

Family portrait sticker

Hair piece is reversed for a different hairstyle from those seen on female figures in Family set (200)

Sloped brick with sticker forms the base of the telephone

Vase made from two transparent 1x1 bricks

Red base plate is unique to this set—it appeared in blue in other sets

Smooth table top features 15 white tiles

< **DISCO DIVAS** With movable arms and hand pieces that can clip together, the happy LEGO figures can be arranged to strike a pose or two.

Gravel Works

1974 • LEGOLAND • #360 • Pieces: 211

Released as Brick Yard in the US, this wonderfully interactive LEGOLAND® set provided the pieces to create an entire quarry scene on a unique base plate. With a factory-like structure, three inventive vehicles, and lots of moving parts and functions, the only thing more fun than building it was playing with it once it was all put together.

Builders can dig up "gravel" pieces (actually 1x1 LEGO® bricks) with the shovel truck's hinged arm, scoop them up with the crane's articulated claw, and turn the winch to hoist them into the air. The crank-powered conveyor belt is used to drop the gravel into the tipper truck, before it is driven away.

∧ **CONVEYOR BELT** Turning a handle on the side of the conveyor belt transports gravel pieces up to the second floor. The gravel drops into the truck at the rear.

BRICK BY BRICK

• The US version of this set, called Brick Yard (580), was released in 1975.

• The yellow brick with black LEGOLAND printing also appeared in blue, white, and red in sets between 1971 and 1975.

• The conveyor belt is made up of red and black pieces. Prior to 1974, it had only been produced in yellow and black.

• The swiveling crane travels along blue train track rails.

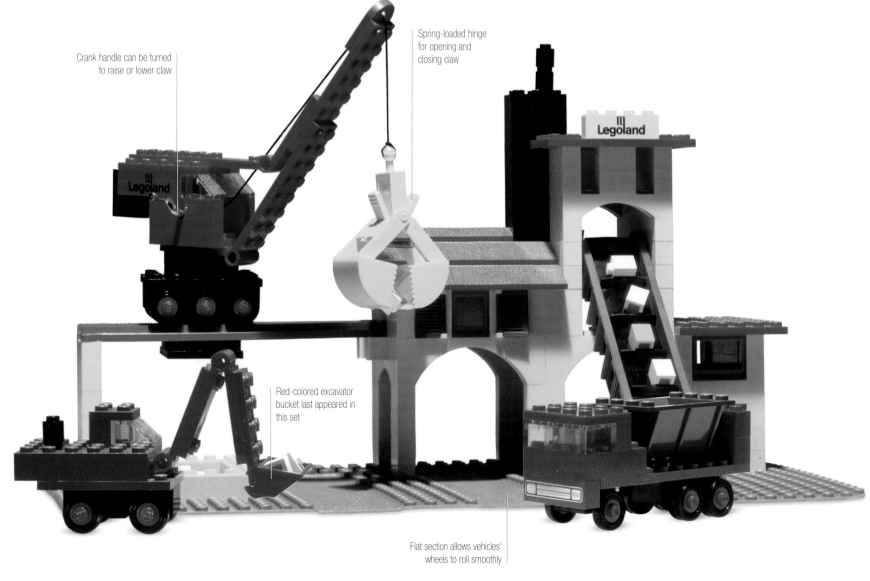

Crank handle can be turned to raise or lower claw

Spring-loaded hinge for opening and closing claw

Red-colored excavator bucket last appeared in this set

Flat section allows vehicles' wheels to roll smoothly

Hospital

1975 • LEGOLAND • #363 • Pieces: 223 • Figures: 7

LEGOLAND® sets featured a new, smaller style of LEGO® citizen in 1975: a featureless figure that came with an assortment of colored legs and torsos and could wear different hat or hair pieces. In the Hospital set, white clothes and red cross stickers distinguish doctors and nurses from their patients, who are surely appreciative of the care despite a lack of facial expressions to show it.

To see the adaptability of LEGO pieces, look no further than this set. Bricks and tiles combine to create a wheelchair and stretcher, and window shutters in white become opening ambulance doors. The figures can even be split in half to make them look like they're sitting down!

- These early figures have arms that are built into their torsos and their legs are joined together.

- The female figure's red hair piece with pigtails is new for this set.

- The hospital stretcher is fitted between each paramedic figure's torso and leg piece to give the impression that they are carrying it.

- On the roof of the hospital is a brick-built red cross.

- This set contains a sticker sheet with 11 red cross stickers—four large and seven small—as well as the Hospital sign sticker.

- The red and white road sign, which signifies "no entry," is a printed piece.

- The base plate is unique to this set.

> ADAPTABLE BUILDING
The wheelchair is built into the paramedic's body and the patient's leg piece is placed in front of her torso to make it look like she is seated.

Sticker on flag piece

Sign over entrance is a sticker on a brick

Gray tiles form a driveway for the ambulance

Tree piece has appeared in more than 100 sets

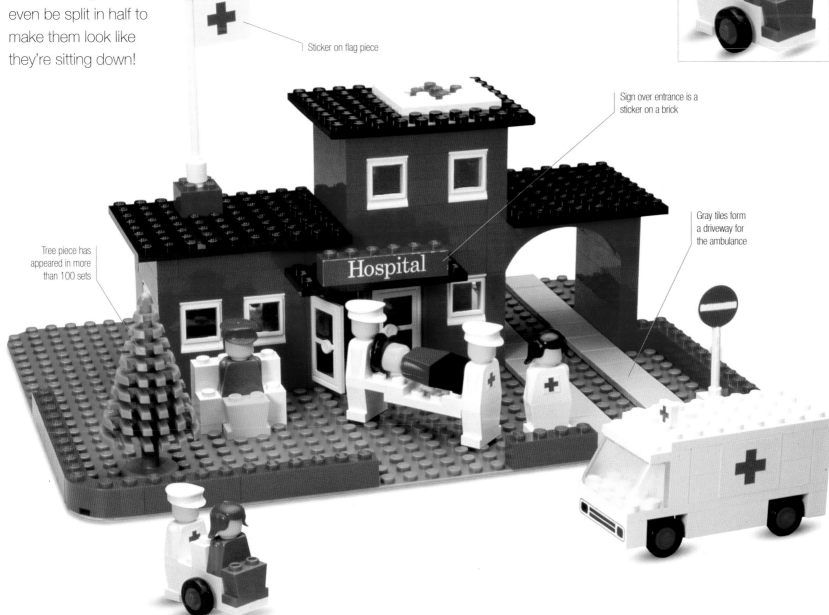

Hospital

Space Module with Astronauts

1975 • LEGOLAND • #367 • Pieces: 364 • Figures: 3

In the 1970s, everybody was crazy about space exploration thanks to the recent Apollo moon missions. The LEGOLAND® Space Module with Astronauts, known as Space Moon Landing (565) in the US, helped builders to relive the excitement that they'd seen on their black-and-white television sets by creating their own lunar landing—in full color! There weren't many space-based LEGO® sets at this point, but that would all change soon…

The Space Module set includes a landing capsule (which can detach from its legs for the return flight to Earth), a rolling lunar rover, and a flag to plant on the moon's surface, as well as three LEGO Family-style astronaut figures.

Guided Tour

KEY

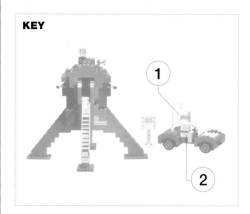

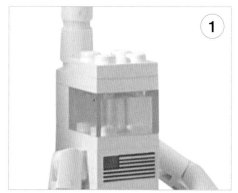

△ **ASTRONAUT HELMET** The helmets are made from white and transparent bricks that are built into the breathing apparatus on their backs.

△ **SITTING ASTRONAUT** The astronaut figures can be built into a seated position for driving the roving vehicle.

Antenna piece with side spokes

16 white 1x1 round bricks represent batteries at the front of the lunar roving vehicle

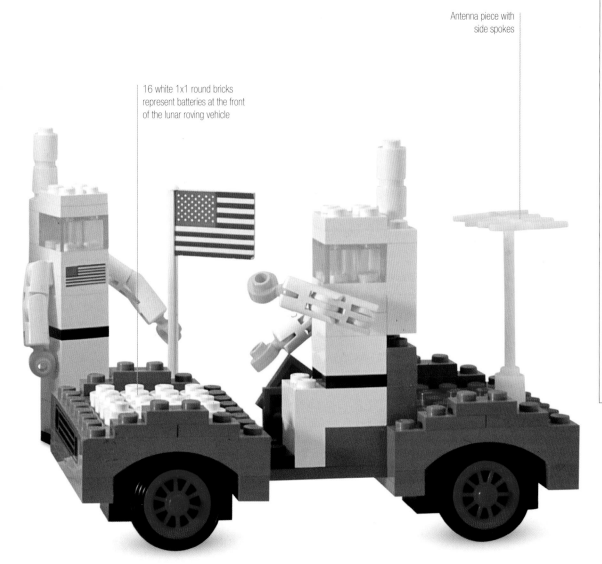

Kristian Reimer Hauge | Culture Mediator

Like many children, Kristian dreamed of working for the LEGO Group. He joined the company in 2010 after completing his history degree. Kristian works in the LEGO Idea House, and is responsible for ensuring that the history and values of the company are conveyed accurately. He gives tours of the LEGO archives, showing employees old sets, such as Space Module with Astronauts (367). He writes articles for publications and helps employees find out information about the company's history. He often has to dig hard to find answers—it's no coincidence that a Sherlock Holmes-style minifigure is pictured on his business card!

BRICK BY BRICK

• The astronauts' brick-built helmets can be swapped for building figure heads and hair pieces when they go indoors.

• A rare blue curved brick is used as a wheel arch on the buggy.

• The delicate antenna piece that is attached to the back of the lunar vehicle was discontinued in 1987.

• The yellow ladder was also produced in light gray. It was less common in the light-gray color.

• The gray hand-held camera is more commonly used as a thruster or jet engine piece. It is also used as a thruster in this set.

• The sticker sheet, with its four large and three small American flags, is unique to the US and European versions of the set.

• The back of the box features alternative builds. These include a helicopter, a television camera, and a gondola!

Landing light is trans-clear slope piece

Thruster appears on both sides of module

Hand-held camera for important lunar research

Radar dish made from white plates

Device for collecting soil samples

37

Thatcher Perkins Locomotive

1976 • LEGO® Hobby Set • #396 • Pieces: 434

In response to the popularity of realistic hobby shop model kits, the LEGO Hobby Set range (also known as Expert models in some countries) featured larger and more detailed building sets. Launched in 1975, each model was based on a specific type of vehicle. One of only eight sets in the range, 1976's Thatcher Perkins Locomotive was modelled after a real steam engine from 1863.

The model's lifelike details include rods that move when it rolls, decorative yellow trim, and even a bell on top. Just like the original, it has a 4-6-0 wheel layout, with four small wheels in front of six big driving wheels in the middle, and none behind.

Guided Tour

KEY

△ **LOCOMOTIVE NUMBER** The "396" sticker on the side of the boiler references the LEGO set number.

◁ **OIL LAMPS** Each of the three oil lamps at the front of the train is made up of a single plain yellow minifigure head and a 2x2 yellow frame piece.

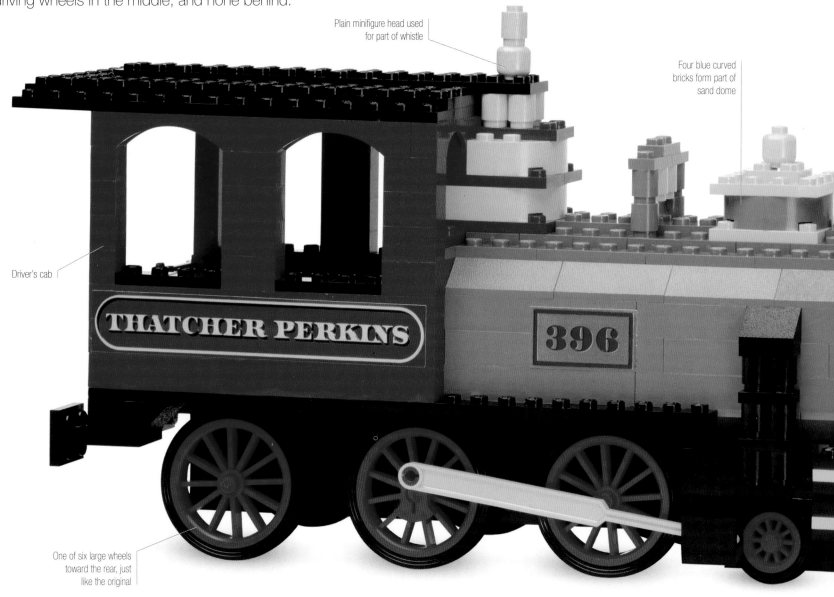

Plain minifigure head used for part of whistle

Four blue curved bricks form part of sand dome

Driver's cab

THATCHER PERKINS

396

One of six large wheels toward the rear, just like the original

- The locomotive is designed to be a model, not a working train on tracks. Its scale is too large for figures to fit inside.

- Two 1x1 round yellow bricks make up the bell, which is located in front of the whistle.

- The locomotive is named after Baltimore and Ohio Railroad engineer Thatcher Perkins.

- There were eight Hobby Sets released from 1975 to 1978. The first of these was LEGO Hobby Set 1913 Cadillac (390).

"The LEGO® Train fan community has a deep level of appreciation for legacy and tradition."

Jamie Berard, LEGO Design Manager Specialist

Brick-built smoke stack

Cowcatcher is made up of sloped bricks

Police Launch

1976 • Model Set – Ships • #314 • Pieces: 53 • Figures: 2

Crewed by a pair of officers in black uniforms and smart white caps, this little police boat packed a fun new feature. Under its three-piece hollow hull was a weighted keel element that let it float upright in a bathtub or pool. String could be tied on a loop at the front of the boat to pull it through the water.

The "Police" text, anchor logos, and life preserver rings on the model's sides are all stickers applied by the builder. The front, middle, and back of the boat are individual pieces, meaning extra center sections can be added in to make a longer ship.

> **NAUTICAL STICKERS**
Ahoy there! Stickers of two anchors and three life preserver rings decorate the boat.

Old-style red bushing connector piece

Stern section of boat fits flush to middle section

- Each of the three large individual boat sections comes fully assembled, complete with a gray deck piece.

- This set contains two old-style policeman figures. They do not have separate arms and their legs are molded together.

- An identical boat appeared in another set in 1978: LEGOLAND Police Boat (709). A single policeman minifigure replaced the two original figures.

- The separate keel piece is colored bright red and has extra long studs for a firm hold.

Dream Cottage
• 1997 • LEGO SCALA • #3270

Log Cabin
• 2011 • LEGO Creator • #5766

Small Cottage
• 2013 • LEGO Creator • #31009

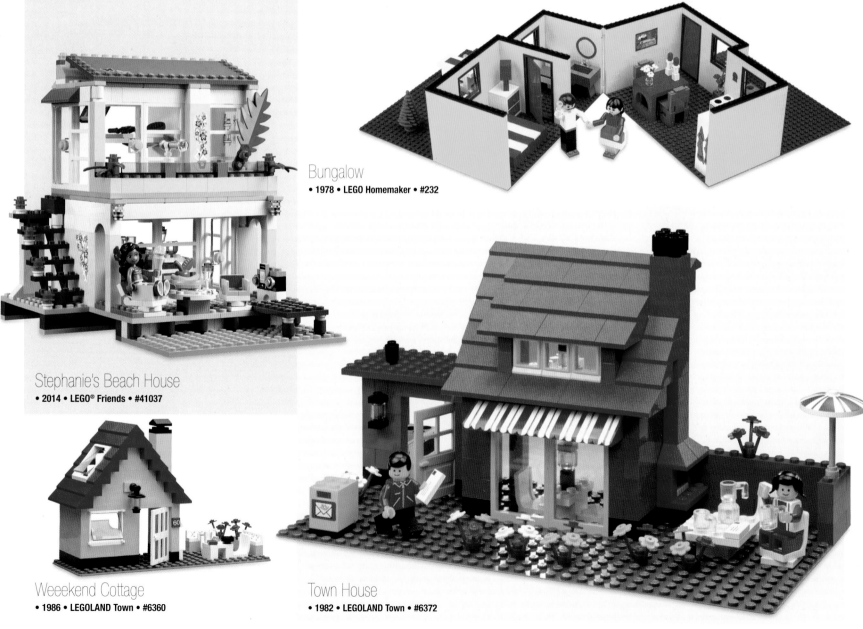

Bungalow
• 1978 • LEGO Homemaker • #232

Stephanie's Beach House
• 2014 • LEGO® Friends • #41037

Weeekend Cottage
• 1986 • LEGOLAND Town • #6360

Town House
• 1982 • LEGOLAND Town • #6372

"Houses are the intuitive thing to start building as a child, and LEGO bricks are a natural material to build them with."

Jamie Berard, LEGO Design Manager Specialist

Mary's House
• 1977 • LEGO DUPLO • #537

Bonnie Bunny's New House
• 1987 • LEGO FABULAND • #3674

My First Playhouse
• 2015 • LEGO® DUPLO® • #10616

HOME SWEET HOME

LEGO® houses through the years

There have been almost as many different types of LEGO houses as there have been people to live in them... and children to put them together! Some are designed for interactive play, such as the early LEGO Homemaker sets with their buildable furniture, and the LEGO® SCALA™ line. Others are realistic brick-built recreations of life in the modern city, country, or suburbs. Even younger builders have been able to get in on the house-constructing fun, thanks to simpler LEGO® DUPLO® and LEGO® FABULAND™ sets.

Family House
• 2013 • LEGO Creator • #31012

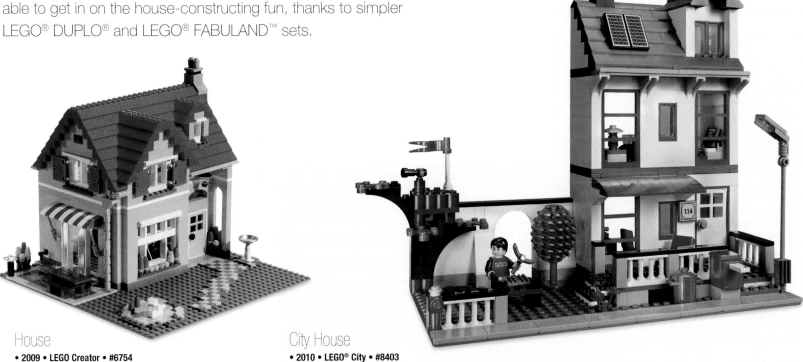

House
• 2009 • LEGO Creator • #6754

City House
• 2010 • LEGO® City • #8403

Universal Building Set with 4.5 Volt Motor

1976 • Universal Building Set • #912 • Pieces: 467 • Figures: 3

Also known as Basic Sets, Universal Building Sets provided builders with an assortment of bricks and pieces that they were encouraged to turn into a multitude of different models, whether one of the many ideas from the box and instructions, or something completely new. This advanced building set was full of parts for making vehicles, plus a motor to bring them to life.

A wire connects the motorized block to a separate battery pack. Builders can either incorporate both into a single large vehicle (such as a tractor towing a trailer), or just use the motor block, leaving the battery pack as a cabled remote control that they can switch on and off at will.

• This set was first released in Europe. An identical version was released in the US a year later with set number 404.

• Interesting pieces include a winch, four nine-tooth gears, and 48 chain links for creating caterpillar tracks.

• Instructions for four builds are included with the set: a crane and truck, bulldozer, hovercraft, and quarry with crane (shown below).

∧ **MOTORING ALONG** The set features a yellow electric motor that is connected to the black battery pack.

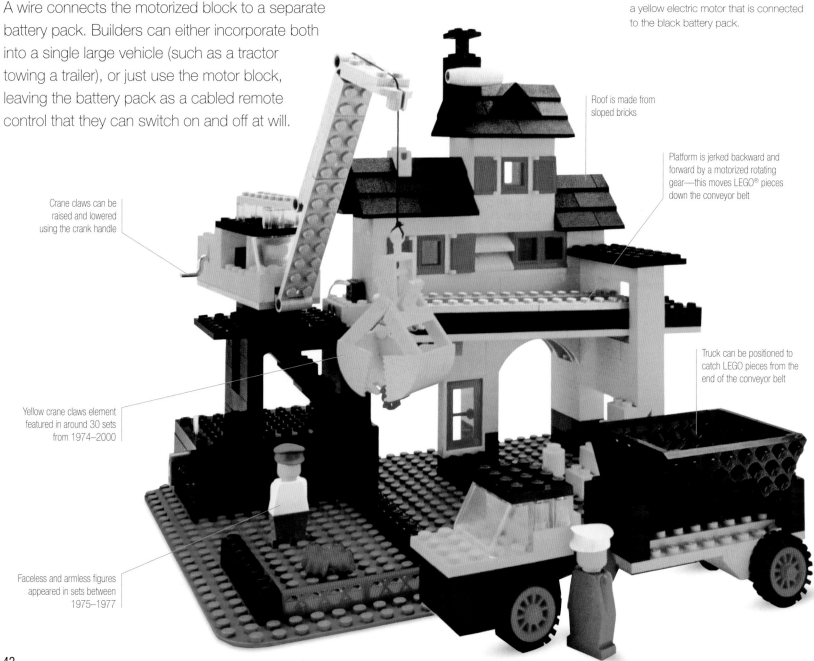

Crane claws can be raised and lowered using the crank handle

Yellow crane claws element featured in around 30 sets from 1974–2000

Faceless and armless figures appeared in sets between 1975–1977

Roof is made from sloped bricks

Platform is jerked backward and forward by a motorized rotating gear—this moves LEGO® pieces down the conveyor belt

Truck can be positioned to catch LEGO pieces from the end of the conveyor belt

INSPIRATIONAL MODELS Build ideas on the front, sides, and back of the box, as well as the inside of the box's lid, include a variety of cars, boats, trains, helicopters, planes, and farm buildings and vehicles.

"Basic sets have always been important to the LEGO Group. Starting with a pile of bricks is where your imagination comes to life."

Jette Orduna, Head of LEGO Idea House

Tractor

1977 • LEGO® Technical Set • #851 • Pieces: 318

By 1977, many experienced LEGO builders were looking for a bigger challenge in their building. Enter the LEGO® Technic set! Born as the Technical Set series in Europe and Expert Builder series in the US, these sets, such as Tractor (851), featured gears, axles, and beams that could be connected to create working mechanical functions.

With built-in rack-and-pinion steering, a spinning thresher, and a lever-activated mechanism for raising its farming tools off the ground, the Tractor is an impressively accurate model of the real thing. Its instructions include steps for adding a 4.5-volt motor, sold separately.

< **THRESHER** The primary model uses a thresher attachment. A sequence of gears rotate the yellow thresher blades as the tractor moves forward and backward.

24-tooth gear wheel can turn to control position of front wheels

Lever can lift and lower thresher at rear

Exhaust stack made from three 1x1 round bricks

Gray bushing piece and black cross-axle piece connect cutting element (gray gear) to the thresher frame

Car Chassis

1977 • LEGO® Technical Set • #853 • Pieces: 601

Containing more than 600 pieces, this detailed automobile interior is one serious "Technical Set." An expert hand and eye are needed to follow the complex instructions for combining the special parts into a steering system and a realistically moving engine block with rear-wheel drive.

Rotating the steering wheel turns the front tires, and rolling the model forward makes the four-cylinder engine start pumping. It even has a multi-speed transmission and adjustable seats. Once the chassis is complete, builders can make up a car body design of their own to go around it, and like the Tractor (851), it can be motorized or rebuilt into other vehicles.

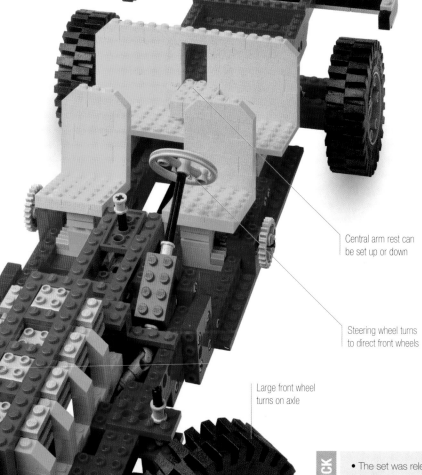

Central arm rest can be set up or down

Steering wheel turns to direct front wheels

Large front wheel turns on axle

Square piece that acts as a cylinder moves up and down as the car moves

Fender

"With LEGO Technic, you get to see how a vehicle works."

Markus Kossman, LEGO Technic Senior Designer

BRICK BY BRICK

- The set was released in the US in 1978 as set number 956.

- An accompanying ideas book shows pictures of a car body that fits onto the chassis. It is made from parts of Helicopter (852).

- The steering wheel piece was introduced in this year.

- The chassis has a three-gear manual gearbox. The shift stick moves back and forward.

Guided Tour

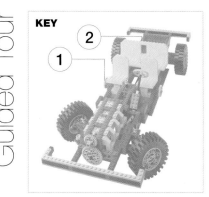

KEY
1
2

1

< **IN THE DRIVING SEAT** By turning a cog on either side of the chassis, the front seats can be moved forward and back. They even recline for a comfortable ride.

2

> **AT THE BACK** There is a space in the rear bench seat where the arm rest can be stowed. Behind the bench, it is possible to see how the wheel axle connects to the drive shaft.

Fire Station

1978 • LEGOLAND® Town • #374 • Pieces: 334 • Minifigures: 4

This year saw a turning point in the world of LEGO sets. Gone were the faceless mini-citizens of earlier LEGOLAND models. In their place came the first LEGO minifigures, with movable arms and legs and painted smiles. They lived in the three different worlds of the classic LEGO play themes, which included Town—the modern home of one busy Fire Station!

When the fire alarm rings, the new minifigure heroes are ready to blaze into action. Rolling out of the Fire Station's numbered garages in an emergency car and fire truck, the fearless firefighters carry tool elements in their clip-like hands. A fire ax, shovel, pickax, and even a set of air tanks help them to vanquish the flames.

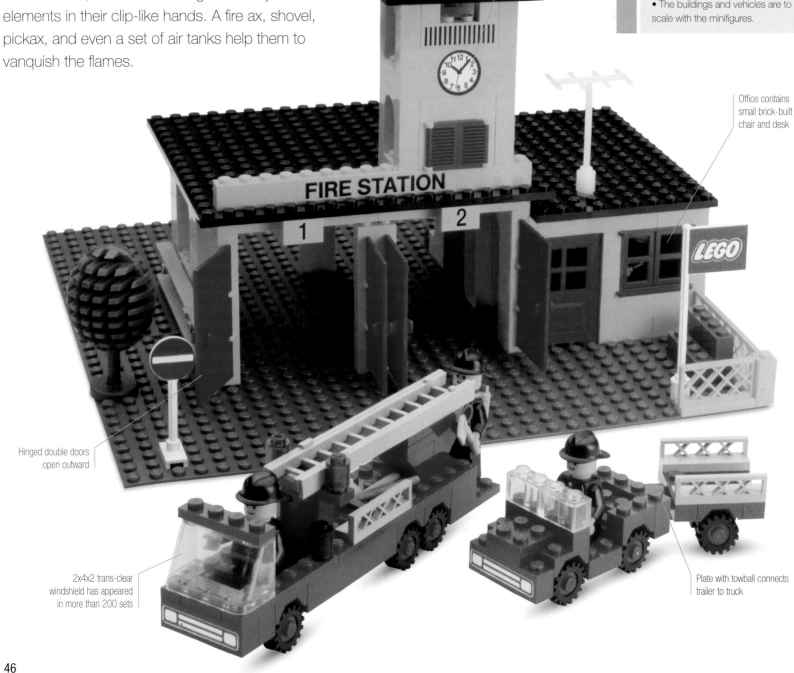

Clock face is a sticker

Office contains small brick-built chair and desk

FIRE STATION

Hinged double doors open outward

2x4x2 trans-clear windshield has appeared in more than 200 sets

Plate with towball connects trailer to truck

Police Car

1978 • LEGOLAND® Town • #600 • Pieces: 23 • Minifigures: 1

Just like today's LEGO® City, the original LEGOLAND Town sets were full of friendly and hard-working civic employees. This police officer may have resembled his blockier ancestors with the addition of a sticker for his uniform details, but now he could wave, walk about on patrol, and sit down. He could not, however, fit inside his tiny Police Car.

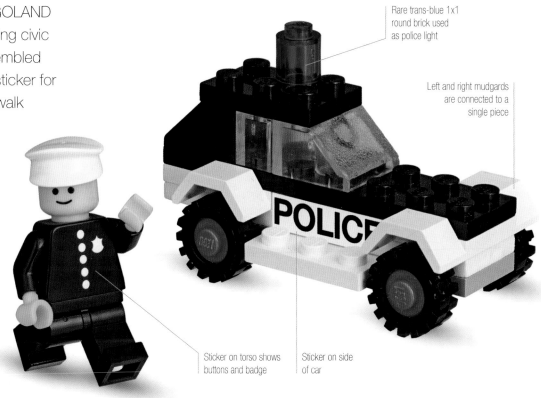

Rare trans-blue 1x1 round brick used as police light

Left and right mudgards are connected to a single piece

Sticker on torso shows buttons and badge

Sticker on side of car

BRICK BY BRICK

• This set was the first to feature a minifigure! Minifigures were created by LEGO designer Jens Nygård Knudsen and his team.

• This police minifigure also appeared in two other LEGOLAND Town sets: Police Boat (709) and Police Car (621) in 1978.

• The minifigure's white cap was introduced in 1975 and has appeared in around 170 sets since.

Ambulance

1978 • LEGOLAND Town • #606 • Pieces: 25 • Minifigures: 1

Hospital sets made a return appearance in the Town setting as well. Mini-sized vehicles like this Ambulance were a hallmark of the earliest play theme models. While they may not have had room for minifigure drivers, they were just the right size for carrying around in a pocket, or for building on the go.

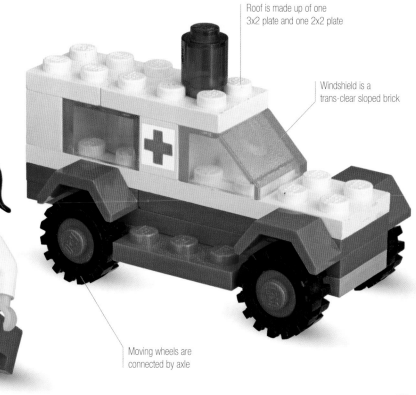

Roof is made up of one 3x2 plate and one 2x2 plate

Windshield is a trans-clear sloped brick

Black pigtail hairstyle first appeared in 1975

Moving wheels are connected by axle

BRICK BY BRICK

• This set featured the first female LEGO minifigure.

• The red crosses on the ambulance and minifigure are stickers.

• The female minifigure appeared in LEGOLAND Town Red Cross Car (623) in the same year.

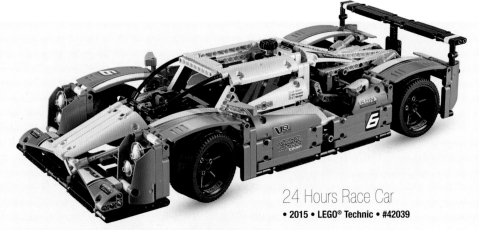

24 Hours Race Car
• 2015 • LEGO® Technic • #42039

Emma's Sports Car
• 2013 • LEGO® Friends • #41013

Family Car
• 1985 • LEGOLAND Town • #6633

Night Driver
• 2007 • LEGO Racers • #8132

IMAGINATION ON WHEELS

LEGO® cars through the years

All builders need are some wheels and a handful of bricks to create a rolling, racing LEGO car or truck model. LEGO autos have been around even longer than minifigures have—in fact, they've been around longer than LEGO bricks! Over the decades, they have included detailed LEGO Hobby Sets, pocket-sized LEGO Racers, complex LEGO Technic models with mechanical functions, cars with remote controls, cars with pull-back motors, and even authentic, large-scaled collector models of licensed real-world vehicles like the iconic Volkswagen Beetle.

Volkswagen Beetle
• 2008 • LEGO® Advanced Models • #10187

Race Car
• 2014 • LEGO® City • #60053

Super Street Sensation
• 1999 • LEGO Technic • #8448

1926 Renault
• 1975 • LEGO Hobby Sets • #391

Terrain Crusher
• 2007 • LEGO Racers • #8130

Car Chassis
• 1980 • LEGO Technical Set • #8860

4-Wheelin' Truck
• 1987 • LEGOLAND Town • #6641

Race Car Number 1
• 1989 • LEGOLAND Town • #1899

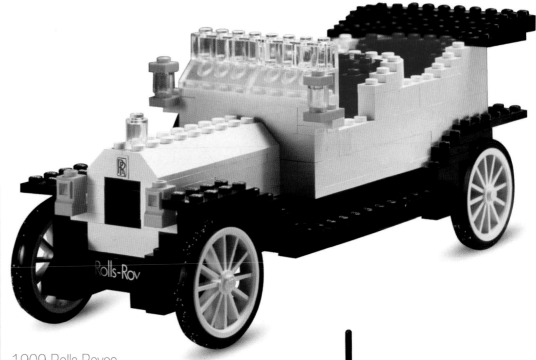

1909 Rolls Royce
• 1976 • LEGO Hobby Sets • #395

Red Go-Kart
• 2015 • LEGO Creator • #31030

Raceway Rider
• 2007 • LEGO Racers • #8131

Small Car
• 2010 • LEGO City • #3177

Roger Racoon with his Sports Car
• 1983 • LEGO FABULAND • #3626

1913 Cadillac
• 1975 • LEGO Hobby Sets • #390

Test Car
• 1988 • LEGO Technic • #8865

Castle

1978 • LEGOLAND® Castle • #375 • Pieces: 767 • Minifigures: 14

The next new LEGO setting to be introduced in 1978 took builders back to the olden days of kings, quests, and chivalry. In the Castle play theme—as represented by this famous and beloved set, nicknamed the "Yellow Castle"—the realm of medieval Europe made its return in living rooms, kitchens, and children's bedrooms all around the world.

The 1978 Castle set had everything a young squire or damsel could wish for: sturdy walls topped with realistic battlements, a tall tower keep, a crank-powered working drawbridge, and a whopping 14 knight minifigures, armored and ready for jousts, duels, and sieges.

Six classic window pieces create a paneled effect

Single stud gaps form crenels (or indentations) in the parapet

One of four brick-built horses

18-piece red drawbridge

BRICK BY BRICK

• The yellow Castle was the first of many minifigure-scaled castles in the Castle play theme. It had the most number of bricks for the price at the time of its release.

• There were no opponents in these early castle models because Godtfred Kirk Christiansen, the President of the LEGO Group at the time, and son of the founder, did not want a war theme in the sets.

• Daniel August Krantz, the set's designer, made the model yellow as there weren't many gray elements at the time. Godtfred Kirk Christiansen didn't like gray bricks because the designers would build tanks out of them!

• The brick-built horse was built in a way that breaks the LEGO Group's modern building rules, due to the way the 1x2 tile is wedged between four studs to form the horse's ears. The LEGO horse figure replaced the brick-built horse in 1984.

• The set was released in the US in 1981, with the set number 6075.

"We researched different types of castles, and built our own simplified versions of any design aspects that struck us."

Daniel August Krantz, LEGO Designer

Guided Tour

KEY

⋀ **KEEPING WATCH** A knight stands guard in one of the towers. His shield and breastplate feature his coat of arms. Each minifigure's breastplate has a sticker with one of four different coat of arms.

< **DRAWBRIDGE** A string piece threads through two holes at the top of the drawbridge. The loose end of the string is secured between two bricks, so that it is pulled taut when the handle is turned.

Crank handle can be turned to raise the drawbridge

OPENED UP

Gray plates serve as a platform for the minifigures to stand on while they defend the castle

Hinges allow the castle to open up for extra playability

Daniel August Krantz | Designer

Hailing from Colorado, USA, Daniel was the first ever international designer to be hired by the LEGO Group, in 1970. His first set was the Blue Windmill (362), and throughout his legendary career, he designed innumerable classics, including the Yellow Castle (375), Guarded Inn (6067), and Message Intercept Base (6987). At the start of his career, it was Daniel and two other designers, Niels Milan Pedersen and Jens Nygaard Nielsen, who designed almost all of the LEGO Group's sets. Daniel retired from the LEGO Group in 1999, but he still lives in Billund, Denmark—in a home filled with his incredible LEGO models.

Space Cruiser and Moonbase

1979 • LEGOLAND® Space • #928 • Pieces: 325 • Minifigures: 4

The last of the three original LEGO play themes, LEGOLAND Space let builders blast off to a universe of colorful minifigure astronauts and intergalactic exploration. Known as the Galaxy Explorer (497) in its US release, the Space Cruiser and Moonbase set showed many well-known features of classic LEGOLAND/LEGO Space: a triangular shape, a gray and blue color scheme, transparent yellow windows, radar dishes, antennas, and the iconic logo of a spaceship circling a moon.

The set includes two base plates, one with a circular landing pad and the other featuring molded crater details. Its crew of astronauts carry walkie-talkies and wear visor-less helmets, with the same air tanks as LEGOLAND Town firefighters. Red and white were the first spacesuit colors, with yellow, blue, and black added later.

Hinged trans-yellow plate opens to reveal the cockpit

Tile secures hinged rear section

Engine is mounted on either side of cruiser

One of five landing feet

LL 928

Guided Tour

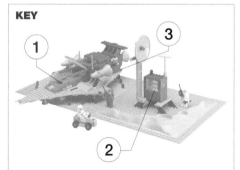

KEY

1
2
3

△ **COCKPIT DETAIL** Inside the cockpit are control panels printed onto two sloped bricks. There is a steering wheel for the pilot and enough space for another two crew members.

△ **CONTROL CENTER** Two printed sloped bricks make up the control panels and a trans-yellow-colored window piece allows a good view of operations on the moon's surface.

△ **SECRET STORE** At the rear of the cruiser is a hidden compartment. Hinged on either side, its double doors open and a ramp lowers to allow access for the moon buggy.

- The gray part of the cruiser is made up of three layers of plates, together with five landing feet and three rocket boosters.

- The set features five bricks printed with the classic LEGOLAND Space logo.

- The astronauts' helmets would often snap. A helmet with thicker chin guard was introduced in 1987—and it is still in use today!

- All four astronaut minifigures come equipped with air tanks.

- Both the European and US sets feature the European set number printed on bricks on the spaceship's sides.

- The molded moon base plate appeared in sets between 1979–1988, including 1979's Two Crater Plates (305), a supplementary base plate set.

Mini Space Cruiser

2015 • LEGO Space • #11910 • Pieces: 102

The LEGO Group created a micro-scale model of the Space Cruiser, which comes exclusively with the trade edition of this book. The original spaceship's features have been lovingly recreated, and include the classic color scheme, yellow cockpit, large engines, and even a miniature moon buggy.

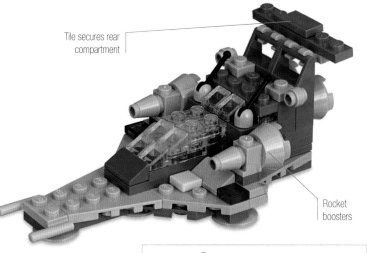

Tile secures rear compartment

Rocket boosters

∧ **CARGO HOLD** Just like the original model, the micro cruiser's two back doors can be opened and a mini moon buggy fits inside.

Walkie-talkie piece was new for 1979

Airplane tail fin piece is used as part of a platform for the control tower

"I wanted this set so much. I would go to my neighbor's house just to play with it. When I was asked to build a retro spaceship for THE LEGO® MOVIE™, I knew exactly which spaceship to base it on."

Raphaël Pierre Roger Pretesacque, LEGO Senior Designer

Police Headquarters

1979 • LEGOLAND® Town • #381 • Pieces: 372 • Minifigures: 4

Before long, sets with minifigures were the biggest little thing on the block. In this Police Headquarters set, the police uniforms were updated with painted torso details instead of stickers, and the vehicles all had space to fit drivers. With bright yellow and green details, its color scheme was a little unusual compared with later police sets.

Stand-out features of this model include lots of transparent colored pieces for lights, an emergency phone outside, see-through garage gates, a cleverly built lamppost on the corner, and a jail cell with a fancy latticed window—a barred window element wouldn't exist until as late as 1996!

Yellow door opens onto walkway

POLICE

Single 2x2 trans-clear brick makes a great streetlight

Guided Tour

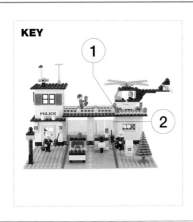

KEY

1

2

1

< **LANDING PAD**
The helicopter is guided toward the brick-built helipad. Three yellow 1x8 plates and four trans-blue 1x1 round bricks mark the landing area on the roof.

2

∧ **ON STANDBY** In front of the double-opening, rare clear doors stand two police vehicles. The convertible car can fit a driver and a passenger, and another cop can ride the motorcycle.

Helicopter blades are attached to rotating base

Tail rotor

POLICE

Jail cell has a yellow bench inside

Telephone is printed onto the brick

- This police officer minifigure with a badge and two zippers first appeared in this set.

- In the US, the set number was 588. It was released in the same year.

- The upstairs and downstairs rooms of the HQ both have desks with red telephones (printed red sloped bricks).

- The police car's steering wheel assembly was the first of its kind.

- The gray base plate with its flat printed road surface and studs was used in sets between 1978–1980.

1980s

With the LEGO® play themes in full swing in the 1980s, the next step was to make them even bigger and better. LEGOLAND® Town collections were enhanced by new airport, postal system, and hospital sets, while the LEGOLAND Castle and LEGOLAND Space themes presented named groups of knights and astronauts who could cooperate or compete as the builder preferred. Electronics added light, sound, and motion to the models, and things got even more exciting at the decade's end, when a surprising new play theme sailed into view!

Basic Set

1981 • LEGO® Basic • #333 • Pieces: 98 • Figures: 2

LEGO Basic sets were still going strong in the 1980s. In 1981, a new Basic figure was introduced in sets for younger builders aged 3 and up. With its hollow, one-piece body and a rotating head with non-removable hair, it looked a lot like a finger puppet. This Basic Set includes two such figures: a girl and a boy.

Like other Basic sets, this one includes lots of general-purpose pieces to supplement a young child's growing LEGO collection. Two pairs of wheels, a door, a window, and a tree can be built together with standard bricks to make houses, vehicles, and as many different creations as young builders could imagine.

BRICK BY BRICK

• The Basic set numbers are based on age markings, for example 333 for 3+, 555 for 5+, and 777 for 7+.

• The boy and girl figures each went on to appear in more than 20 sets.

• The green single-piece tree first appeared in 1978.

• This set came with suggestions for building models, including a dog, a boat, a truck, and a tortoise!

• The yellow 2x2 brick with eyes printing was new in 1981. It was also produced in red and white. It featured in more than 100 sets in all three colors between 1981 and 2002, but it is rarer in red and white.

19 bright-blue bricks come with this set

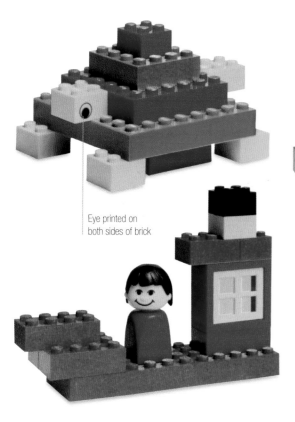

Eye printed on both sides of brick

Single 8x8 green brick can act as a base plate

"Basic sets provide inspiration for building on your own."

Jette Orduna, Head of LEGO Idea House

> BASIC FIGURE
The figures have cute sculpted noses and ears, and eyes and mouths that are printed in black. The hair piece comes in two designs.

Post Office

1982 • LEGOLAND® Town • #6362 • Pieces: 135 • Minifigures: 1

No town would be complete without a trusty post office to handle the mail! While not as common as police, firefighting, or construction, the postal service has made occasional appearances in LEGO Town and City sets over the years. The Post Office was the first of these, establishing the looped post horn logo that has decorated LEGO postal models ever since.

The Post Office is full of play options. The printed 1x2 "letter" tiles can be slid through the slots in the mailboxes for drop-off, and townspeople can pick up their packages from the shelves on the side. There's even a mail truck so the mailman can make his daily deliveries.

BRICK BY BRICK

- This was the first set to feature the 1x2 printed envelope tile. There are six in this set.

- The back of the set is open. The Post Office contains a desk and chair, table, and gated postal sorting area.

- The mail truck has an open back for storing packages and letters.

- The sticker sheet, with seven Post Office logo images and two sets of opening times, is exclusive to this set.

- The happy mailman minifigure appeared in a further five sets, including LEGOLAND® Town Mail Truck (6651) in the same year, and Steam Cargo Train Set (7722) from the LEGO® Trains theme in 1985.

> MAILMAN DEBUT Where else would the mailman make his debut but in his very own post office? The yellow, two-part opening mailbox was also introduced in 1982.

Large Post Office logo sticker covers three 1x4 bricks

Package sits on shelf, awaiting collection

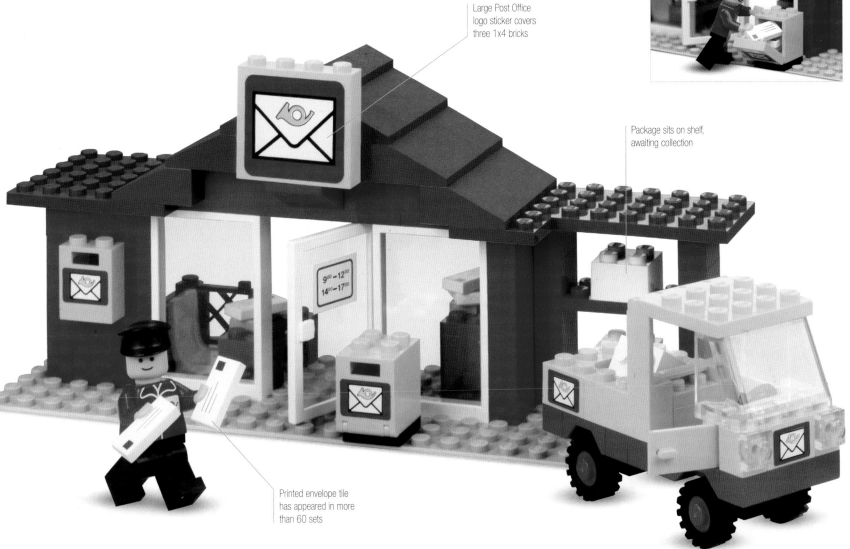

Printed envelope tile has appeared in more than 60 sets

Holiday Home

1983 • LEGOLAND® Town • #6374 • Pieces: 256 • Minifigures: 2

Where could you go for a nice weekend away when you lived in a LEGOLAND Town? If you were this minifigure couple, you'd drive out to the Holiday Home, a peaceful countryside cottage with a big front yard for getting lots of rest and relaxation. Built on a grass-green base plate with a printed stone walkway, it had all the comforts of a home away from home.

The Holiday Home has a grill for cookouts and a porch with a striped awning. The interior is furnished with a kitchen and stove, a dining room with a "glass" table, and a second-story bedroom with a small window for gazing at the stars at night.

BRICK BY BRICK

- The blue sloped brick with "74" printed on it is exclusive to this set. "74" makes up part of the set number.

- The chair piece was introduced in 1980 and it is still used in sets today.

- The base plate, with printed cobblestone driveway, also appeared in LEGOLAND Town Holiday Villa (6349) in 1988.

- The female minifigure is unique to this set. The male minifigure went on another adventure in Push-Along Passenger Steam Train (7715) in 1985.

- The six-paned, red kitchen door was new for this year.

- There is a bedroom upstairs, which includes a bed.

∧ **OUTSIDE DINING** The happy minifigure couple relax at the outdoor table. The patio awning behind them has a stripy detail made up of two stickers.

Rare cypress tree

Upper-floor bedroom window tilts open

Front part of the car's roof can lift up

Entrance light is made up of trans-clear and red 1x1 round bricks

Hamburger Stand

1983 • LEGOLAND® Town • #6683 • Pieces: 69 • Minifigures: 2

Minifigures need to eat, too... at least in our imaginations. Staffed by a friendly cook in a chef's hat, the Hamburger Stand is ready to serve up brick-built burgers and other tasty, plastic snacks to all the hungry customers who pass by. At closing time, owners can fold up the window shutters until it is time to re-open again the next morning.

While the burger stand has no name, the picture on the roof makes it clear what can be found inside. Blue pieces give the yellow walls an eye-catching trim, and a sticker on the door displays more snacks for sale. The cook even has a cash register to ring up his latest order.

BRICK BY BRICK

- The customer minifigure with the all-red outfit is exclusive to this set. Her zippered jacket torso piece first appeared in 1980.

- The rare, striped printed dish element that is used as a parasol first appeared in sets in 1982.

- Translucent doors are found on many LEGOLAND Town buildings, but this door's blue trim is unique to this set.

- There are two stickers in this set: the burger sign on the roof and the popsicle and cup pictures on the door.

- The burger sticker later appeared in LEGOLAND Airport (6399) in 1990.

- The inverted, sloped yellow bricks that make up the serving counter have appeared in more than 200 sets since they were introduced in 1976.

∧ **KA-CHING!** The printed sloped brick cash register was introduced in 1979. It was first used as a LEGOLAND Space computer panel, and it came in blue, light gray, and white.

Burger sticker covers two 1x4 bricks

Gray 1x1 tile makes a handy burger box

Chef minifigure can also be found selling popcorn in Main Street (6390), released in 1980

Galaxy Commander

1983 • LEGOLAND® Space • #6980 • Pieces: 427 • Minifigures: 5

The classic LEGOLAND Space armada got a new flagship when the Galaxy Commander was released in 1983. The biggest spacecraft model in the entire theme at the time, it was one of several classic LEGO spaceships with a blue and white color scheme instead of the usual blue and gray.

The mighty Galaxy Commander boasts twin cockpits, a detachable landing module in the back, and a pair of wheeled rovers for surveying the terrain of alien planets. All that and a landing pad, too! It even has an extra surprise: remove a pair of tiles, and you can unlock the landing module to deploy a laboratory station with a flip-up roof and radar dish.

BRICK BY BRICK

- The Galaxy Commander was also known as Starship "Explorer" in the UK, Space Command Ship in Canada, and Phase 3 Command Ship in Australia.

- The Galaxy Commander was the first LEGO spacecraft to feature two cockpits—each with its very own steering wheel!

- The set contains 56 transparent pieces, some of which are rare. The large quantity of transparent pieces was rare, too.

- Five astronaut minifigures (two white, two yellow, and one red) make up the spaceship's crew. The yellow minifigures were uncommon at the time.

- The rover with the hose element has a hinged door at the back that can be used for storage.

- The set came with ideas for alternative builds, including a landing base, refueling station, and a communications center, as well as other spacecraft and rovers.

REAR VIEW

Nozzle and hose elements on buggy are used for refueling

"I got it at Christmas the year it came out. It is still my favorite set because of the nostalgia. I thought it was awesome!"

Mark John Stafford, LEGO Senior Designer

Guided Tour

KEY

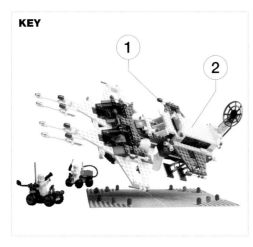

∧ **DETACHABLE MODULE** The back section of the spacecraft comes apart from the front. Remove two 2x1 gray tiles and push back the hinged blue sides to release the research lab.

∧ **RESEARCH LAB** The mobile laboratory has a hinged roof that lifts up to reveal a chair and two printed sloped bricks for computer screens. A walkie-talkie can be clipped to the wall.

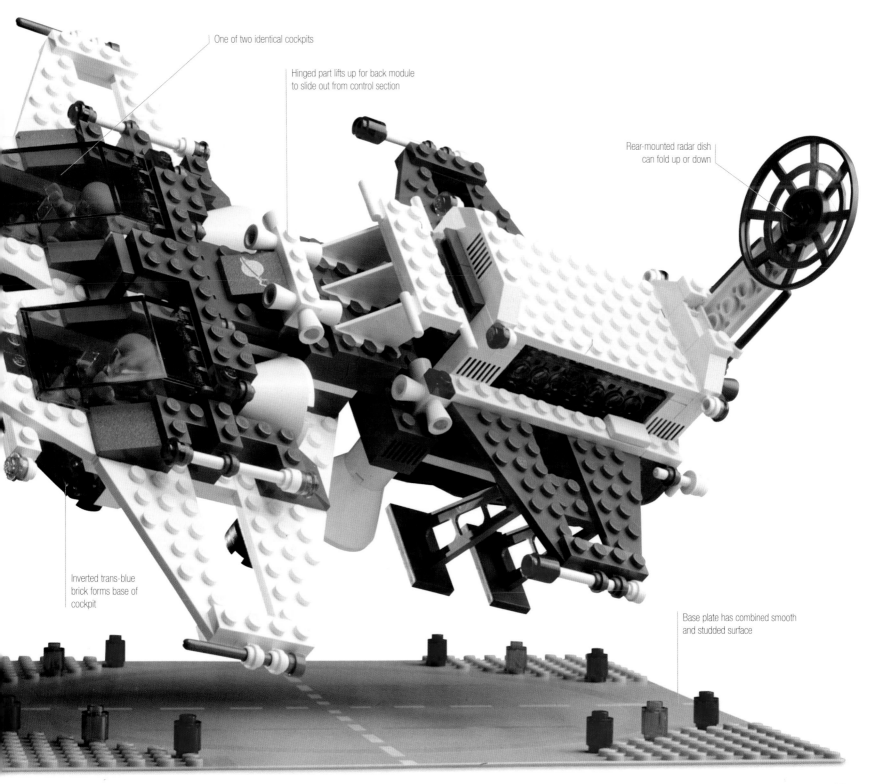

One of two identical cockpits

Hinged part lifts up for back module to slide out from control section

Rear-mounted radar dish can fold up or down

Inverted trans-blue brick forms base of cockpit

Base plate has combined smooth and studded surface

King's Castle

1984 • LEGOLAND® Castle • #6080 • Pieces: 687 • Minifigures: 12

The 1984 LEGOLAND Castle sets marked the debuts of several new factions of LEGO knights—one bearing lion-symbol shields and the other with crossed axes symbols on their shields. The castle's gray stone walls, well defended by a quartet of loyal archers, are hinged to swing open for inside play.

In addition to a working drawbridge and portcullis gate, the King's Castle has waving pennants, printed stone detailing, and a prison cell inside a tower. One thing that it doesn't include is an obvious king—there wouldn't be a royal minifigure with a crown until 1995.

Lance piece first appeared in 1978—it was new in dark gray for 1984

Shield printed with lion symbol

Drawbridge is made from two black plate pieces

• The string for the portcullis gate is tied to a looped brick, which can be placed on the castle wall or on the base plate to either raise or lower the gate.

• The horses all come with saddle pieces that fit into the groove in their backs.

• The castle was designed so that other castles could be attached to it, with pins, to make a huge castle.

• The large castle wall pieces (some printed with stone details) were created to make this set easier to assemble than 1978's Yellow Castle (375).

"We did everything in those days—I made all the decorations, the horses, the weapons…"

Niels Milan Pedersen, LEGO Designer

Guided Tour

KEY

1

2

1

∧ **NO ESCAPE** The dungeon under the rear right tower is just large enough to fit a couple of captured minifigures inside. A bar fits across the door to lock it.

2

∧ **ON GUARD** The castle swings open on its hinges. In the open position, the set forms a long wall for the minifigure soldiers to patrol.

Bow and arrow piece was new for this year

Waving pennant pieces were new for this year

New horse element with movable head and neck was introduced this year

Niels Milan Pedersen | Designer

A LEGO legend, Niels has worked for the LEGO Group since 1980, and has designed countless iconic sets across many themes, including LEGO Space, Castle, Pirates, and Adventurers, to name just a few. He sculpted many "firsts," such as the LEGO horse, monkey, crocodile, and skeleton. He originally designed the skeleton a decade before it appeared in a set, but was scolded at the time for creating a dead minifigure! He loved working on the castles, but Black Seas Barracuda (6285) is his favorite set, because he designed the pirates' detailed faces and new elements, including the monkey and the peg-leg.

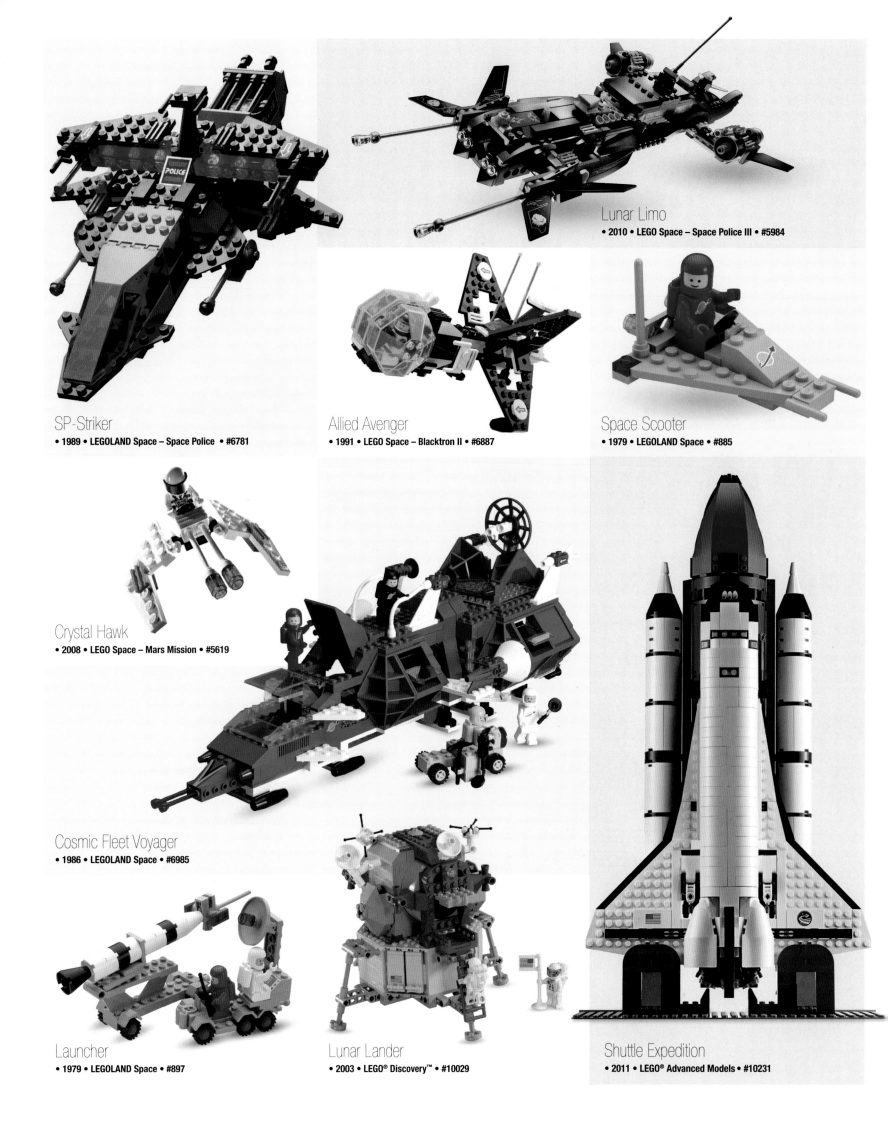

SP-Striker
- 1989 • LEGOLAND Space – Space Police • #6781

Lunar Limo
- 2010 • LEGO Space – Space Police III • #5984

Allied Avenger
- 1991 • LEGO Space – Blacktron II • #6887

Space Scooter
- 1979 • LEGOLAND Space • #885

Crystal Hawk
- 2008 • LEGO Space – Mars Mission • #5619

Cosmic Fleet Voyager
- 1986 • LEGOLAND Space • #6985

Launcher
- 1979 • LEGOLAND Space • #897

Lunar Lander
- 2003 • LEGO® Discovery™ • #10029

Shuttle Expedition
- 2011 • LEGO® Advanced Models • #10231

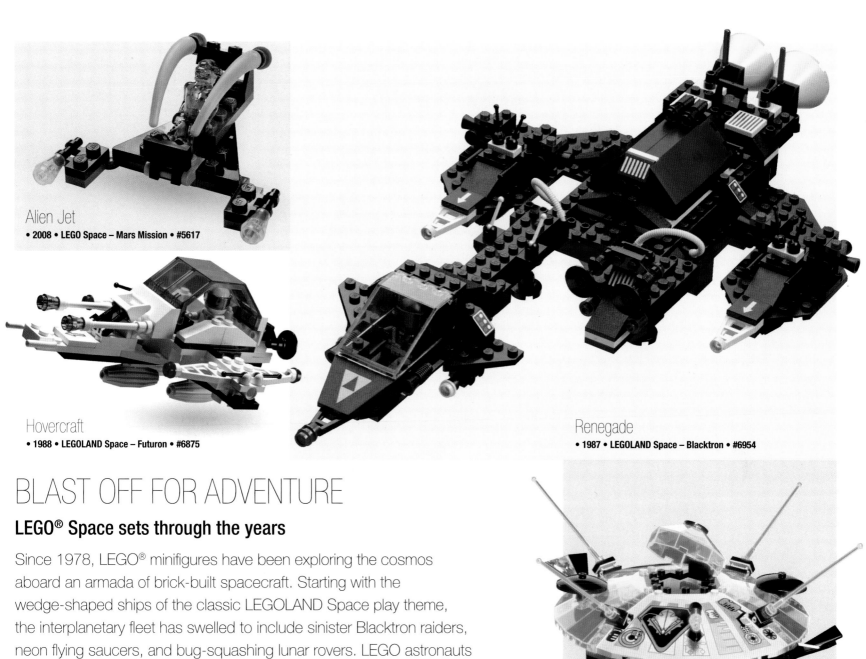

Alien Jet
• 2008 • LEGO Space – Mars Mission • #5617

Hovercraft
• 1988 • LEGOLAND Space – Futuron • #6875

Renegade
• 1987 • LEGOLAND Space – Blacktron • #6954

BLAST OFF FOR ADVENTURE

LEGO® Space sets through the years

Since 1978, LEGO® minifigures have been exploring the cosmos aboard an armada of brick-built spacecraft. Starting with the wedge-shaped ships of the classic LEGOLAND Space play theme, the interplanetary fleet has swelled to include sinister Blacktron raiders, neon flying saucers, and bug-squashing lunar rovers. LEGO astronauts have dug up extraterrestrial ice crystals with transparent orange chainsaws, battled aliens—or teamed up with them—and explored the frontiers of outer space in models that stretch from the familiar designs of real rockets to the furthest flights of science fiction.

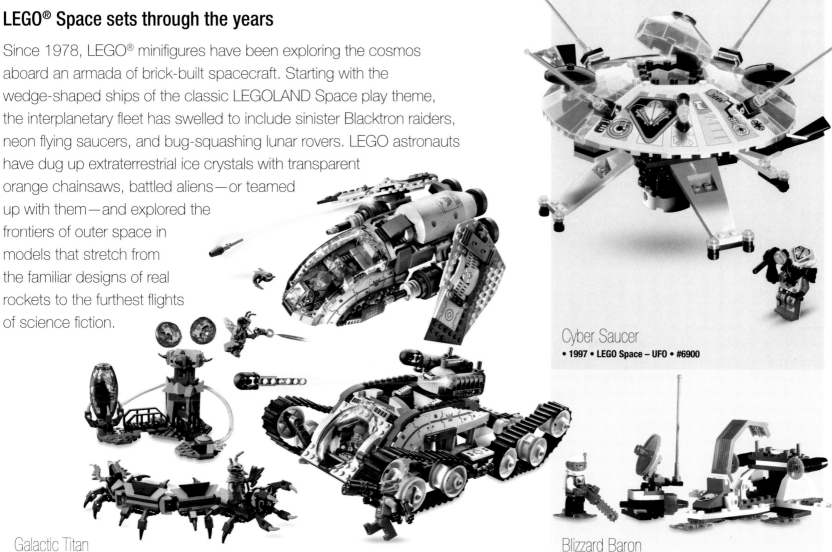

Cyber Saucer
• 1997 • LEGO Space – UFO • #6900

Galactic Titan
• 2013 • LEGO Space – Galaxy Squad • #70709

Blizzard Baron
• 1993 • LEGO Space – Ice Planet 2002 • #6879

Airport

1985 • LEGOLAND® Town • #6392 • Pieces: 533 • Minifigures: 8

The LEGOLAND Town play theme got its first airport in 1985. Finally, the citizens of LEGOLAND could travel to far-off places—or at least to other rooms in the house. Built on specially decorated runway base plates, the set includes a passenger plane, a helicopter, an airport building with a control tower, and a baggage cart for transporting luggage to and from the aircraft.

Builders can re-enact the entire 1980s airport experience, from buying a ticket to loading bags into the X-ray machine under the policeman's watchful eye. While passengers wait for their flight in the departure lounge, the air traffic controller up in the tower keeps everything running (and flying) smoothly.

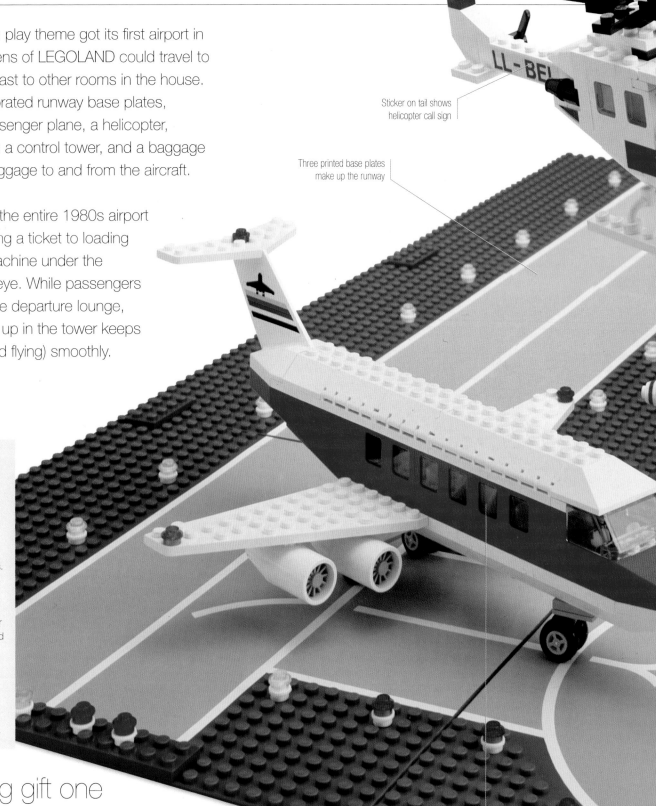

Sticker on tail shows helicopter call sign

Three printed base plates make up the runway

BRICK BY BRICK

• The planes in the LEGOLAND Town Airport subtheme usually came with two engines. This plane has four.

• The runway in this set is four studs narrower than runways in later airport sets.

• The male and female airport worker minifigures are unique to this set. Their co-worker, who wears a red cap, is in two other sets.

• The front wheel piece on the airplane is fixed to a turntable, letting it maneuver easily when on the ground.

Plane had space inside for four minifigure passengers and cargo

Heli-pad printed onto base plate

"It was my big gift one Christmas but I still asked for it again the following Christmas! My parents were scratching their heads."

Jamie Berard, LEGO Design Manager Specialist

The light-gray radar dish first appeared in LEGOLAND Space sets

Helicopter roof can swing up to fit the minifigure pilot inside

Guided Tour

KEY

1

2

3

4

> **CONTROL TOWER**
Three windshield pieces, which were new for this year, form the control tower. The controller minifigure's red seat has appeared in around 100 sets.

1

> **AIRPORT CAFÉ**
Below the control tower is a café with a table and enough space for two minifigures to sit down. Their red cups have featured in more than 150 sets.

2

3

∧ **SECURITY CHECKS** The security officer checks passengers' luggage in the X-ray machine, which features rare trans-blue panels. The suitcases are loaded onto the baggage cart on the other side.

4

∧ **AIRPLANE** The plane introduced new elements to builders, including the white and gray engine pieces. It features the striped LEGO Airport logo on its fin, which is also seen on the building and workers' torsos.

Mobile Police Truck

1985 • LEGOLAND® Town • #6450 • Pieces: 84 • Minifigures: 1

Town sets went electric in 1985. Together with a similar fire truck, the Mobile Police Truck was the first LEGO model to utilize the new "Light & Sound System." Powered by a 9-volt battery box, the police truck turned on its lights and played a siren noise when activated... making it quite popular among young builders, but a bit less so with their parents!

The set can be customized to match the police vehicles of the builder's home country. Turning the dial on top of the truck switches between two different siren sounds, and extra transparent bulb filters in blue, red, and yellow let builders change the colors of its glowing lights.

"It just blew my mind. To make simple plates and bricks come alive—even today, I still think this was the most imaginative use of electronics."

Jamie Berard, LEGO Design Manager Specialist

• The printed inn sign, depicting two goblets and some grapes, is exclusive to this set (and its Legends re-release: set number 10000).

• Although the barmaid minifigure with the red hennin headdress is unique to this set, the same minifigure appeared wearing a white hennin in LEGO Castle Maiden's Cart (6023) in the same year.

• In addition to the bow and arrows, other weapons in this set include a spear, lance, and battleax.

• The inn's wall can connect to other LEGOLAND Castle sets released at the time using a pin element.

Colored pennants attach to black antenna piece

Hinged cab roof lifts up

Round brick controls electric sound and light

Policeman minifigure has appeared in around 20 sets

• The police officer minifigure in this set first appeared in sets in 1979.

• Each road sign, made with a printed tile fitted to a 1x2 plate, can stand up.

• The set comes with a blue megaphone, red stop paddle, a walkie-talkie, and two white road barriers. These can attach to the side of the vehicle.

• The main body of the vehicle accommodates the battery. There is room for the two road signs behind it in the trunk.

• The minifigure can access the driver's cab through the side door, or via the hinged roof.

• The police sign on the side of the truck is a sticker.

Guarded Inn

1986 • LEGOLAND® Castle • #6067 • Pieces: 248 • Minifigures: 4

The Crusaders and the Black Falcons found common ground and hospitality at the Guarded Inn, one of the most famous classic Castle sets. Featuring an elegant medieval inn attached to a section of castle wall, this set is cherished for both its colorful design and its usefulness for civilian minifigures. It was re-released in 2001 as a LEGO Legends set.

While knights stand guard on the wall outside, the entire front of the inn swings open on hinges to provide access to the dining area, tended by a friendly maiden. The unique red and black timber frame wall pieces are exclusive to this set and its reissue.

Battlement is built into inn roof

Small side window is made from two yellow headlight bricks

Torso piece with printed necklace has appeared in around 20 sets since its debut in 1986

Guided Tour

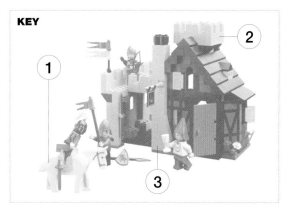

KEY

∧ **TRUSTY STEED** The white horse, which bears a Black Falcon knight, has a removable saddle element, which can be replaced with a white brick and plate to fill the gap.

∧ **LOOKOUT TOWER** With a quiver of arrows and a bow, a Crusader keeps a watchful eye from his lookout post. All the minifigures are exclusive to the set and its reissue.

∧ **THE INN WITHIN** The brick-built chimney is hinged so that the entire front of the inn can open out. The interior of the inn contains a table, two stools, and two goblets.

Monorail Transport System

1987 • LEGOLAND® Space • #6990 • Pieces: 715 • Minifigures: 5

LEGOLAND Space followed the lead of the Castle theme in 1987 in spinning off its first official teams. Futuron featured a group of planetary colonists whose vehicles retained the blue and white colors of some classic Space models. The astronauts of Futuron traveled in suitably futuristic style aboard the one set that every child wanted: the awesome electric Monorail Transport System.

The working monorail train has two cars, with a motor powered by a 9-volt battery in between. Controlled by two knobs on the track, it can automatically drive forward and back, or stop at a station to pick up cargo.

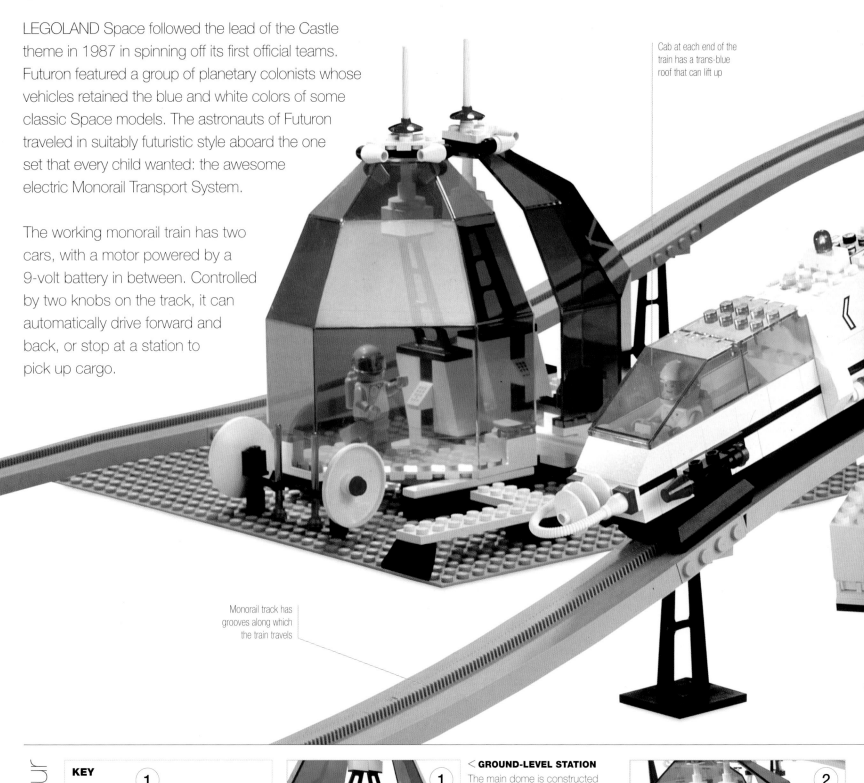

Cab at each end of the train has a trans-blue roof that can lift up

Monorail track has grooves along which the train travels

Guided Tour

KEY

1
2
3
4

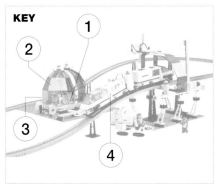

< GROUND-LEVEL STATION
The main dome is constructed from two futuristic-looking trans-blue quarter domes on a gray base plate. The dome pieces were new for this set.

> MOVING STATION Turning a gear piece moves the station's loading bay into position for sending and receiving cargo.

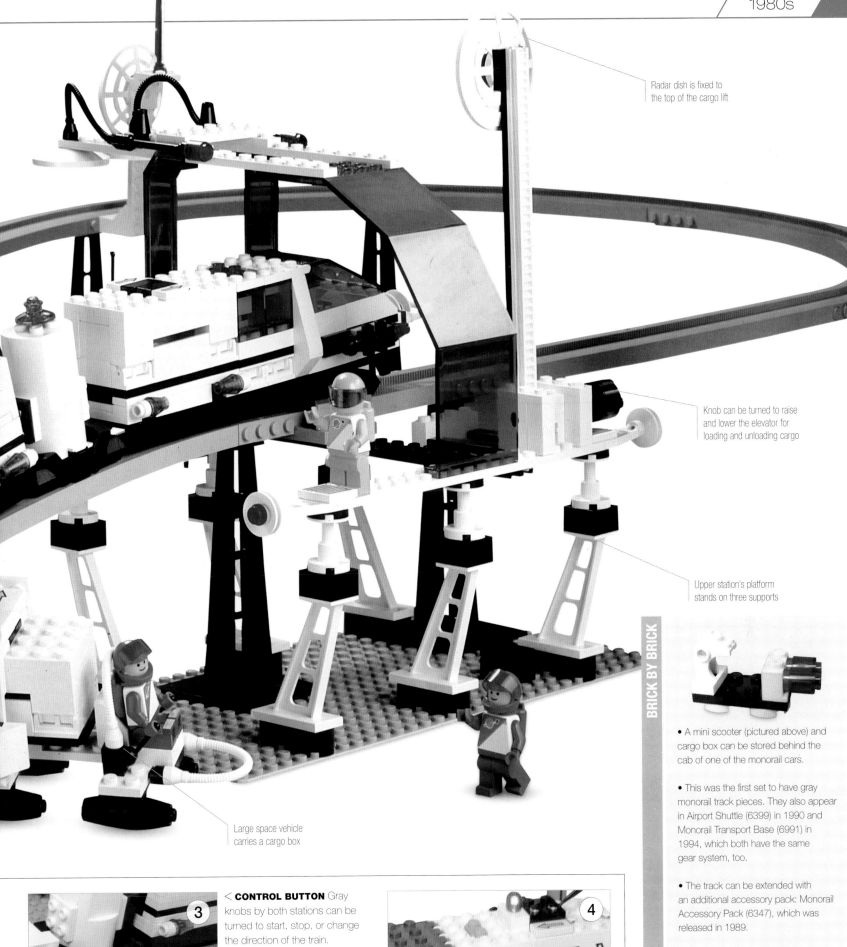

Radar dish is fixed to the top of the cargo lift

Knob can be turned to raise and lower the elevator for loading and unloading cargo

Upper station's platform stands on three supports

Large space vehicle carries a cargo box

BRICK BY BRICK

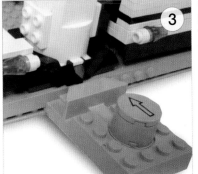

- A mini scooter (pictured above) and cargo box can be stored behind the cab of one of the monorail cars.

- This was the first set to have gray monorail track pieces. They also appear in Airport Shuttle (6399) in 1990 and Monorail Transport Base (6991) in 1994, which both have the same gear system, too.

- The track can be extended with an additional accessory pack: Monorail Accessory Pack (6347), which was released in 1989.

- The set includes an exclusive printed card backdrop that shows a star field over a grid.

- Two blue and three yellow astronaut minifigures appear in the set. They wear helmets with trans-blue visors, which were new for the Futuron subtheme.

③ **< CONTROL BUTTON** Gray knobs by both stations can be turned to start, stop, or change the direction of the train.

> BATTERY CAR The 9-volt battery is housed here—the red light lights up when the power is on. A short black cable takes power to the motor in the central connector car.

④ ⟨ 9V ⟩

Emergency Treatment Center

1987 • LEGOLAND® Town • #6380 • Pieces: 308 • Minifigures: 5

One of only a handful of doctor-themed sets released for LEGOLAND Town, 1987's Emergency Treatment Center included a modern hospital and an ambulance. Its angled architecture, big windows, and cast of minifigures make it easy to see how far things had come in the world of LEGO medical care since Hospital (363) in 1975.

Inside the Emergency Treatment Center are a reception office, an operating theater, and a recovery ward upstairs. To help the doctors in their work, the hospital has a water cooler, a swiveling light, an oxygen tank, and two stretchers with wheels that fold so that they can be placed inside the ambulance.

Transparent sticker with white stripes on window

Tree comes as a single piece

Stretcher with wheels can double up as a hospital bed

- All of the minifigures are exclusive to the set. The torso of the medic minifigure with the stethoscope appears in five other sets.

- The side-part hair piece was first introduced in 1979. It comes in different shades of brown, gray, black, yellow, orange, and tan.

- The green base plate with gray road pattern is featured in two other sets: LEGOLAND Town Space Shuttle (1682) in 1990, and Metro PD Station (6598) in 1996.

- The four window decals with white stripes and red cross patterns are exclusive to this set.

Radar dish piece is also
used as a trash
can lid in this set

Door of ambulance
can open for
easy access

Guided Tour

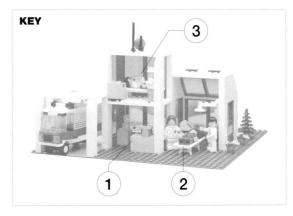

⋀ **WELCOMING RECEPTION** A minifigure sits at a desk with
a telephone and a cup. The water cooler is made up of a
transparent minifigure head piece fixed to a cup with a handle.

⋀ **OPERATING THEATER** With oxygen tanks at the ready,
a doctor prepares to operate. Above the patient is a swiveling
light. Behind the doctor, a computer monitors progress.

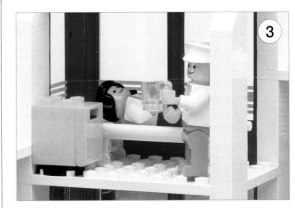

⋀ **RECOVERY WARD** Tended by a smiling hospital worker,
the minifigure patient recuperates in the upstairs ward.
There is an opening bedside cabinet for storing belongings.

Black Monarch's Castle

1988 • LEGOLAND® Castle • #6085 • Pieces: 665 • Minifigures: 12

A new challenger arrived in the land of LEGOLAND Castle in 1988. With their black stone fortresses and fearsome wyverns on their shields, the Black Knights were definitely a force to be reckoned with. The first of two castles for the group, the large Black Monarch's Castle had a foreboding appearance that must have intimidated any enemies who dared approach.

Like 1984's King's Castle (6080), the Black Monarch's Castle has walls that can swing out to the sides to create a wider fortification. Also like the earlier castle, it does not come with the king of the Black Knights himself... though a spookily glowing "Black Monarch's Ghost" would appear in a 1990 set.

Wheel turns to raise or lower the drawbridge

The sides of the castle can be opened up for greater playability

Single panel piece with gray stone pattern is unique to this set

Guided Tour

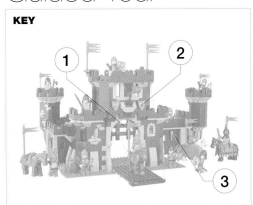

∧ **PLATED PORTCULLIS** The portcullis is made of 10 black plates and a special 3x2 plate with a hole at its apex for the string to pass through. A pulley system raises and lowers it.

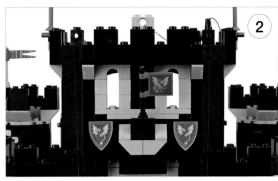

∧ **HERALDIC SIGNS** The flag and shields with a printed dragon made their debut in this set. They also appeared in LEGO Castle Sea Serpent (6057) and Black Knight's Castle (6086) in 1992.

∧ **CASTLE CELL** The rear jail features a latticed single-piece door that was new in dark gray for this set. It first featured in yellow in LEGO FABULAND's Police Station (3664) in 1984.

Castle jail

Castle is built on three green base plates

• The horses' red and blue barding with its dragon design made its debut in this set. It appeared in one other set: LEGOLAND Castle Black Knight's Castle (6086) in 1992.

• The castle has hinges and pins, allowing it to be connected to other sets, such as LEGOLAND Castle Knight's Stronghold (6059), released in 1990.

• Of the six different designs of minifigure knights in this set, five of them are unique to Black Monarch's Castle. The knight with black legs made his first appearance four years earlier, in LEGOLAND Castle Knight's Castle (6073).

The Mermaid Castle
• 2005 • LEGO BELVILLE • #5960

Dark Forest Fortress
• 1996 • LEGO Castle • #6079

Vladek's Dark Fortress
• 2005 • LEGO KNIGHTS' KINGDOM II • #8877

Wolfpack Tower
• 1992 • LEGO Castle • #6075

KING AND CASTLE

LEGO® castles through the years

There have been many castle and fortress sets since the LEGO® play themes began in 1978. Some look like historical medieval architecture, while others could have popped off the illustrated pages of a book of fairy tales. There are castles that are schools for wizards, and castles that are the undersea abodes of mermaids. They may be ruled by good monarchs, wicked tyrants, or the occasional vampire lord. And whether their strong walls and tall towers are made of stone, wood, or seashells… they're really all built from bricks!

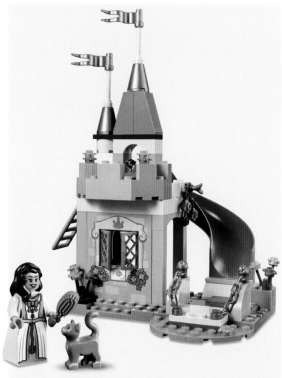

The Princess Play Castle
• 2014 • LEGO® Juniors • #10668

Trolls' Mountain Fortress
• 2009 • LEGO Castle • #7097

King's Castle
• 2013 • LEGO Castle • #70404

Kingdoms Joust
• 2012 • LEGO Castle • #10223

"When we design a castle,
we think about elements a real
castle contains—a drawbridge,
a tower, a prison…"

Bjarke Lykke Madsen, LEGO Design Master

Hogwarts Castle
• 2001 • LEGO® Harry Potter™ • #4709

Big Royal Castle
• 2014 • LEGO® DUPLO® • #10577

Vampyre Castle
• 2012 • LEGO Monster Fighters • #9468

Message Intercept Base

1988 • LEGOLAND® Space • #6987 • Pieces: 572 • Minifigures: 5

Launched in 1987, the Blacktron subtheme introduced the first group of bad guys into LEGOLAND Space (rivaling the Futuron good guys). Blasting through the cosmos in black spaceships with hints of yellow, the Blacktron fleet taught the galaxy to beware their "triangle-in-a-triangle" symbol. The 1988 Message Intercept Base gave the raiders somewhere to hang out between battles—and to spy on their fellow space explorers, too!

The roof-dome of the elevated base splits open with the help of LEGO® Technic parts, allowing the small spaceship to land inside. A tunnel leads to the nearby observation post, which slides back and forth at the turn of a yellow cone as its instruments home in on Futuron signals.

Yellow plates with clips form a storage rack for tools

Wings of the spaceship fold in, allowing it to fit into the hangar

Black support piece was later used as a part for grandstands in LEGO Sports sets

BRICK BY BRICK

• The opening-roof mechanism design first appeared a year earlier in Futuron Cosmic Laser Launcher (6953).

• The black panels that make up the sides of the hangar are printed with the Blacktron logo. They are unique to this set.

• The model includes various minifigure tools, such as a metal detector, radio, and megaphone.

• The black balloon tires on the space buggy have appeared in more than 40 LEGO sets between 1982 and 2004.

• Designers of LEGOLAND Space sets were not allowed to add weapons to their models as Godtfred Christiansen, then owner of the LEGO Group, did not want violent conflict in the sets. The designers added studs or other round pieces to weapon-like parts of their models to get around this restriction, aware that children would still see these parts as weapons.

Guided Tour

KEY

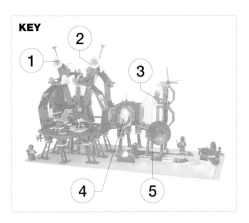

ROOF MECHANISM When a yellow cone piece on the side of the hangar is turned, the yellow rack piece slides up, pushing the hinged black plates up and outward, and opening the roof.

READY FOR ACTION With the roof open, the radar dishes are now on either side of the hangar, and there is room for the spaceship to blast off.

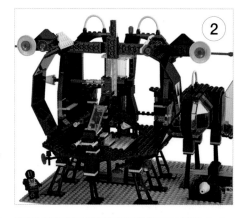

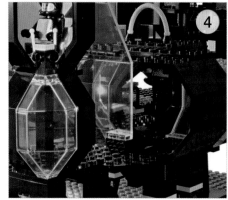

Quarter-dome piece is exclusive to this set in trans-yellow

CONTROL TOWER The elevated control desk of the observation center contains levers, printed tiles, and a swiveling chair.

SPACIOUS BASE Turning another yellow cone piece moves the control tower backward and forward along tracks, either connecting it to the main base or setting it apart.

SPACE TUNNEL The Blacktron minifigures can move from the hangar to the control tower via the connecting walkway. Two hinged trans-yellow pieces open up for access inside the tunnel.

Blacktron astronauts have black suits with opaque black visors, and gray printing on their torsos

Molded lunar base plate was last seen in this set

Amusement Park

1988 • LEGO® FABULAND™ • #3683 • Pieces: 95 • Figures: 4

The first LEGO theme to feature characters with individual names and stories, the LEGO FABULAND series of sets took place in a charming everyday world of walking, talking animals. Designed for younger builders, FABULAND models mixed standard LEGO pieces with larger, simpler elements for quick and easy assembly.

The Amusement Park is full of fun rides and activities for its cast of playful FABULAND figures. Freddy Fox, Lucy Lamb, Maximillian Mouse, and Clive Crocodile can spin on the merry-go-round, splash around in the rowboat, and take in the view from the top of the rotating Ferris wheel. They can even visit the gaming booth to win fabulous FABULAND prizes!

Merry-go-round roof is decorated using three stickers with a colored dot pattern

Prize booth displays 2x2 printed tile prizes

Dish printed with colored numbers sits on red turntable

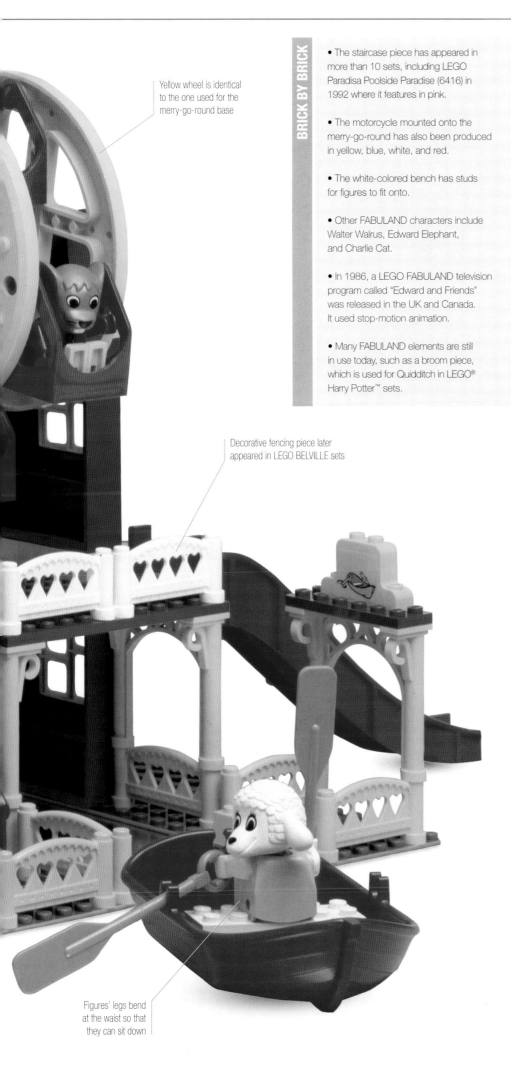

Yellow wheel is identical to the one used for the merry-go-round base

Decorative fencing piece later appeared in LEGO BELVILLE sets

Figures' legs bend at the waist so that they can sit down

• The staircase piece has appeared in more than 10 sets, including LEGO Paradisa Poolside Paradise (6416) in 1992 where it features in pink.

• The motorcycle mounted onto the merry-go-round has also been produced in yellow, blue, white, and red.

• The white-colored bench has studs for figures to fit onto.

• Other FABULAND characters include Walter Walrus, Edward Elephant, and Charlie Cat.

• In 1986, a LEGO FABULAND television program called "Edward and Friends" was released in the UK and Canada. It used stop-motion animation.

• Many FABULAND elements are still in use today, such as a broom piece, which is used for Quidditch in LEGO® Harry Potter™ sets.

Guided Tour

KEY

1
2
3

1

△ **FERRIS WHEEL** The wheel is driven by turning the axle. Small rods either side of each seat fit into holes in the wheels, enabling the seats to swing as the ride goes round. Wheee!

2

△ **ROWBOAT RIDE** Fun-seekers must line up beneath the yellow arch with the boat sticker for a turn on this river ride. The boat passes along the gap between the two base plates.

3

△ **WHEEL OF FORTUNE** In front of the merry-go-round is a roulette-style game. Players choose a number, spin the wheel, and if they win, they can claim a prize—a printed tile!

Black Seas Barracuda

1989 • LEGOLAND® Pirates • #6285 • Pieces: 865 • Minifigures: 8

Pirates! In 1989, the boisterous buccaneers hit the world of LEGO building in a big way. The scurvy scallywags who sailed aboard the Black Seas Barracuda and its fellow ocean-going sets were the first minifigures to have different facial features, including eyepatches, whiskers, and even lipstick for the lady swashbucklers.

Commanded by the hook-handed and peg-legged Captain Redbeard, the Black Seas Barracuda has a crew of seven, a brand-new monkey and parrot, and a half-a-minifigure figurehead on its prow. Its masts and fabric sails are designed to resemble those of real historical ships of the era.

"As a child, it was the set that you had to have. Everyone wanted the Black Seas Barracuda."

Michael Thomas Fuller, LEGO Design Manager

Striped pattern on sail is typical of many LEGO pirate ships, such as Shipwreck Island (6296) in 1996

Brick-yellow goblet has also appeared as part of a firehose in LEGOLAND Town

---

BRICK BY BRICK

• The monkey figure, with minifigure hands for clasping, first appeared in this set. It was sculpted by set designer Niels Milan Pedersen.

• The parrot figure also made its debut in this set.

• Almost all LEGO pirates wear their eye patches over the left eye. An exception includes a 1996 female pirate.

• Due to its popularity, this set was re-released 13 years later, in 2002, as a LEGO Legends set (10040).

• The ship's figurehead is made up of a rare brick-yellow minifigure torso with no printing, a female minifigure head, a red bandana, and a yellow goblet.

• The ship's five striped fabric sails are exclusive to this set and its 2002 re-release.

Jolly Roger printed flag piece warns others that this is a pirate ship

Overlapping plates can be a walkway for the pirate as he adjusts the rigging

The quarterdeck can lift up to reveal the captain's cabin below

Brown row boat comes as single piece and can be towed

Guided Tour

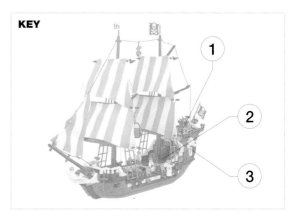

KEY

△ **HELM** On the tiered quarterdeck, a crew member steers the ship while another consults a printed map tile. Both the steering wheel and map were created for the LEGO Pirates theme.

△ **GUN DECK** Two pirates load the four cannons on the gun deck—these cannons were new for this set. There are 24 cannonballs (black 1x1 round bricks) in the set.

△ **CAPTAIN'S CABIN** The stern, with its latticed windows, folds down to reveal the cabin. Captain Redbeard admires his booty—gold colored coins, which first appeared in this theme.

1990s

More play themes arose to join the classics throughout the 1990s, as LEGO® sets sent builders back to the Wild West and to a world deep beneath the ocean waves. New sets and themes sought to catch the imaginations of creative girls, and advanced builders were introduced to a world of robotic models that they could program and bring to life themselves. And one of the biggest LEGO themes of all time made its appearance at last, sweeping fans young and old off to a famous galaxy far, far away.

Mega Core Magnetizer

1990 • LEGO® Space • #6989 • Pieces: 503 • Minifigures: 3

In 1990, magnets were an exciting new attraction for LEGO Space sets—which, like the other play themes, dropped the "LEGOLAND" branding from their boxes that year. The red, black, and trans-neon green vehicles of M:Tron incorporated magnetic pieces to attach and transport small vehicles and containers. The largest set in the line was the Mega Core Magnetizer, a giant six-wheeled vehicle that served as the M:Tron team's mobile base. From 1991, they faced off against some updated enemies in the shape of Blacktron Future Generation.

A magnet at the end of the Mega Core Magnetizer's gear-extended crane lets it pick up its equipment, cargo pods, a pair of space buggies, and a mini-flyer, all of which can be stored in the model's compartments. Many of the set's parts feature elaborately detailed printed decorations.

BRICK BY BRICK

- This is the only set to feature the quarter-dome piece, which forms the huge windshield, in trans-neon green.

- The model has a hinge under the black dish, two hinges connecting the main part of the vehicle to the back, two under the crane's base, and one for the rear hatch.

- The hinged, printed panel that forms the radar dish at the vehicle's rear was new for 1990. It last appeared in 2004's LEGO City Airport (10159).

- The three minifigure astronauts all have matching M:Tron uniforms, as well as identical smiley faces.

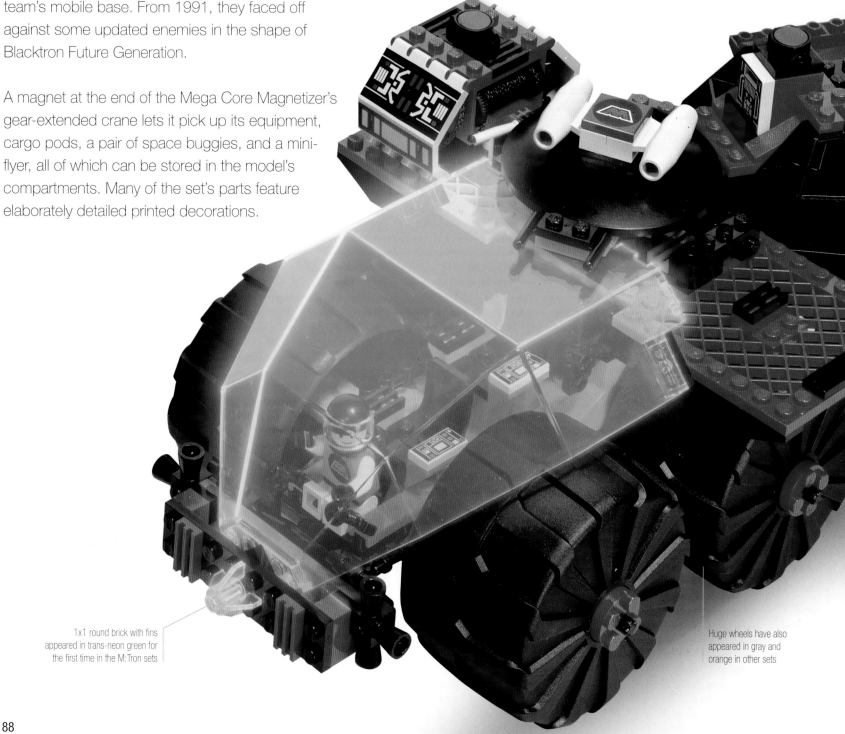

1x1 round brick with fins appeared in trans-neon green for the first time in the M:Tron sets

Huge wheels have also appeared in gray and orange in other sets

Knob for lengthening
and shortening the crane

"Jet-powered," one-seater
mini-flyer allows one minifigure to
blast off on a solo scouting mission

Magnet for picking
up containers and
smaller vehicles

One of two space
buggies that can be
stored on either side
of the Magnetizer

Space buggy has a
swiveling magnet so it can
be picked up by the crane

Guided Tour

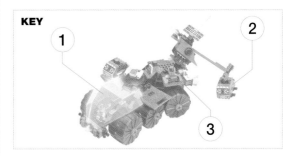

KEY

1

2

3

1

∧ **BUCKLE UP** The three minifigure astronauts sit one behind
the other in the cockpit. The neon windshield clips securely
into place when it's time to roll.

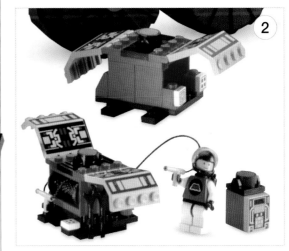

2

∧ **CONTAINERS** The storage containers have magnets on
top and detailed printed lids. The minifigures store wrenches,
hammers, and hoses in the large containers.

3

∧ **CARGO BAY** The mini-flyer fits snugly into the cargo bay at
the rear of the Magnetizer. The supervising minifigure keeps in
touch with the rest of the crew using a walkie-talkie.

Airport Shuttle

1990 • LEGO® Town • #6399 • Pieces: 767 • Minifigures: 9

Utilizing the same motorized technology as 1987's Monorail Transport System (6990) from LEGOLAND Space, the Airport Shuttle brought monorails back to the modern day with a speedy five-passenger transit vehicle for the Town play theme. An accessory set released the following year included the first LEGO monorail switch-track elements, letting builders create even more complex branching layouts.

The Airport Shuttle set has two stations, each with a ticket scanner, a monorail map, and an airplane departure schedule. One of the stations features a snack kiosk with the same burger logo as 1983's Hamburger Stand (6683), so that travelers can grab a quick bite before their trip.

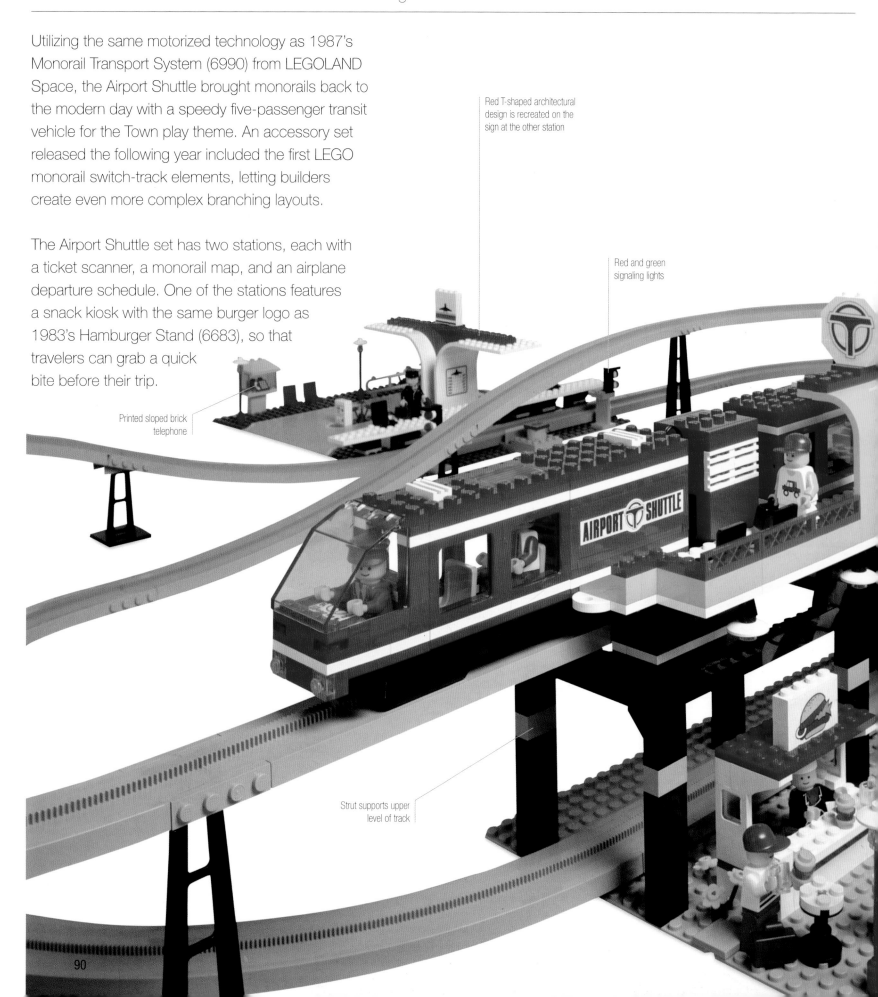

Red T-shaped architectural design is recreated on the sign at the other station

Red and green signaling lights

Printed sloped brick telephone

Strut supports upper level of track

OVERHEAD VIEW

9-volt battery is stored
in the passenger carriage

Airport station

Monorail station

Guided Tour

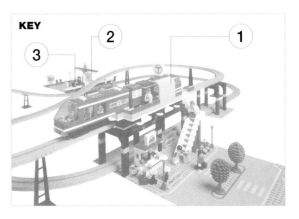

KEY

3   2   1

7725 8
7755 2
7720 . . . .
7815 . . . .
7819 . . . .
7821 . . . .

• The numbers on the flight departures
stickers refer to LEGO train sets from
the 1980s, such as 7725—1981's
Electric Passenger Train.

• Of the nine minifigures, six are unique
to this set. The pilot, shuttle driver,
and minifigure with airplane logo on his
torso have all appeared in other sets.

• The shuttle's motor sits between
the two passenger carriages.

• This is the only monorail set created
for LEGO Town. The two other monorail
sets belong to the LEGOLAND/LEGO
Space theme: 1987's Monorail
Transport System (6990) and 1994's
Monorail Transport Base (6991).

• The base plate with crosswalk
printing, which supports the staircase,
is exclusive to this set.

∧ **MONORAIL STATION** All aboard! The pilot and other
minifigure passengers wait to board the shuttle train.
The station's curved panels are unique to this set in yellow.

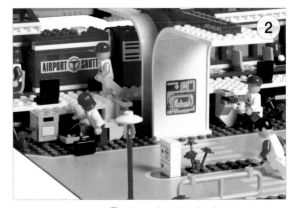

∧ **AIRPORT STATION** The busy airport station has two
yellow and gray ticket punches and two yellow and gray
lockers for storing luggage.

∧ **SAFETY FIRST!** With a crosswalk and the help of a map
and two sign stickers, jetlagged minifigures can navigate
their way to and from the airport safely.

Breezeway Café

1990 • LEGO® Town • #6376 • Pieces: 183 • Minifigures: 5

A new decade brought a four-star dining establishment to LEGO Town's minifigure citizens—and to LEGO fans, too! The stickers on the café's curved windows provide a hint at the style of cuisine served inside, and indeed, the set was also released under the name "Ristorante Italiano" in some countries.

LEGO fans loved this set so much that it was re-released 12 years later, and it's not hard to see why. The airy and charming café atmosphere is made even more romantic by a flower bed, a second-story balcony with a palm tree, and a colorful parrot.

• Breezeway Café was re-released as a LEGO Legends model (10037) under the same name in 2002.

• This set was the first to feature the formal waiter, dressed in black vest and tie. A variant of the minifigure, sporting a mustache, appears in four sets in LEGO Paradisa, beginning with Poolside Paradise (6416) in 1992.

• Main Street (6390), released in 1980, has an earlier version of the chef—he has black hips and legs instead of white.

• The red and yellow faucet pieces act as ketchup and mustard dispensers.

• The fence piece that forms the balcony was first introduced in 1967—in red and white.

> IN THE KITCHEN
Carrying a glass and tray, the waiter heads behind the counter to place an order with the chef. The kitchen is equipped with a stove, grill, skillet, and pot.

Diners sit on the balcony behind rare curved trans-clear panels with exclusive decorative stickers

Tropical palm is made from 12 pieces, including six sections of trunk and four large palm leaves

Lights (trans-red and yellow 1x1 round plates) decorate the underside of the arbor

Pair of lights mark the café entrance—each light is made up of three 1x1 trans-yellow plates

Metro Station

1991 • LEGO® Trains • #4554 • Pieces: 612 • Minifigures: 8

LEGO Trains returned in a major way in 1991. Now operating on a 9-volt electric system, instead of the 4.5-volt and 12-volt systems that preceded it, the new LEGO Trains ran on dark-gray tracks with metal rails that conducted power to their built-in motors. They all made stops at the Metro Station, a classic yellow depot on a trackside platform.

A favorite among the small number of LEGO Train stations, the Metro Station has indoor and outdoor waiting areas, a luggage-hauling vehicle, ticket and snack booth windows, a phone booth, a mailbox, and lamp posts to keep the edge of the platform safe at night. All builders needed to do was add a train!

BRICK BY BRICK

- The set comes with eight suitcases—one in black, three in white, and four in brown.

- The railway employee's white signal paddle first appeared in LEGOLAND Town Police Station (6384) in 1983.

- The trolley wheels piece used for the handcart also forms part of a skateboard in other sets.

- In 1996, the LEGO Group released a similar set called Train Station (2150). It has different minifigures and a few other differences: the building is red, not yellow; the handcart is yellow; and the fences are black.

Guided Tour

KEY

1

2

∧ **STATION OFFICE** One employee consults the printed screens on his computers while the other sorts through the shiny coins in the petty cash case.

∧ **BOOTH WINDOWS** The snack booth chef has appeared in seven other sets. The railroad employee in the adjoining ticket booth is exclusive to this set.

Round tile with printed clock pattern first appeared in Railway Station (7824) in 1983

Lamp post is topped with a round 2x2 trans-yellow brick and a white 4x4 radar dish piece

Red handcart frame and trolley wheels first appeared this year

Sign displays sticker with train schedule

Black Knight's Castle

1992 • LEGO® Castle • #6086 • Pieces: 569 • Minifigures: 12

Who needs just one castle when you can have two? In 1992, the Black Knights got their second fortress home in the Black Knight's Castle, which shared the imposing color scheme of 1985's Black Monarch's Castle (6085), but was built on an elevated base.

The Black Knight's Castle has not only a drawbridge in front (protecting LEGO Castle's first single-piece portcullis gate), but also a small fold-down ramp at the back for making sneaky escapes. It includes a glow-in-the-dark ghost behind a hidden tower door, and a captured member of the Wolfpack renegades in the dungeon.

- In the US and Canada, this set was originally named "Dungeon Master's Castle," but in 1994 it was changed to Black Knight's Castle in line with the UK.

- In the tower at the rear, there is a brick-built door that can be opened to reveal the resident ghost.

- Of the nine Black Knight minifigure designs featured, eight are unique to this set.

- The molded base plate, with its printed rock pattern also appeared in LEGO Castle King's Mountain Fortress (6081) in 1990.

- From 1992, when this set was released, set packaging carried a new LEGO System logo that would remain on boxes until the end of the decade.

Single panel piece with stone pattern printed around window

Knight's dragon plume piece was new in 1992

Guided Tour

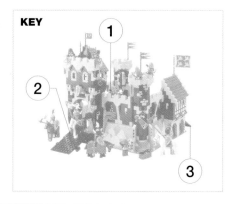

KEY

① ② ③

∧ **DUNGEON** The base plate is molded to create a well and dungeon. The dungeon, with hinged, lattice hatch, is a great place for holding Wolfpack captives.

< **DRAWBRIDGE** The drawbridge can be operated by turning the crank wheel at the side of the entrance. The portcullis piece is lowered using a pulley system.

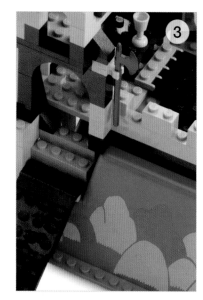

> **REAR BRIDGE** At the back of the castle, the knights can make a quick getaway by lowering a hinged bridge. Quick! A Wolfpack bandit is on his way!

94

"From the right angle, there is an amazing profile of the gate, corner tower, and wooden house."

Bjarke Lykke Madsen, LEGO Design Master

Glow-in-the-dark ghost minifigure has appeared in seven LEGO Castle sets

Printed flag design is unique to this set

Hinged roof can open to reveal secret storage area

Rare timber pattern gives the effect of a medieval tavern

Air Tech Claw Rig

1992 • LEGO® Technic • #8868 • Pieces: 954

In the years since the first Expert Builder models of the 1970s, LEGO technical sets became ever more complex. Now officially called LEGO Technic, they were built largely out of studded beams and connectors, incorporating fewer traditional bricks. In 1992, the motorized Air Tech Claw Rig was a giant among LEGO vehicles, but what really made it stand out was its working pneumatic system, powered by a 9-volt motor and compressor.

In this detailed set, air is pushed through a complex series of flexible tubes and pistons to operate the rig's multi-jointed crane and gripper claw arm. Other mechanical functions control the steering and the movement of the V6 engine and fan.

> "We live by innovation. We try to innovate all the time."

Markus Kossman, LEGO Technic Senior Designer

Twisting this knob steers the front wheels

Three-blade piece rotates as a fan

Sticker beside switch indicates movement of crane arm

- The dimensions of the claw rig are: 58in (147cm) x 16in (40cm) x 24in (60cm).

- The set comes with around 14ft (4.2m) of pneumatic tubing.

- The small, yellow pneumatic cylinder and pump were new in 1992. They also appeared in Pneumatic Excavator (8837).

- The rig is compatible with the large LEGO Technic figures. They can sit on any of the three red seats.

- This was the last set to feature the old-style 0.8x1.2in (20x30mm) tires. It was also the only set to contain six of them.

- The sticker sheet, with its four sets of graphical instructions, is unique to this set.

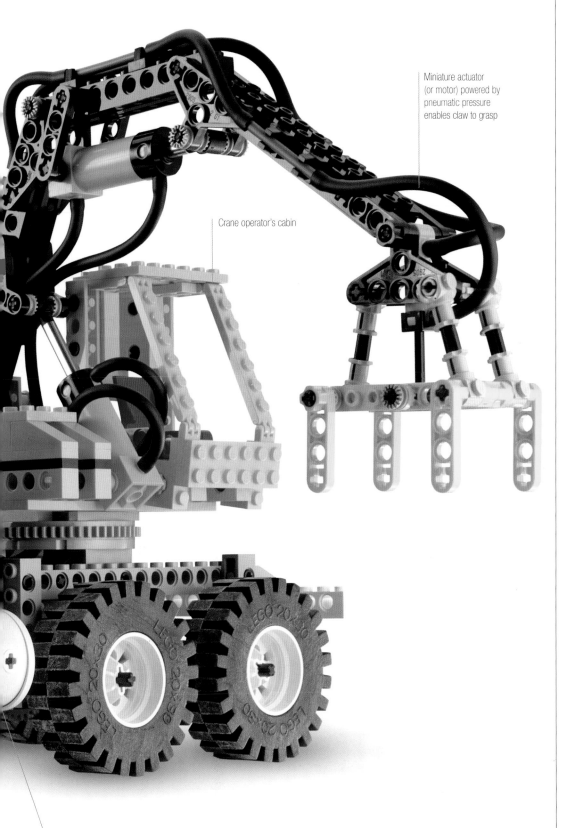

Miniature actuator (or motor) powered by pneumatic pressure enables claw to grasp

Crane operator's cabin

Fuel tank made from cylinder pieces, which are exclusive to this set in white

Guided Tour

KEY

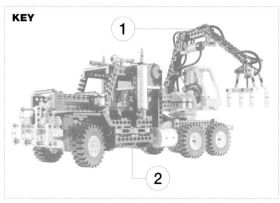

∧ **PNEUMATIC POWER** The pneumatically driven turntable element enables the crane to move through 180 degrees. Yellow pumps are used to extend the boom and jib.

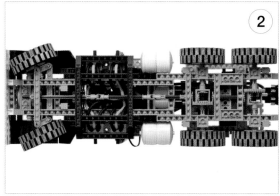

∧ **UNDERNEATH** The two sets of rear wheels have differential gears, which enable the wheels to turn at different angles. They are also used to drive the engine and fan via a long drive shaft.

∧ **ALTERNATIVE BUILD** With its battery box on top, the Claw Rig can be rebuilt into a material handler truck that picks up objects and drops them into its rear bucket.

"It's the simplest functions that the younger children love: opening and closing windows, or having a little box to put pieces inside."

Elisabeth Kahl-Backes, LEGO Design Manager

My First Police Set
- 2014 • LEGO DUPLO • #10546

Delivery Van
- 1980 • LEGO DUPLO • #2623

Musical Apple
- 2000 • LEGO Baby • #2503

Fun with LEGO Duplo Bricks
- 2009 • LEGO DUPLO • #5486

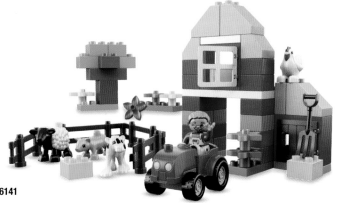

My First Farm
- 2012 • LEGO DUPLO • #6141

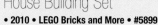

Tanker Truck
- 2003 • LEGO 4+ • #4654

House Building Set
- 2010 • LEGO Bricks and More • #5899

Garbage Truck
- 2005 • LEGO DUPLO • #4659

Elisabeth Kahl-Backes | Design Manager

Elisabeth is the creative lead for the LEGO DUPLO My First and licensed themes, but she has also worked on LEGO DUPLO Town (including Castle). A parent herself, she believes in the importance of her sets acting as a learning tool as well as a playful toy, and providing opportunities for interaction between parent and child. Elisabeth says the key to designing sets for young children is to figure out the icons that make a model instantly recognizable as, for example, a castle or a train, and then create them with a simplistic design. She says, "Often, children's drawings show you how simple it can be".

Ricky Racoon on his Scooter
• 1979 • LEGO FABULAND • #324

Pirate Building set
• 2009 • LEGO Creative Building • #6192

My First QUATRO Figure Set
• 2006 • LEGO QUATRO • #5470

Freight Train Set
• 1983 • LEGO DUPLO • #2700

SMALL HANDS, BIG IMAGINATIONS

LEGO® sets for younger builders through the years

Since 1969, LEGO® DUPLO® sets have inspired early creativity with their big, toddler-safe bricks and simpler building style. Over the years, LEGO DUPLO has been joined by other themes for young builders, including LEGO DUPLO PRIMO, LEGO QUATRO, and LEGO Baby for preschoolers, and LEGO FABULAND and LEGO 4+ to bridge the gap between LEGO DUPLO and standard LEGO System sets. More recently, LEGO Juniors sets (previously Bricks and More) have offered easy builds using classic pieces and minifigures as an introduction for builders aged 4–7 to the construction concepts of more advanced sets.

Big City Zoo
• 2009 • LEGO DUPLO • #5635

Supermarket Suitcase
• 2015 • LEGO Juniors • #10684

My First Plane
• 1999 • LEGO Primo • #2071

Bus
• 2009 • LEGO DUPLO • #5636

Poolside Paradise

1992 • LEGO® Paradisa• #6416 • Pieces: 229 • Minifigures: 4

The LEGO Paradisa theme ran from 1992 to 1997 and was set on a tropical island full of beaches, horseback riding, and sailing trips. Paradisa sets may have been designed to appeal especially to girls, but LEGO fans of all kinds celebrated their new and rare brick colors and minifigure parts. Poolside Paradise is one of the island's many vacation destinations, offering a tranquil spot to relax in the sun.

The palatial set is the only one to include this base plate with its molded swimming pool. Along with a shady tree, it has an indoor viewing area, a waiter to serve drinks to the guests, and a small mailbox for sending letters back home. Who would ever want to leave?

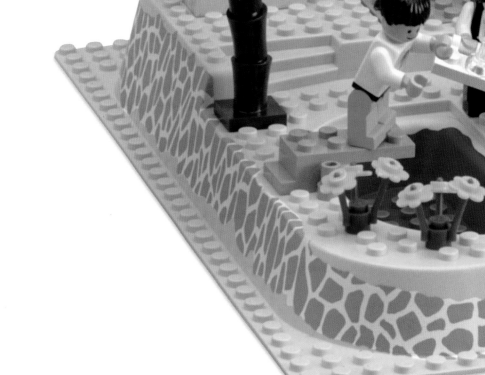

Palm tree trunk
is made of six
dark-brown pieces

Two rare convex, transparent panels provide a great view for diners inside

"Paradisa had so many cool colors and bricks... I went shopping in secret to buy these sets!"

Jamie Berard, LEGO Design Manager Specialist

Steps are molded into the base plate

Open-top sports car with trans-light blue windshield—cool!

Printed crazy paving drive

Printed blue pool water

Guided Tour

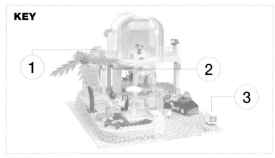

1 2 3

1

∧ **STAIRWAY TO PARADISE** The staircase piece was first introduced in 1987, but this was the first time it appeared in pink. Two male and two female minifigures come with the set.

2

∧ **WHAT'S COOKING?** In the kitchen at the back of the house, the waiter uses the coffee machine and frying pan. The cupboard door and drawers can open and close.

3

∧ **POST FROM PARADISE** The little mailbox at the end of the driveway has a flip-down door with printed envelope detail. The set comes with three printed envelope tiles.

Imperial Trading Post

1992 • LEGO® Pirates • #6277 • Pieces: 608 • Minifigures: 9

In 1992, the LEGO Pirates' old enemies, the Imperial Soldiers, were replaced by the Imperial Guards. Recognizable by their red uniforms and flags, the Guards reigned over the seas from their grand Imperial Trading Post, welcoming merchants but chasing off any pirates who tried to sail into port with a fusillade of their cannon fire. But even the Imperial Guards could not rule the waves forever, and they were supplanted in turn by the conquistador-like Imperial Armada in 1996.

The Imperial Trading Post is the largest of the classic Imperial Guards models, and includes both a medium-sized merchant ship and a small pirate sailboat, along with nine minifigure guards and crew. Two cranes transport treasures and trade goods from vessel to port and back again, and a covered pit in the raised base holds spare provisions or pirate prisoners.

Cannon (one of three) snaps onto red base

Turntable at base of mast allows steering

White torso with brown vest printing appeared in one other set, LEGO Pirates Skull's Eye Schooner (6286) in 1993

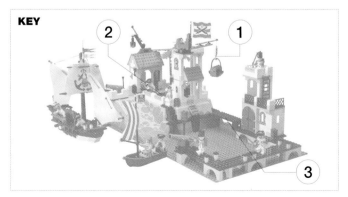

KEY

< **CARGO CRANE** This crane rests on a 4x4 turntable that enables it to swivel. Once the cargo is hooked on, the winch is turned to hoist it up and deposit it in the correct place.

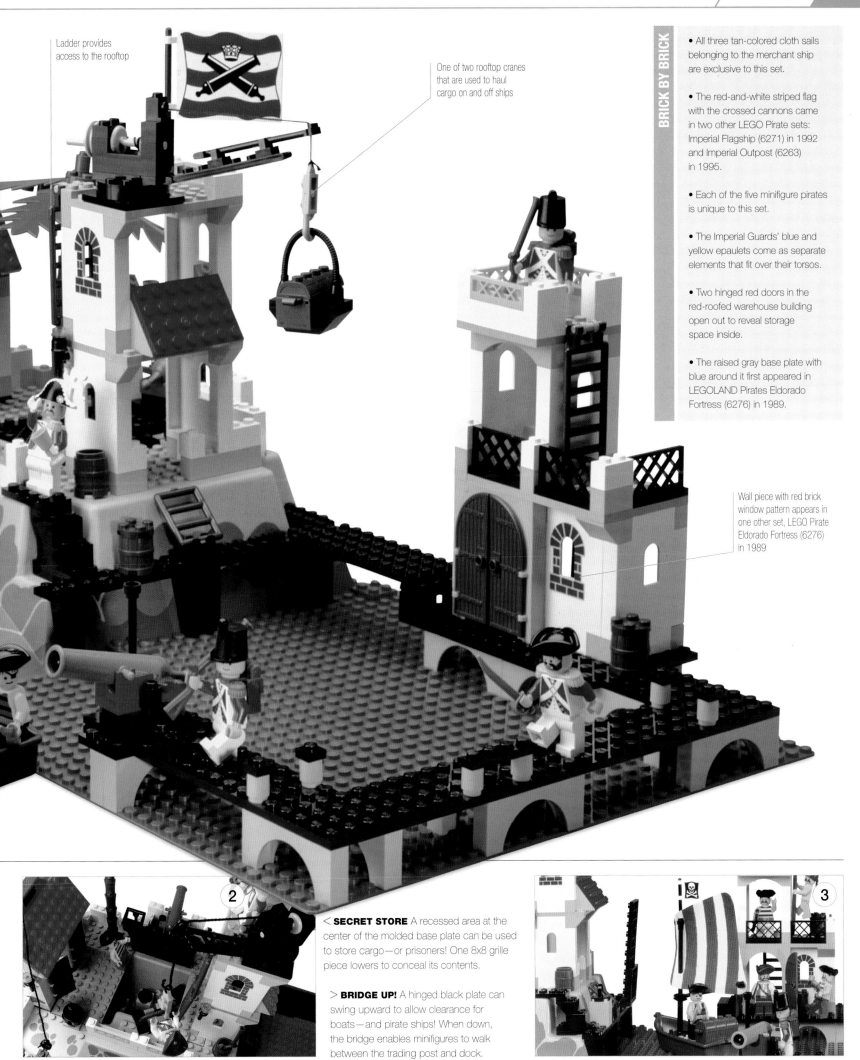

Ladder provides access to the rooftop

One of two rooftop cranes that are used to haul cargo on and off ships

BRICK BY BRICK

• All three tan-colored cloth sails belonging to the merchant ship are exclusive to this set.

• The red-and-white striped flag with the crossed cannons came in two other LEGO Pirate sets: Imperial Flagship (6271) in 1992 and Imperial Outpost (6263) in 1995.

• Each of the five minifigure pirates is unique to this set.

• The Imperial Guards' blue and yellow epaulets come as separate elements that fit over their torsos.

• Two hinged red doors in the red-roofed warehouse building open out to reveal storage space inside.

• The raised gray base plate with blue around it first appeared in LEGOLAND Pirates Eldorado Fortress (6276) in 1989.

Wall piece with red brick window pattern appears in one other set, LEGO Pirate Eldorado Fortress (6276) in 1989

< **SECRET STORE** A recessed area at the center of the molded base plate can be used to store cargo—or prisoners! One 8x8 grille piece lowers to conceal its contents.

> **BRIDGE UP!** A hinged black plate can swing upward to allow clearance for boats—and pirate ships! When down, the bridge enables minifigures to walk between the trading post and dock.

Pizza To Go

1994 • LEGO® Town • #6350 • Pieces: 142 • Minifigures: 3

Who's ready for some pizza? In 1994, a new eatery moved into LEGO Town. Pizza To Go was a small but well-detailed set featuring a pizzeria and a delivery van. The iconic 2x2 round tile with printed pizza decoration first appeared in this model—which came with five of them! Pizza To Go was released again in 2002 as a LEGO Legends set.

Inside the pizzeria, the chef uses an oar as a pizza paddle while he works at the double-shelf oven, which has a grille piece for a vent on the outside of the building. He hands his pizzas to the driver to deliver all across town.

BRICK BY BRICK

- The printed pizzeria sign that sits on top of the van is exclusive to this set and its LEGO Legends re-release (10036).

- The white dish with red and green printing, which is used here as a parasol, first appeared in this set.

- The delivery van driver's cab roof is hinged so it can lift up, as can the trans-blue sunroof within it.

- The set comes with a garbage can with separate lid, a trans-clear cup, and a walkie-talkie that clips to the van.

- The lady and delivery man minifigures are unique to this set and its re-release. The chef appears in two other sets.

- A total of 10 classic LEGO sets were re-released in the LEGO Legends line from 2001–2004.

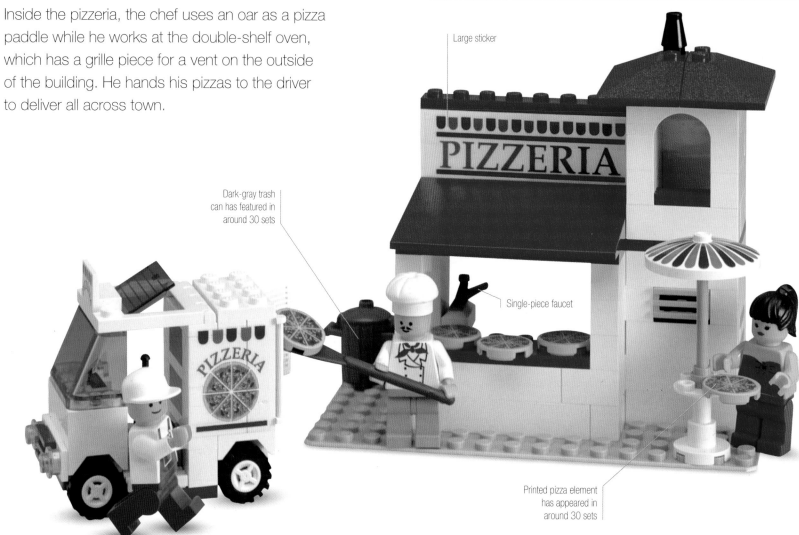

Large sticker

Dark-gray trash can has featured in around 30 sets

Single-piece faucet

Printed pizza element has appeared in around 30 sets

Guided Tour

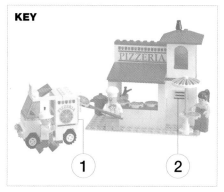

KEY

1
2

1

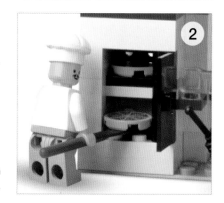

2

< PIZZA VAN Two shuttered doors open to reveal two shelves at the back of the van. Each shelf can fit a single pizza.

> PIZZA OVEN There are two shelves in the oven, so two delicious pizzas can be cooked at any one time.

Pretty Playland

1994 • LEGO® BELVILLE™ • #5870 • Pieces: 92 • Figures: 2

LEGO BELVILLE sets offered a larger scale of build and play that was reminiscent of the 1970s LEGO Homemaker and LEGO Family models. The sets, such as Pretty Playland, starred doll-like characters who could be posed, played with, and even dressed in fabric clothing. The long-lived theme lasted all the way from 1994 until 2011, branching out into worlds of fantasy and fairy tales such as Thumbelina and the Snow Queen.

The Pretty Playland set provides its boy and girl figures with a full playground in which to play. They can go down the slide, sit on the seesaw, and spin on the merry-go-round. There is even a skateboard, a teddy bear, and a friendly dog to keep them company!

∧ **SIT TIGHT** BELVILLE figures have jointed elbows and ankles, making them easy to pose. Their seesaw is made of two blue plates and bar elements.

BRICK BY BRICK

- The LEGO BELVILLE boy figure is unique to this set.

- The pink, patterned fabric skirt that the girl figure wears is removable.

- The boy's skateboard with separate wheels first appeared in LEGO FABULAND Clive Crocodile (3721) in 1988, but in red with yellow wheels.

- The girl's pink suitcase with butterfly sticker can open and close.

- The rare chrome-silver-colored bucket has appeared in six other LEGO BELVILLE sets.

- The teddy bear element was first introduced in 1994 in LEGO BELVILLE sets. It has been made in many different colors, including yellow, pink, and brown.

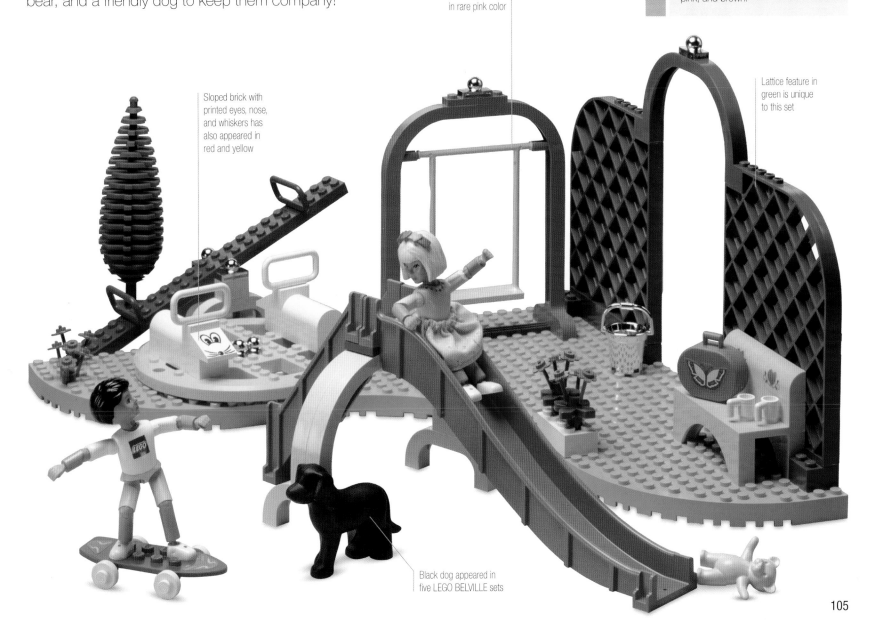

Swing element in rare pink color

Sloped brick with printed eyes, nose, and whiskers has also appeared in red and yellow

Lattice feature in green is unique to this set

Black dog appeared in five LEGO BELVILLE sets

Neptune Discovery Lab

1995 • LEGO® Aquazone • #6195 • Pieces: 492 • Minifigures: 4

LEGO Aquazone, the futuristic underwater adventure theme, starred the heroic Aquanauts, a team of deep-sea miners who competed against the villainous Aquasharks over rare oxygen-producing Hydrolator crystals. The Aquanauts operated out of the Neptune Discovery Lab, a research and mining facility built on the ocean floor.

The Neptune Discovery Lab includes a submersible vehicle for collecting crystals, and a crane that transfers them to a working conveyor belt, which can either take them to the lab or deposit them into a magnetic box that the sub can carry. A new octopus can menace the divers, or just hang out.

Submarine is powered by a propeller and four jets at the rear

Guided Tour

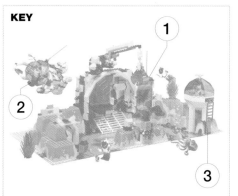

KEY
1
2
3

Spiky plant first appeared in LEGO Aquazone sets

1

∧ **CRYSTAL DELIVERY** The crane can swivel to pick up crystals from the sub and deposit them onto the two-way conveyor belt. A black wheel is turned to move the crystals into the base—where they appear behind the base's ramp.

2

∧ **SUPER SUB** The submarine has two posable arms (one with a rotating, hinged claw, and the other with a magnet), an orange antenna, and a compass that sits just in front of the propeller. Central hatches and windows fold back, allowing access.

3

< **CONTROL TOWER** The tower can be entered via a ladder. The dome lifts up, and inside there is room for a minifigure to operate the navigation screen, and clips for stowing harpoons and knives.

One of two large, trans-blue opening doors—these are exclusive to the set

Control tower's octagonal base piece is unique to this set in yellow

Magnet on top of the box enables it to be carried by the sub

Black octopus has appeared in around 15 LEGO sets so far

• This set was also known as LEGO Aquazone Aquanauts Aqua Dome 7.

• There are four Aquanaut minifigures in this set. The Aquanaut with the black helmet and headset printing is unique to this set, although his head piece has appeared in around 50 LEGO sets.

• The sub's working compass appeared in eight Aquazone sets from 1995–1998.

• The two identical molded base plates with blue underwater printed patterns are exclusive to this set.

• This is the only set with spring-loaded crane claws in trans-blue. They are solid yellow in all other sets.

• This is the largest of the Aquazone sets, and the only one to feature a base for the Aquanauts.

Bandits' Secret Hideout

1996 • LEGO® Western • #6761 • Pieces: 238 • Minifigures: 5

LEGO Western galloped into town in 1996. With models based on the legendary American Old West, its sets were populated by cowboys, sheriffs, and plenty of horses for canyon chases and round-ups. The Bandits' Secret Hideout set featured a desert gold mine taken over by outlaws, along with the cavalry soldiers who were sent to root them out and bring the desperados to justice.

If the skull on the signpost isn't enough to convince trespassers to stay away, then the Secret Hideout's many booby traps will probably do the trick—from a tripwire-triggered cannon that rolls down the mine cart rails, to a collapsing water barrel. That vulture up on the roof is looking a little peckish, too…

Vulture is a parrot element in gray

Rotating base houses three shotguns

Printed door of safe appeared in three other LEGO Western sets

Dynamite stick is
a printed tile

REAR VIEW

Cannon on tracks is
part of a booby trap for
the cavalrymen

Rocks are hollow with
space for bandits to
play cards or hide out
on the other side

• Beneath the "KEEP OUT" skull sign
is a secret stash of gold coins.

• The black staircase can easily
be removed to foil the cavalry! This
single piece was introduced in 1996.

• The chrome-gold-colored bugle
was created in 1996 and first
appeared in this set and LEGO
Western Fort Legoredo (6769).

• Inside the hideout at the top of the
staircase is a yellow chair and a set
of shuttered windows.

• The base plate with its printed
hoof marks, rocks, and wheel ruts
is exclusive to this set.

• The blue, printed cavalry flag
appears in two other sets: LEGO
Western Frontier Patrol (6706)
and Fort Legoredo (6769).

Guided Tour

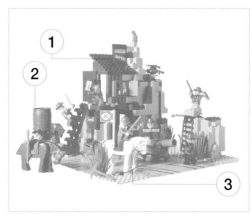

∧ **BARREL BATTERY** A barrel perches behind the
hinged Gold Mine sign. It takes just one bandit to raise
the sign and release the barrel onto a target below.

∧ **TIPPING BARREL** If it looks like a cavalryman is
about to climb the stairs to the hideout, a sneaky
bandit can tip a barrel onto him.

∧ **TRIP WIRE** A wire is attached to a brick that props
up a cannon on tracks. When an unsuspecting horse
triggers the wire, the brick moves, and the cannon
rolls toward the cavalrymen!

Robotics Invention System

1998 • LEGO® MINDSTORMS® • #9719 • Pieces: 727

Sure, you could use your LEGO bricks to build any kind of invention that you could imagine, but could you make them walk, roll, pick up objects, and put on a show at your command? In 1998, the answer was finally yes, thanks to the LEGO® MINDSTORMS® series of kits. The first Robotics Invention System set included a computerized RCX (Robotic Command eXplorer) brick, along with sensors, wires, and motors to let builders design and assemble their own moving, reacting robotic creations.

An infrared transceiver helps the RCX intelligent brick receive programming instructions from a computer, telling it when and how to operate up to three motors and three sensors at the same time. Extra kits and accessories can be added to the basic Robotics Invention System to give it even more capabilities.

"The aim is to help people create their own technology."

Lars Joe Hyldig, LEGO Design Manager

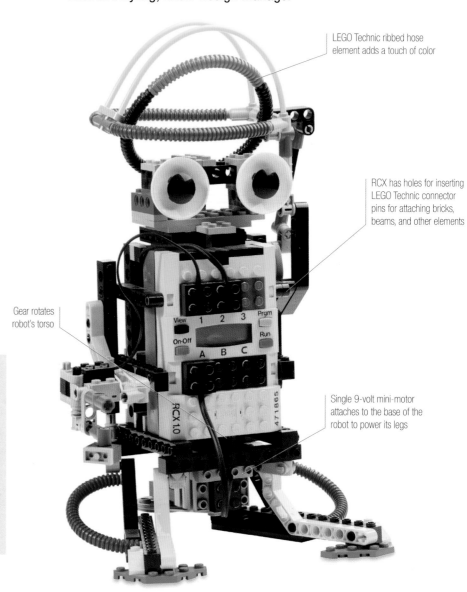

LEGO Technic ribbed hose element adds a touch of color

RCX has holes for inserting LEGO Technic connector pins for attaching bricks, beams, and other elements

Gear rotates robot's torso

Single 9-volt mini-motor attaches to the base of the robot to power its legs

• Users "build" a program on their computers and download it to the RCX brick using the infrared transceiver. The program tells the motors and sensors plugged into the RCX brick how to bring the robot to life.

• A blue light sensor brick can be positioned face-down to detect a line drawn on the ground. The robot can be programmed to move away from it.

• An accompanying CD-ROM includes ideas for building six sub-assemblies, including two robots, two pathfinders, and two acrobots.

• Following updates in 1999 (9747) and 2001 (3804), the Robotics Invention System got two huge upgrades: LEGO MINDSTORMS NXT (8527) in 2006 and EV3 (31313) in 2013. Each new generation had a sleeker look and added even greater programming options.

KEY

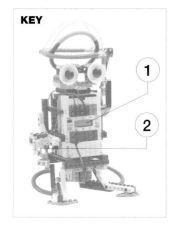

1

2

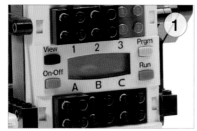

∧ **RCX CONTROLS** The LCD window displays information such as battery charge, program download, and which input/output ports are active.

∧ **SENSITIVE ARM** The robot can be programmed to move away from an object if it comes into range of the sensor brick (positioned here on top of the robot's arm).

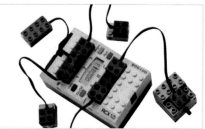

∧ **INPUT/OUTPUT** Output ports (labeled by letter) can connect to motors and lights. Input ports (labeled by number) can connect to light, temperature, touch, and rotation sensors.

Sonic Stinger

1998 • LEGO® Space • #6907 • Pieces: 96 • Minifigures: 1

Crewed by cyber-detailed minifigures called Zotaxians and their robotic droid assistants, the LEGO Insectoids were a fleet of alien spacecraft and ground vehicles that resembled giant Earthly insects and arachnids. The 1998–1999 LEGO Space subtheme premiered new mechanical leg and wing parts, and a few sets, such as Sonic Stinger, included a special Light and Sound component that made the models glow and emit electronic sci-fi noises when their buttons were pressed. The Sonic Stinger was flown by Gypsy Moth, the Zotaxian queen herself.

With its bulbous, transparent neon-green eyes and long antennae, the Sonic Stinger looks like a gigantic robot wasp, although its light-up abdomen gives it qualities of a firefly, too. Its articulated wings have printed circuitry patterns, and its booster-equipped rear has a magnet that lets it pick up a Voltstone energy orb using its magnetic sticker.

• The Gypsy Moth minifigure wears a trans-neon green helmet. This element was also used for Mr. Freeze's helmet in the LEGO® Batman™ theme, although in a trans-clear color.

• Including the helmet, Light and Sound brick, and Volstone orb, the set features 17 trans-neon green elements. The helmet and eye pieces are rare.

• The trans-neon green rock piece with the silver-colored magnetic sticker is exclusive to the Insectoid theme, and represents their Voltstone orb power source. It was only ever produced in this color.

• The stinger Light and Sound brick is exclusive to the Insectoid subtheme, and it appeared in two other sets in 1998.

• A promotional version of the set (6909) included a wearable insect mask for children.

Wing elements help Insectoids disguise themselves as giant bugs

Voltstone orb element sits on top of the craft

Magnet to pick up Voltstone orb

∧ **STING IN THE TAIL** A Light and Sound brick flashes orange and produces sci-fi sounds. Pressing each of the three buttons starts a different combination of light and sound patterns.

Buttons to activate the Light and Sound brick

Yoda
- 2002 • LEGO *Star Wars* **Ultimate Collector Series** • **#7194**

Trade Federation MTT
- 2007 • LEGO *Star Wars* • **#7662**

Motorized Walking AT-AT
- 2007 • LEGO *Star Wars* • **#10178**

TIE Fighter & Y-wing
- 1999 • LEGO *Star Wars* • **#7150**

Obi-Wan's Jedi Starfighter
- 2010 • LEGO® *Star Wars*® **Ultimate Collector's Series** • **#10215**

Clone Trooper Battle Pack
- 2011• LEGO® *Star Wars*® **Clone Wars**™ • **#7913**

Sandcrawler
- 2014 • LEGO *Star Wars* **Ultimate Collector's Series** • **#75059**

Jabba's Palace
- 2012 • LEGO *Star Wars* • **#9516**

"Licensed sets are a test of your abilities as a builder… You can't just change the design if it's structurally unsound."

Michael Thomas Fuller,
LEGO Design Manager

Mos Eisley Cantina
- 2014 • LEGO *Star Wars* • **#75052**

R2-D2
- 2012 • LEGO *Star Wars* **Ultimate Collector Series** • **#10225**

Jabba's Sail Barge
• 2006 • LEGO *Star Wars* • #6210

A BRICK GALAXY FAR, FAR AWAY...

LEGO® *Star Wars*® sets through the years

In 1999, the *Star Wars* galaxy returned to movie screens all around the world… and LEGO® *Star Wars*® sets arrived on toy store shelves for the very first time! With hundreds of sets released since then, the popular and successful theme has let fans build all of their favorite starships and vehicles from the epic films and TV shows, from giant LEGO *Star Wars* Ultimate Collector Series models to tiny LEGO *Star Wars* Microfighters. Populating the brick-built galaxy is a massive cast of minifigure Jedi Knights, Sith warriors, troopers, rebels, aliens, and droids.

Imperial Star Destroyer
• 2006 • LEGO *Star Wars* • #6211

Millennium Falcon™
• 2014 • LEGO *Star Wars* Microfighters • #75030

Ewok Village
• 2013 • LEGO *Star Wars* • #10236

Wookiee™ **Gunship**
• 2015 • LEGO® *Star Wars* Rebels™ • #75084

AAT
• 2009 • LEGO *Star Wars* Clone Wars • #8018

Jedi Starfighter & Vulture Droid
• 2005 • LEGO *Star Wars* • #7256

Republic Attack Gunship
• 2008 • LEGO *Star Wars* Clone Wars • #7676

Tunnel Transport

1999 • LEGO® Rock Raiders • #4980 • Pieces: 349 • Minifigures: 2

At the end of the last millennium, a spaceship was hurled across the universe to the mysterious Planet U, a world rich in Brickonium energy crystals… and giant, hostile rock monsters. The ship's crew were the LEGO Rock Raiders, and their sets were geared up with drills, saws, and other sci-fi mining equipment. Their biggest vehicle was the Tunnel Transport, a propeller-powered flier that explored subterranean caverns in search of the precious crystals that the Rock Raiders needed to repair their ship and get back home.

With the mighty Tunnel Transport, veteran geologist Docs and courageous pilot Jet can dig out crystal deposits using their small digger vehicle's chainsaws, or load boulders into a large bucket. Both have magnets so that the Tunnel Transport can pick them up and fly them back to base.

Magnet for attaching the contrainer to the main vehicle

Element first used as a tail fin in 1986—it is exclusive to this set in dark turquoise

Two-piece boulder splits apart to reveal a trans-neon green crystal

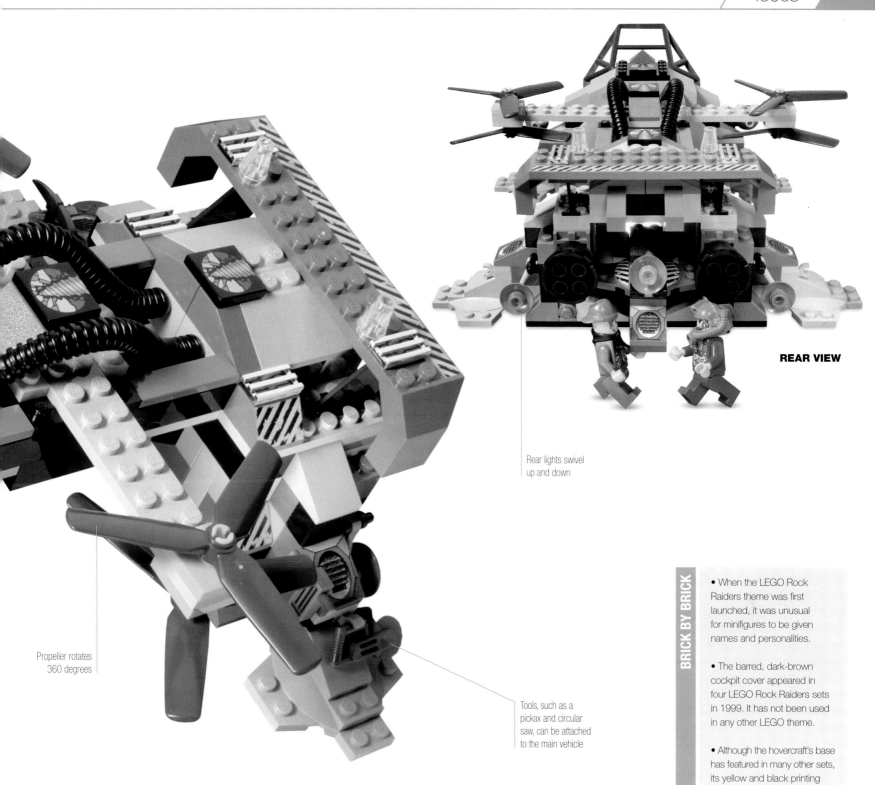

REAR VIEW

Rear lights swivel
up and down

Propeller rotates
360 degrees

Tools, such as a
pickax and circular
saw, can be attached
to the main vehicle

• When the LEGO Rock
Raiders theme was first
launched, it was unusual
for minifigures to be given
names and personalities.

• The barred, dark-brown
cockpit cover appeared in
four LEGO Rock Raiders sets
in 1999. It has not been used
in any other LEGO theme.

• Although the hovercraft's base
has featured in many other sets,
its yellow and black printing
make it exclusive to the Rock
Raiders theme. It also featured
in Helicopter Transport (1276).

Guided Tour

KEY

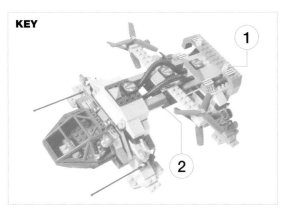

< **HOVERCRAFT** The set
includes a small hovercraft
for scouting missions. It can
be stored in a compartment
at the rear of the Tunnel
Transport vehicle.

> **LAND DIGGER** The small
digger has a tipper bucket
for transporting boulders.
A magnet behind the seat
attaches the digger to the
Tunnel Transport.

2000s

Following the incredible success of LEGO®
Star Wars®, the first decade of the new millennium
saw the rise of themes based on popular movies,
sports, and super heroes. Even original LEGO
sets branched out into epic adventures that took
builders from the days of Viking warriors to a
futuristic world of battling mechs. And for the
fans who had grown up building LEGO models,
advanced sets designed for older builders offered
more pieces, more building steps, and bigger,
more detailed models than ever before.

Dino Research Compound

2000 • LEGO® Adventurers • #5987 • Pieces: 612 • Minifigures: 6

The LEGO Adventurers made their first appearance in a 1998 Egyptian archaeology theme, and returned in 1999 for an expedition into the Amazon jungle. In 2000, Dino Island marked the third excursion for Johnny Thunder and his intrepid crew, who built the Dino Research Compound to help them capture and study the island's dinosaurs… hopefully before the sneaky Sam Sinister could steal them!

The Adventurers can explore on land, sea, and air with the help of the set's vehicles, or look out for danger from the watchtower, which hides a communications dish beneath its opening roof. A working zip line transports supplies down to the ground, and the various nets and snares are great for catching giant prehistoric reptiles.

BRICK BY BRICK

• The gray sloped brick with printed rusty steel pattern, which is used for the building's roof, is exclusive to this set.

• The set includes four dinosaur figures: a flying Pteranodon, a Tyrannosaurus rex, a baby Tyrannosaurus rex, and a Stegasaurus.

• The Tyrannosaurus rex's upper jaw can be raised or lowered, its arms can move up and down, and its hinged tail moves from side-to-side. The Stegasaurus also has a hinged tail.

• The minifigures featured in the set are Adventurers Johnny Thunder, Pippin Reed, Dr. Kilroy, and Mike, and villains Sam Sinister and Mr. Cunningham.

• Several characters have appeared under different names in other Adventurers subthemes, for example, Sam Sinister has been called Lord Sam Sinister, Baron Von Barron, Mr. Hates, and Evil Eye.

• Minifigure accessories include Dr. Kilroy's magnifying glass, Pippin Reed's gem, and the Adventurers' white pith helmets.

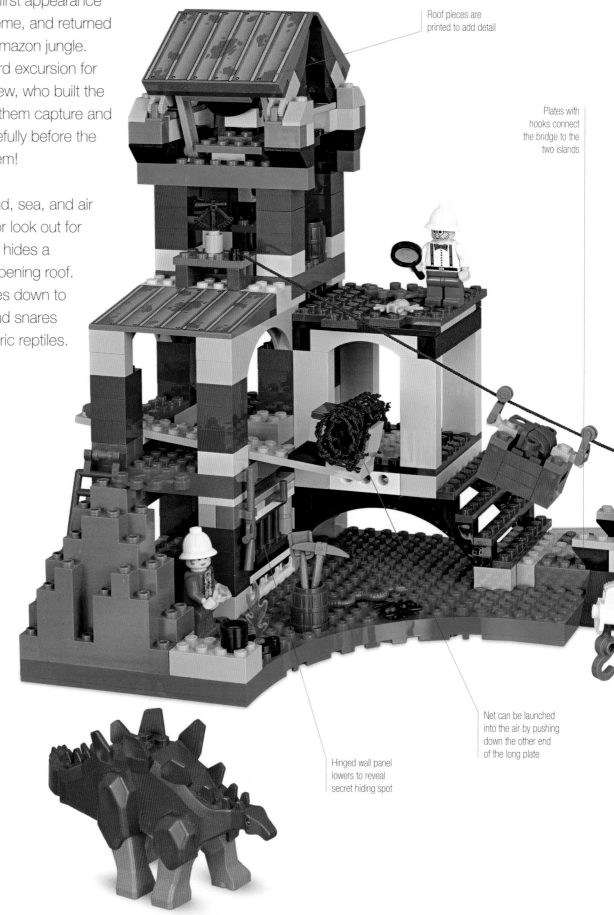

Roof pieces are printed to add detail

Plates with hooks connect the bridge to the two islands

Net can be launched into the air by pushing down the other end of the long plate

Hinged wall panel lowers to reveal secret hiding spot

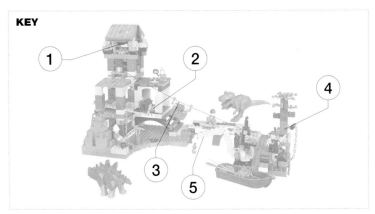

Net can be released
from the underside
of Sam Sinister's and
Mr. Cunningham's plane

Brown rowboat first
appeared in LEGOLAND
Pirates in 1989

Guided Tour

KEY

∧ **UNDERCOVER COMMUNICATIONS**
As the sides of the tower's roof open
outward, the radar dish is raised from
its hiding place.

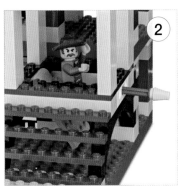

∧ **WALKING INTO A TRAP** The tower
is protected by a trapdoor. Just pull out
the yellow LEGO Technic axle to catch
the intruder by surprise!

∧ **ZIP LINE** A zip line connects the top
of the tower and the crane. This could be
a quick way to transport equipment, or a
hasty means of escape for a minifigure!

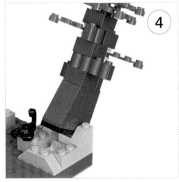

∧ **SECRET STASH** Beneath the tree is
a secret compartment for hiding small
objects. The tree sits on a 1x2 hinge
that allows it to be moved up and down.

∧ **HEAVY LIFTER** Johnny Thunder
operates the crane to raise the rowboat
out of the water. The crane can be
rotated 360 degrees.

∧ **RESEARCH VEHICLE** The car is
armed with a lance and chain, which
can be raised and lowered, for
catching dinosaurs.

X-wing Fighter

2000 • LEGO® *Star Wars®* **Ultimate Collector Series• #7191** • Pieces: 1304 • Figures: 1

The long-running Ultimate Collector Series of LEGO® *Star Wars®* sets kicked-off in 2000. Featuring huge models with massive piece counts for maximum detail, the series began with the famous starfighter flown by rebel hero Luke Skywalker. Made up of approximately 1,300 pieces, the X-wing Fighter was released alongside an equally impressive model of the evil Galactic Empire's TIE Interceptor (7181).

The UCS X-wing is as accurate to the on-screen original as it was possible to make with the LEGO elements of the time. A system of internal gears opens the wings into their iconic X-shape, and their marking stripes identify the ship as Luke's Red Five fighter. The brick-built support stand has a plaque with information about the movie vehicle.

"We had the idea that we wanted to create LEGO sets for skilled builders and adults. Where better to start than with the X-wing and TIE Fighter?"

Henrik Andersen, LEGO Senior Designer

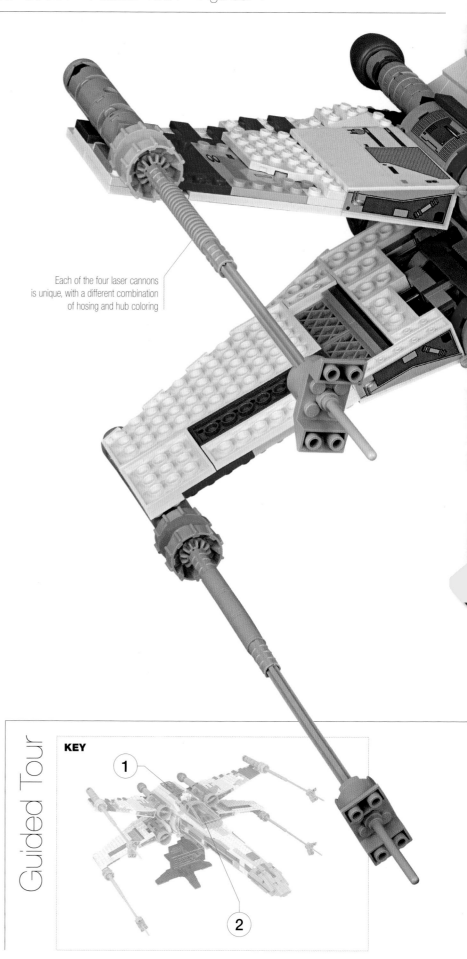

Each of the four laser cannons is unique, with a different combination of hosing and hub coloring

BRICK BY BRICK

• During the research process for UCS models, the design team visited a toy store in Hamburg to investigate if there was a market for models aimed at adults and skilled builders.

• There have been 22 LEGO *Star Wars* UCS sets released so far.

• There wasn't a suitable LEGO element that could be used as the cockpit windshield. Henrik Andersen, the set's designer, found that the mold for a battery box from an old 4.5-volt LEGO train set fit the shape he needed, so he used it to create a new element for the set.

• Henrik remembers creating around 60 versions of the set before the final model was approved. He was a new designer at the time, so he was also learning how to build official LEGO sets.

• The R2-D2 figure in this set has appeared in 13 other sets. There have been seven other variants of this figure.

• There have been 13 LEGO X-wing models so far. These include the first X-wing model released in 1999 (7140) and another UCS model, Red Five X-wing (10240) in 2013.

Guided Tour

KEY

1

2

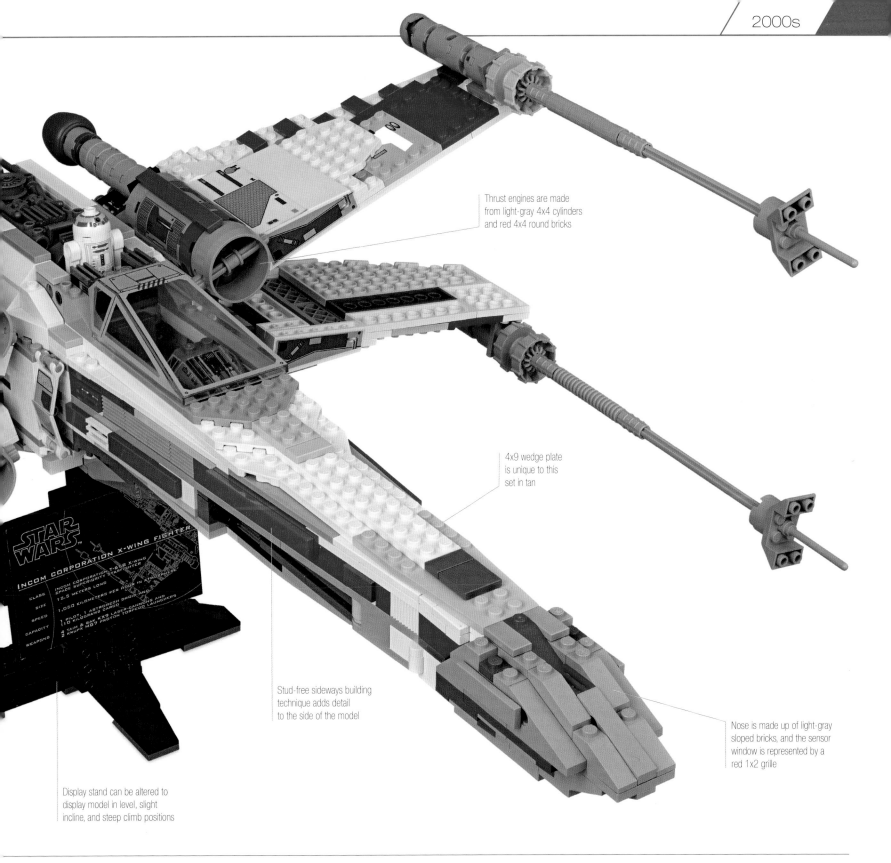

Thrust engines are made from light-gray 4x4 cylinders and red 4x4 round bricks

4x9 wedge plate is unique to this set in tan

Stud-free sideways building technique adds detail to the side of the model

Nose is made up of light-gray sloped bricks, and the sensor window is represented by a red 1x2 grille

Display stand can be altered to display model in level, slight incline, and steep climb positions

STAR WARS

INCOM CORPORATION T-65B X-WING SPACE SUPERIORITY STARFIGHTER

CLASS	INCOM CORPORATION T-65B X-WING SPACE SUPERIORITY STARFIGHTER
SIZE	12.5 METERS LONG
SPEED	1,050 KILOMETERS PER HOUR IN ATMOSPHERE
CAPACITY	1 PILOT, 1 ASTROMECH DROID AND 110 KILOGRAMS CARGO
WEAPONS	4 TAIM & BAK KX9 LASER CANNONS AND 2 KRUPX MG7 PROTON TORPEDO LAUNCHERS

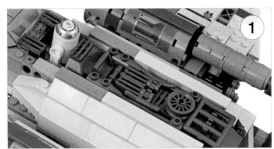

△ **DEFLECTOR SHIELD GENERATOR** Dark-gray elements, including a bar window and a spoked wheel, make up the details on the top of the starfighter. R2-D2, the set's only figure, sits in the astromech socket behind the cockpit.

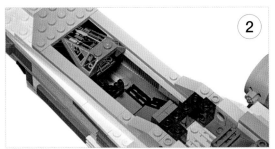

△ **COCKPIT** The X-wing cockpit has extensive detailing, including a moving joystick and a targeting display screen showing Luke's Death Star trench run in Episode IV. The pilot's seat can also be adjusted.

△ **"X" FORMATION** The sand-colored knob on the rear of the model is connected to the internal gearbox that opens and closes the S-foil wings. The "X" formation is for attack, and the flat formation is for cruising.

Sopwith Camel

2001 • LEGO® Advanced Models • #3451 • Pieces: 577

A large and fantastically realistic recreation of the historic British World War I fighter biplane, the Sopwith Camel was one of the first sets in a new line of advanced models for skilled builders, aged 12 and up.

The LEGO Sopwith Camel has a rotating engine made out of minifigure megaphones and radar dishes, double wings built with brown plates, and a pair of binoculars mounted on the cockpit for the pilot. Strings represent the wing control cables of the original plane.

"This was a tricky build… it was a challenge to use the struts to make the biplane stable."

Henrik Andersen, LEGO Senior Designer

BRICK BY BRICK

• This was one of the first sets to be sold online. It was initially packaged in black and white boxes, because no one would see the packaging before they received the model, but the company later decided to make all box art colored.

• The plane's wheels are made from two large LEGO Technic steering wheels and two tan-colored radar dishes.

• This model measures 15in (38cm) in width and 11in (28.5cm) in length. The original Sopwith Camel had a 28ft (8.5m) wingspan and measured 18ft 9in (5.7m) in length.

• Two other LEGO versions of the Sopwith Camel were released in 2012: a LEGO Creator set (10226) with 883 pieces, and a miniature version (40049) with 65 pieces.

"Hump" with machine guns gave the Camel its name

LEGO Technic axle is used as a strut to support the upper wing

Footplate built into fuselage

Engine cowling is made up of four curved fence elements, introduced in 1996

Guided Tour

KEY

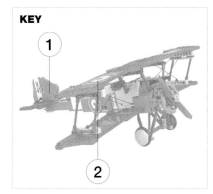

1

2

1

< **TAILFIN** The rounded edge of the tailfin is created using curved arches and bricks. The set number is included in the aircraft designation code on a red, white, and blue sticker.

> **RAF STICKERS** The large Royal Air Force roundel stickers on the wings are split to allow easy positioning over the two levels of the wing plates.

2

Blacksmith Shop

2002 • LEGO® My Own Creation • #3739 • Pieces: 622 • Minifigures: 2

The Blacksmith Shop was a novel experiment: an official set made by a LEGO fan. It was produced under the LEGO "My Own Creation" label, and was available for purchase directly from the company's website. Designed in the style of 1986's classic LEGOLAND Castle Guarded Inn (6067), it featured a medieval building that opened on hinges to reveal a detailed and fully furnished interior.

Inside the blacksmith's workshop, the forge and anvil sit at the base of the hinged chimney near a rack of weapons and tools. A staircase leads up to the simple home that the smith shares with his wife, including a bed and dining area.

"This was groundbreaking. It gave me the idea that maybe something I built could be good enough to become an official LEGO set."

Jamie Berard, LEGO Design Manager Specialist

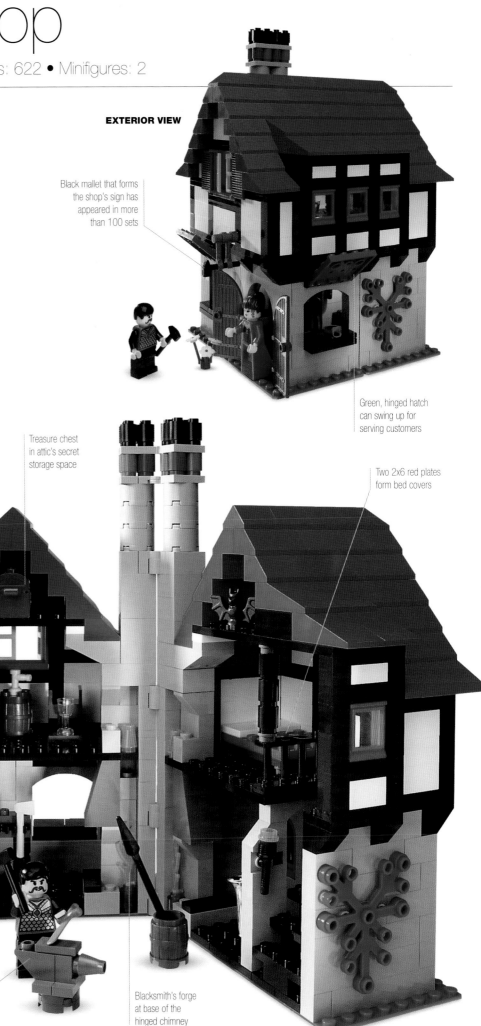

EXTERIOR VIEW

Black mallet that forms the shop's sign has appeared in more than 100 sets

Green, hinged hatch can swing up for serving customers

Treasure chest in attic's secret storage space

Two 2x6 red plates form bed covers

Brick-built anvil

Blacksmith's forge at base of the hinged chimney

123

Arctic Snowmobile
• 2014 • LEGO City • #60032

Emma's Splash Pool
• 2012 • LEGO Friends • #3931

Street Sweeper
• 2005 • LEGO® City • #7242

Turtle's Little Oasis
• 2013 • LEGO® Friends • #41019

WITH JUST A FEW BRICKS

Small LEGO® sets through the years

You don't need to have a lot of bricks in order to build a great LEGO® model. Some of the most fun and colorful sets around are made out of fewer than 100 pieces! From miniature monsters to micro-scale vehicles, these tiny titans include speedy chases, intergalactic explorers, and scenes from the worlds of pirates, the Wild West, or the movie studio stunt-stage. Portable and affordable, they can be carried around with you, packed in your knapsack for holiday trips, or assembled together into wild displays on your dining room table. The possibilities are endless!

Sismobile
• 1983 • LEGOLAND Space • #6844

Jawg
• 2014 • LEGO® Mixels™ • #41514

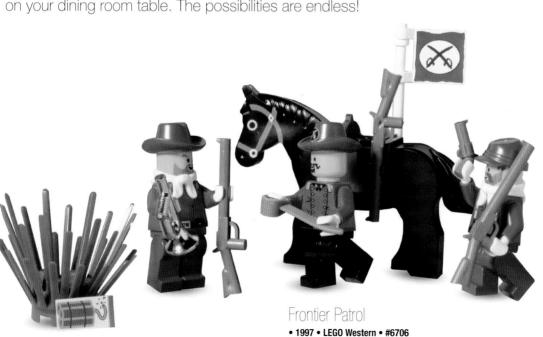

Frontier Patrol
• 1997 • LEGO Western • #6706

Big Wheels Digger
• 1999 • LEGO® DUPLO® – Town • #2807

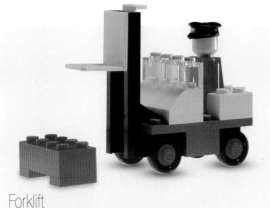

Forklift
- 1975 • LEGOLAND • #615

"A lot of people's childhood memories of LEGO sets are the small ones."

Jette Orduna, Head of LEGO Idea House

Stuntman Catapult
- 2001 • LEGO Studios • #1356

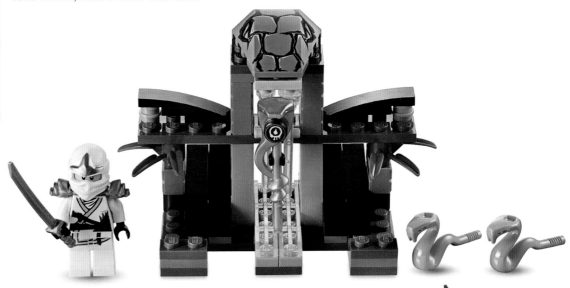

Venomari Shrine
- 2012 • LEGO® NINJAGO™ • #9440

Frost
- 2000 • LEGO® Technic • #8511

Ring of Fire
- 2013 • LEGO® Legends of Chima™ • #70100

Riverside Raid
- 2014 • LEGO Agents • #70160

Treasure Surprise
- 1996 • LEGO Pirates • #1747

Magic Shop
- 1993 • LEGO Castle • #6020

Ice Cream Cart
- 1985 • LEGOLAND Town • #6601

Aeroplane and Pilot
- 1974 • LEGO Building Set With People • #250

The Chamber of Secrets®

2002 • LEGO® Harry Potter™ • #4730 • Pieces: 591 • Minifigures: 5

After a 2001 launch accompanying the first film in the blockbuster *Harry Potter*™ series, the LEGO Group produced a second wave of sets for the 2002 sequel, *Harry Potter and the Chamber of Secrets*. The titular Chamber of Secrets set recreates the hidden room beneath Hogwarts™ castle where the movie's final showdown takes place between student wizard Harry and the monstrous Basilisk.

The model unfolds to reveal a trapdoor entrance inside the Hogwarts girls' bathroom; the stone face of Salazar Slytherin (through which the glowing-toothed Basilisk can slither); and two half-sections of the snake-festooned Chamber of Secrets, with collapsing and swinging walls. Good thing there's also the fiery Fawkes™ the phoenix to assist Harry in his moment of need!

• The lilac-suited Gilderoy Lockhart™ minifigure is unique to this set. He appears in green in LEGO® Harry Potter™ The Dueling Club (4733).

• Minifigures of red-haired Ginny Weasley™ and the sinister-looking Tom Riddle™ first appeared in this set. Two more variants of Ginny have appeared in other LEGO Harry Potter sets.

• The red Fawkes the phoenix figure is exclusive to this set.

• A digital version of the Basilisk later appeared in the Well of Souls level of the LEGO® *Indiana Jones: The Original Adventures* video game in 2008. It is less detailed than the Basilisk in this set.

• Tom Riddle's diary, with lock and ink spots printing, also featured in LEGO Harry Potter Dobby's Release (4731).

• The LEGO Harry Potter theme ran until 2011. The design team visited the movie set for one of the models in the theme's final year, Diagon Alley™ (10217).

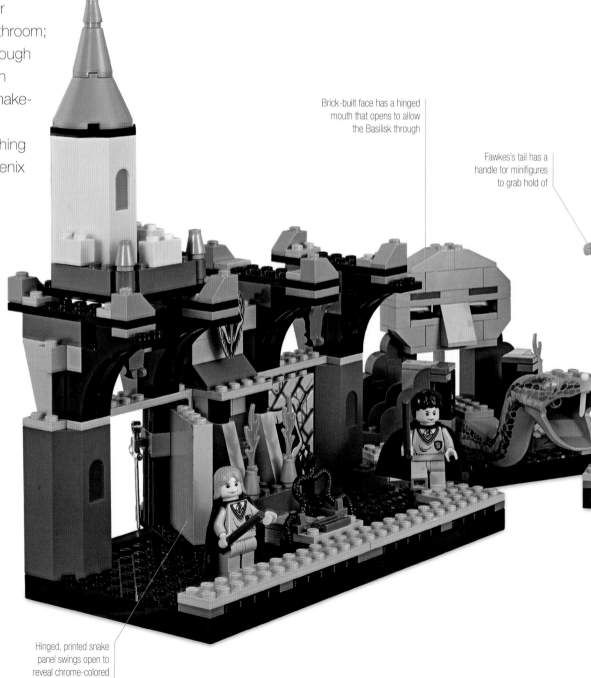

Brick-built face has a hinged mouth that opens to allow the Basilisk through

Fawkes's tail has a handle for minifigures to grab hold of

Hinged, printed snake panel swings open to reveal chrome-colored Sword of Gryffindor

Guided Tour

KEY

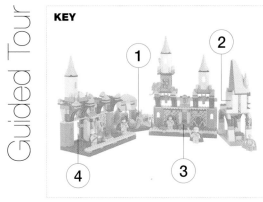

∧ **BASILISK BITE** Two glow-in-the-dark knife pieces make fantastic fangs for the basilisk. Its body is made up of eight sand-green parts with green, printed scales.

∧ **SECRET PASSAGEWAY** Pushing the wall beneath Moaning Myrtle's bathroom releases the trapdoor so that minifigures can slide down into the Chamber of Secrets.

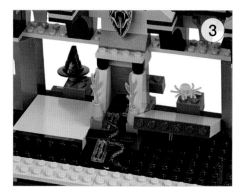

∧ **TUMBLING WALLS** A trans-blue grille tile beneath the fireplace on the right wall can be pushed to knock down the wall panels on either side, revealing the Sorting Hat™ and a spider.

∧ **SWORD OF GRYFFINDOR** Pressing down the grille tile on the left wall causes the wall panels to swing open. The Sword of Godric Gryffindor is clipped to the inside of one panel.

∧ **CLOSED-UP** The sides of the set can be folded in so that it more closely resembles the Chamber of Secrets as seen in the *Harry Potter* movie.

Oval shield with printed snake head is exclusive to this set

Tom Riddle's diary, stained with ink

Each wall of this set can be fitted together, or opened up for extra playability

Scorpion Palace

2003 • LEGO® Adventurers • #7418 • Pieces: 337 • Minifigures: 5

The LEGO Adventurers returned in 2003 for one more globe-trotting adventure, embarking on an Orient Expedition that took Johnny Thunder and friends across India, up snowy Mount Everest, and finally to China, on a quest to find the lost treasures of Marco Polo. Sets in the line came with cards and board pieces that let builders use models, including the grand Scorpion Palace, to play a board game.

The Scorpion Palace is home to the tyrannical Maharaja Lallu, an ally to the Adventurers' foe Lord Sinister. The coveted Golden Shield treasure is hidden inside, but Johnny and Dr. Kilroy had better watch out—moving the scorpion statue's claws releases a giant LEGO boulder that rolls after anyone who tries to steal the Maharaja's treasure.

Scimitar sword was introduced in this theme

Tail piece is identical to the small trunk piece

BRICK BY BRICK

- The Maharaja Lallu minifigure with white turban is exclusive to this set.

- The palace guard's printed blue torso is unique to this set.

- The elephant's body was made from the same mold used for a dinosaur in 2001's LEGO Dinosaurs theme.

- Getting the trap with the boulder just right was a struggle for the design team at first— the set's designer Henrik Andersen recalls the balls flying everywhere during the model's development!

- A special promotional edition of this set, which came packaged with a foam toy scimitar, was also released in 2003.

Lord Sam Sinister minifigure comes with a hook hand

The Maharaja's treasure chest is protected by a giant scorpion

"The team dressed up the project room with a rope bridge, palms, tables covered in cloth, and suitcases with travel stickers. Tropical bird noises were played through speakers."

Henrik Andersen, LEGO Senior Designer

ALTERNATIVE BUILD

The ball rolls down the tracks onto a raider

The palace can be rebuilt with three stories

Printed oriental rug pattern hangs in doorway

Johnny Thunder carries a printed tile with exclusive map design

Guided Tour

KEY

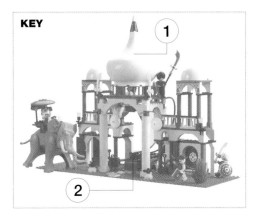

1

2

1

∧ **HALF-DOME** The onion-shaped half-dome was developed with the LEGO® BELVILLE™ team, who used it in dark-violet in their sets. It is hollow to accommodate the ball.

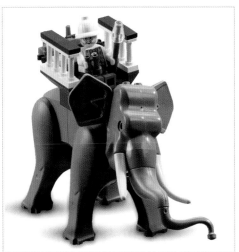

∧ **EXCLUSIVE ELEPHANT** The light-gray Asian elephant is unique to the Scorpion Palace set. In this alternative build, white balcony pieces are used to build a howdah seat.

2

∧ **SCORPION TRAP** If anyone tries to take the treasure chest from the scorpion, the movement triggers a mechanism, causing the boulder—hidden in the dome—to roll down onto the thief.

Main Street

2003 • LEGO® Legends • #10041 • Pieces: 616 • Minifigures: 8

Talk about a blast from the past! In 2003, the LEGO Legends series of recreated and reissued classic sets saw the return of a fan-favorite model that first appeared in 1980. The original Main Street was an expansion for LEGO Town that brought the whole play theme together in a street scene bustling with buildings and activity. A hotel, an auto dealership with a cowboy-hatted salesman, a construction crew, and a working crane made sure that something was always happening in this busy burg.

Like the 1980 version, the re-release has a pair of base plates that can be rearranged to make different road configurations, eight minifigures, two vehicles, a collection of traffic signs, and a park bench and street-side popcorn cart.

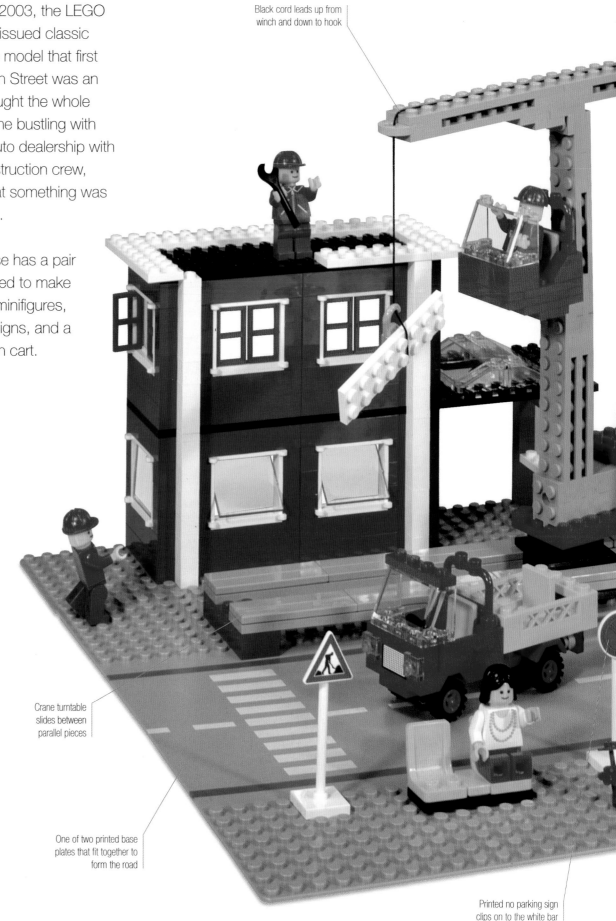

Black cord leads up from winch and down to hook

Crane turntable slides between parallel pieces

One of two printed base plates that fit together to form the road

Printed no parking sign clips on to the white bar

• Although the set is very close to the original, some previously painted parts now have stickers. A few pieces that were no longer in production (such as the female minifigure's hair piece) were also replaced with modern versions.

• Sharp-eyed fans may also notice that the green markings on the base plate are more rounded in the update.

• All eight minifigures have classic smiley faces to match the head pieces used in the original.

• The car dealership has two floors. Downstairs, there are car brochures (stickers on tiles) and there is room for a car. Upstairs, there is a desk with two chairs and a sloped brick with a printed computer screen.

Guided Tour

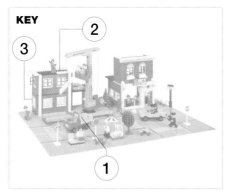

< **WINDOW DELIVERY**
The truck, with its roofless driver's cabin, delivers eight sets of red-framed windows destined for the top floor of the hotel. Mind your step!

∧ **FINISHED BUILDING** Elements from the crane are used to make the hotel sign, so the hotel cannot be completed until the crane is taken apart. A yellow sticker adds the final touch.

∧ **FURNISHED HOTEL** Once the crane has been dismantled, several of its elements can be used to create hotel furniture, such as a chair and two beds with pillows.

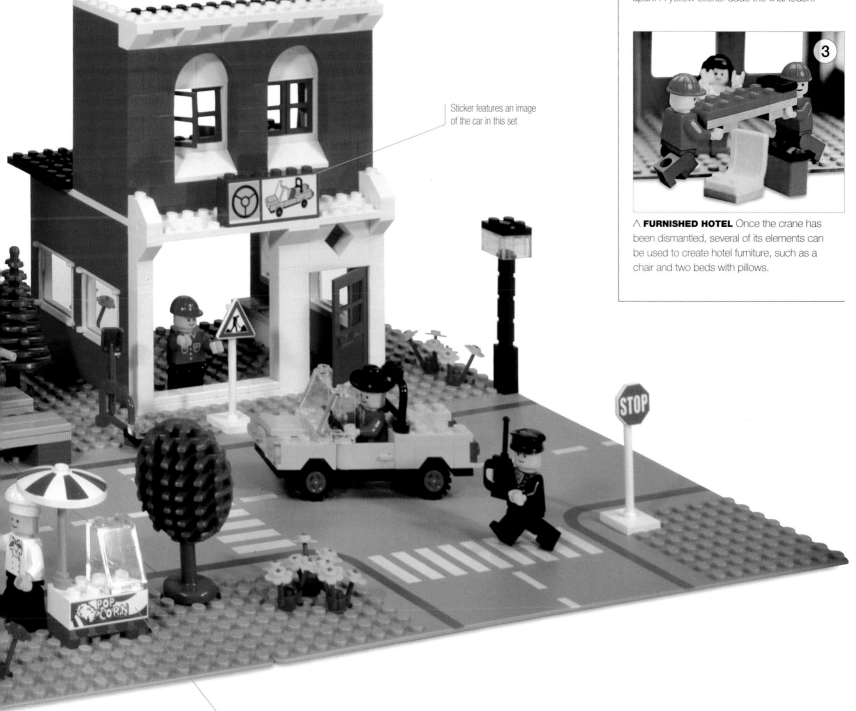

Sticker features an image of the car in this set

Sticker detail on popcorn cart

Viking Fortress against the Fafnir Dragon

2005 • LEGO® Vikings • #7019 • Pieces: 1019 • Minifigures: 6

In the historical-but-fantastical spirit of LEGO Castle came the LEGO Vikings—fierce warriors with horned helmets who battled legendary creatures from Norse mythology in seven sets released between 2005 and 2006. They made a big impact with their new minifigure faces, decorations, weapons, and armor pieces, and their impressively long model names—such as the Viking Fortress against the Fafnir Dragon, the largest set in the line.

The Fafnir Dragon is quite posable thanks to ball-jointed elements from the BIONICLE® line of buildable action figures. When he lays siege to the fortress walls (made with palisade bricks to mimic wooden poles), the Viking defenders can fight back with swords, axes, and firing catapults.

"This is a very unusual shape for a LEGO castle. We took inspiration from four Danish ring fortresses from the Viking age."

Bjarke Lykke Madsen, LEGO Design Master

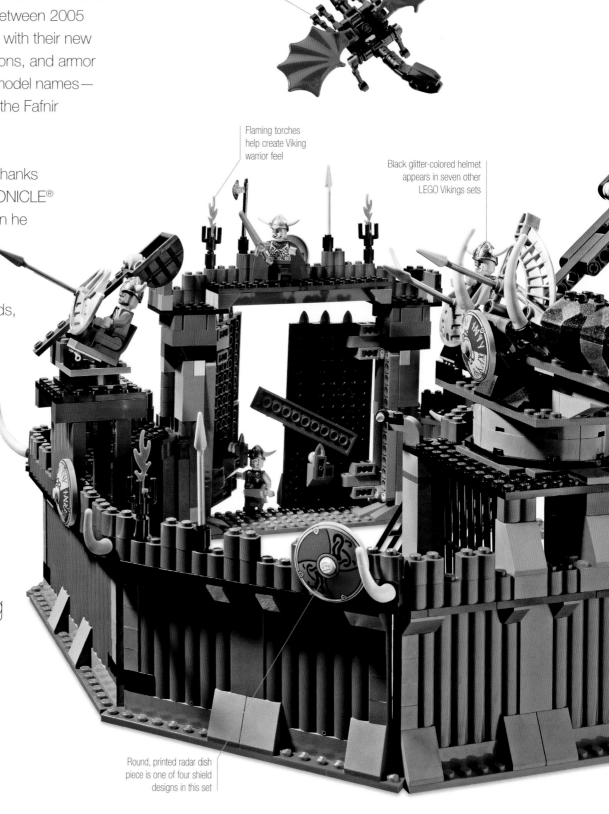

Baby dragon has six legs

Flaming torches help create Viking warrior feel

Black glitter-colored helmet appears in seven other LEGO Vikings sets

Round, printed radar dish piece is one of four shield designs in this set

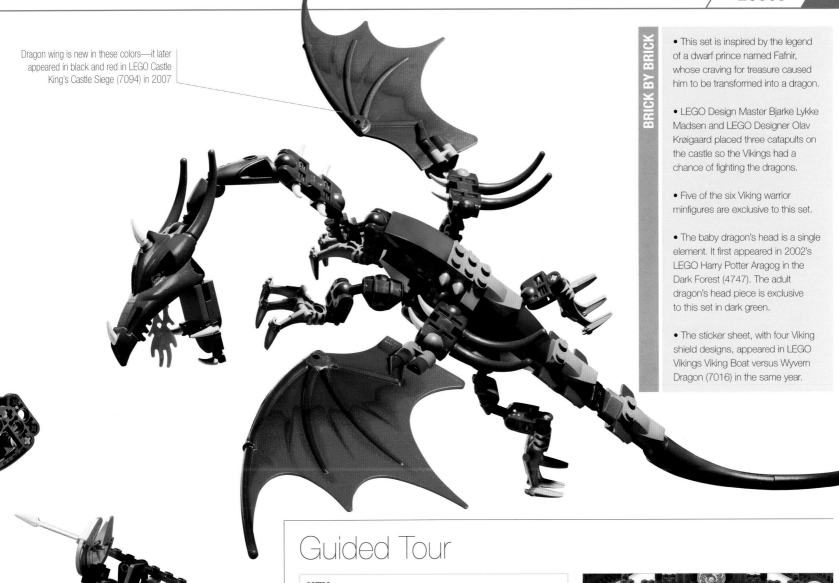

Dragon wing is new in these colors—it later appeared in black and red in LEGO Castle King's Castle Siege (7094) in 2007

• This set is inspired by the legend of a dwarf prince named Fafnir, whose craving for treasure caused him to be transformed into a dragon.

• LEGO Design Master Bjarke Lykke Madsen and LEGO Designer Olav Krøigaard placed three catapults on the castle so the Vikings had a chance of fighting the dragons.

• Five of the six Viking warrior minifigures are exclusive to this set.

• The baby dragon's head is a single element. It first appeared in 2002's LEGO Harry Potter Aragog in the Dark Forest (4747). The adult dragon's head piece is exclusive to this set in dark green.

• The sticker sheet, with four Viking shield designs, appeared in LEGO Vikings Viking Boat versus Wyvern Dragon (7016) in the same year.

Brown palisade walls first appeared in LEGO Western Fort Legoredo (6769) in 1996

Guided Tour

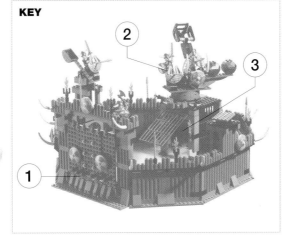

KEY

∧ **ARMORED FRONT DOOR** There is only one way in and one way out of the Viking fortress. Once shut, the double doors can be secured with a plate behind the doors.

∧ **AIM AND FIRE** Two types of catapult come with this set. The smaller version (of which there are two) fires unpainted gray minifigure head elements used as shots. The larger, heavily armored catapult fires metallic rocks. Both types are mounted on turntables and can rotate for accurate shooting.

∧ **BEAST BEHIND BARS** The hinged, single-piece cage door can lift up and down. A 2x12 brown plate can be lodged across the entrance to ensure there is no escape!

Kit Fisto
• 2007 • LEGO® *Star Wars*® • #7661

LEGO Family
• 1974 • LEGO Figures • #200

Kai DX
• 2011 • LEGO® NINJAGO™ • #2507

Skeleton Warrior
• 2007 • LEGO Castle • #7094

Professor Quirrell
• 2001 • LEGO® Harry Potter™ • #4702

Andrea
• 2012 • LEGO® Friends • #3932

Red Spaceman
• 1980 • LEGOLAND Space • #6901

Mom
• 2015 • LEGO® DUPLO® • #10585

Tara Wike | Design Manager

Tara began her career in architecture before joining the LEGO Group in 2009 as an element designer. She was placed in the collectible LEGO Minifigures team, and is now the creative lead. Unusually, Tara has worked solely on minifigures, and has become somewhat of a minifigure expert, or as she puts it, the "minifigure police!" Tara likes to think about how new elements in the Minifigures line can be used in other sets, for example the waiter's tray could be used as a sign on the side of a building. The Diner Waitress is based on Tara. As a joke, the designers gave her a "judgey" face on the other side as she is known for always having opinions!

Bernard Bear
• 1979 • LEGO FABULAND • #329

Lady Robot
• 2013 • LEGO Minifigures • #71002

Diner Waitress
• 2013 • LEGO Minifigures • #71002

Giant Troll
• 2008 • LEGO Castle • #7048

Captain Redbeard
• 1989 • LEGOLAND Pirates • #6285

Cowboy
• 1976 • Model Sets • #210

Chicken Suit Guy
• 2013 • LEGO Minifigures • #71000

Wyldstyle
• 2015 • THE LEGO® MOVIE™ • #70819

MINIFIGURES AND MORE

LEGO® characters through the years

LEGO® figures have come a long way since the brick-built, round-headed LEGO Family members of 1974. From them evolved the first true minifigure, with two dot eyes, a simple smile, and movable arms and legs. Nowadays, LEGO characters can be aliens or ninja, spacemen or skeletons. They may wear peg-legs, animal heads, or chicken suits. Their sizes range from mini-dolls to giant trolls. Some are even familiar characters from TV shows and movies—and every one of them is packed with personality!

Laval
• 2013 • LEGO® Legends of Chima™ • #70010

Ha-Ya-To
• 2006 • LEGO EXO-FORCE • #7709

Bombur the Dwarf
• 2012 • LEGO® The Hobbit™ • #79003

Fangdam
• 2012 • LEGO NINJAGO • #9445

Marge Simpson
• 2014 • LEGO® The Simpsons™ • #71006

Darth Vader
• 2008 • LEGO Star Wars • #10188

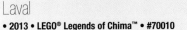

Farmer
• 2009 • LEGO® City • #7637

Sailor
• 1978 • LEGO DUPLO • #534

Mobile Crane

2005 • LEGO® Technic • #8421 • Pieces: 1884

With one of the highest piece-counts of any LEGO® Technic set, the Mobile Crane was one big, yellow chunk of heavy-duty construction machinery when it was released in 2005. It can take 10 hours or more to assemble from its nearly 1,900 elements, but the building time is well worth it! When finished, the crane is loaded with working functions and mechanisms that make it feel just like a (slightly) smaller version of the real thing.

A steering knob on the back controls six of the crane's eight giant wheels for tight turns, and another extends and locks the side outriggers to brace it against heavy loads. Pneumatics raise the boom, and its motorized double-telescoping arm and hook work with the push of a button.

Markus Kossmann | Senior Designer

Markus has been designing LEGO Technic sets and elements since he joined the LEGO Group in 1998. He enjoys creating challenging builds, and he strives to ensure all LEGO Technic models have "AFC": "authenticity," "functionality," and "challenge." As well as mentoring other designers, creating new elements using 3D printers, and working with the building instructions team to make the instructions as simple as possible, Markus occasionally gets to ride the real versions of the vehicles he builds, such as the Mercedes-Benz Unimog U 400 (all in the name of research, of course).

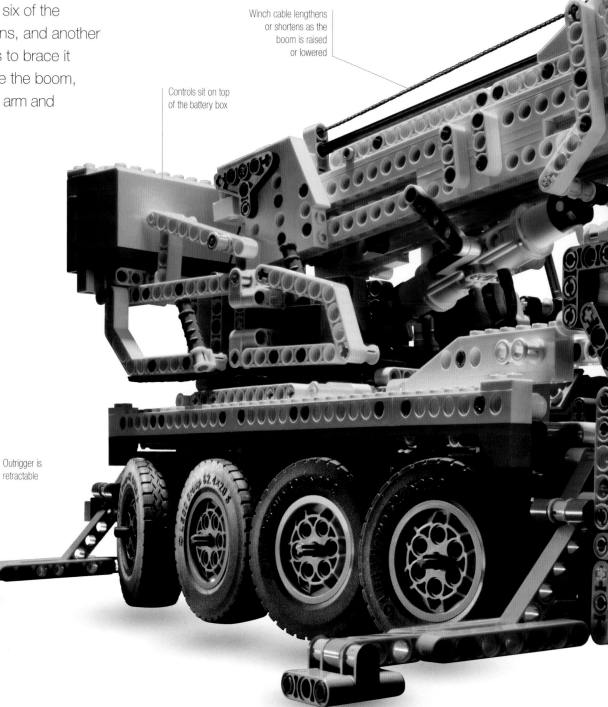

Winch cable lengthens or shortens as the boom is raised or lowered

Controls sit on top of the battery box

Outrigger is retractable

"With play themes, you have to make a story. With LEGO Technic, our vehicles are the story."

Markus Kossman, LEGO Senior Designer

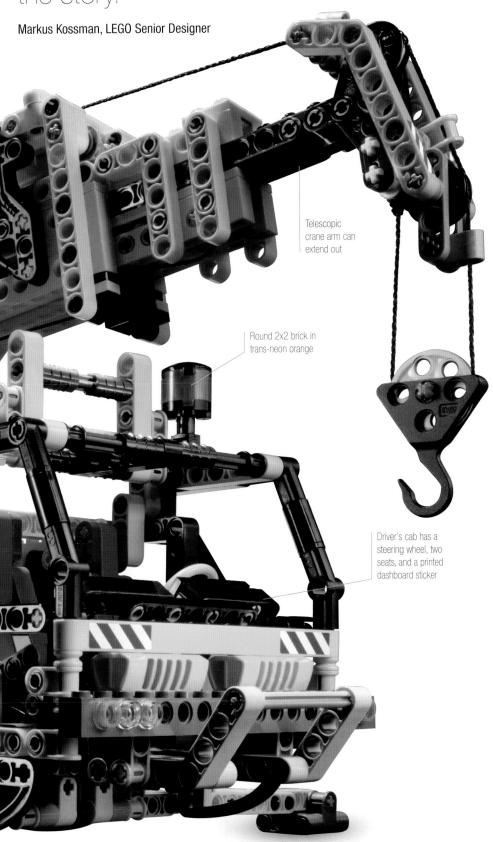

Telescopic crane arm can extend out

Round 2x2 brick in trans-neon orange

Driver's cab has a steering wheel, two seats, and a printed dashboard sticker

Guided Tour

KEY

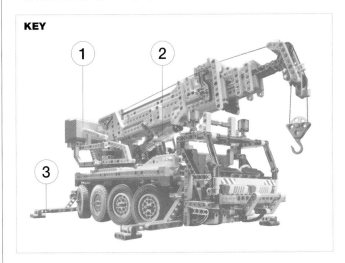

> **BATTERY BOX**
At the push of a red button, the 9-volt battery drives the motor to extend the telescopic arm of the boom and to raise or lower the winch. It also acts as a counterweight.

∧ **PNEUMATIC ACTION** To raise the boom, a manual pneumatic pump drives the air via LEGO Technic tubing into two pneumatic cylinders. The hook that hangs from the telescopic arm has appeared in 10 other sets.

∧ **REAR CONTROLS** The light-gray knob can be turned to enable the outriggers to extend down. The larger, black knob below is turned to change the direction of the wheels.

The Batcave: The Penguin and Mr. Freeze's Invasion

2006 • LEGO® Batman™ • #7783 • Pieces: 1075 • Minifigures: 7

What super hero could be more suited to LEGO bricks and building than Batman? Swinging into action in 2006, the LEGO Batman play theme let builders create the black (and very dark gray) comic-book world of the Dark Knight. The centerpiece of the collection was The Batcave: The Penguin and Mr. Freeze's Invasion, which packed a dynamic degree of heroes, villains, vehicles, and crime-fighting equipment into one epic set.

The Batcave has it all, from a mini-sub and hench-birds for the Penguin to a block of ice in which Mr. Freeze can trap loyal butler Alfred. Batman and Robin get vehicles for missions on ice or water, as well as a crime-tracking computer, a Bat-Signal and net-launcher, and a quick-change capsule that switches the billionaire Bruce Wayne to his secret identity of the Caped Crusader.

A geared elevation mechanism rotates and tilts the defense turret

The Penguin's sub has a periscope that moves up and down

Knob rotates the turntable 360 degrees for launching the Bat-Blade vehicle

Guided Tour

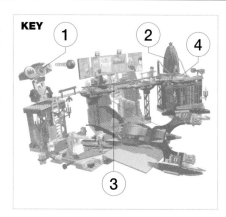

KEY ① ② ④ ③

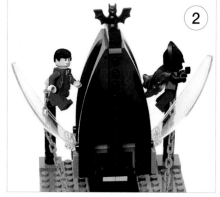

△ DEFENSE TURRET The tower has a Bat-Signal spotlight, net launcher—the net shoots out by pushing a round brick at the back—and spring-loaded rocket, which is activated by pulling the red cone back.

◁ TRANSFORMATION CHAMBER Both Bruce Wayne and Batman minifigures fit inside the pod. Simply spin it around and Bruce changes into the Caped Crusader (and vice versa).

Detailed stickers show that Two-Face and the Joker are being tracked on the Bat-Computer

Chris Bonven Johansen | Design Master

Chris has worked as a graphic designer for the LEGO Group since 1997. He designs graphics for printed decorations on minifigures and models, stickers, and comics. The themes he has had most fun working on include LEGO Studios, Batman, *Star Wars*, The Simpsons, and the collectible Minifigures line. He picks archetypal characteristics to ensure his minifigure subjects are instantly recognizable, and works hard to make sure that the facial expressions show the personalities of the characters. When he can, he likes to add humor, such as an "I love Gotham" sticker on the Joker's ice-cream van in 2008's LEGO Batman The Tumbler: Joker's Ice Cream Surprise (7888).

Batman's workout bench

Robin's jetski has a rotating cannon

< CONTROL CENTER This hi-tech area includes the Batcomputer, the Batphone, a fingerprint analysis area, comfy swivel chairs, and Batarangs and Bat-cuffs hidden under the table.

> HOLDING CELL Pulling out a round brick behind the jail opens a trapdoor to drop intruders into the cell below. Fortunately for them, the jail has a sewer escape pipe!

∧ HENCH-BIRDS The mini penguins have a clip on one side for holding guns. The plate with tooth piece used for the beak also appears on a bird and duck in 2009's LEGO Castle Medieval Market Village (10193).

Grand Titan

2006 • LEGO® EXO-FORCE™ • #7701 • Pieces: 196 • Minifigures: 1

Activated in 2006, the LEGO EXO-FORCE theme took inspiration from the mecha action of Japanese comics and animation. It created a futuristic world in which a pitched battle was taking place between brave humans and destructive robots for control of the split Sentai Mountain. One of the main defenders of humanity was the green-haired and hot-tempered Takeshi, pilot of the mighty Grand Titan battle machine.

Strong joints in the Grand Titan's legs allow the mech to be posed for action while fighting robot forces. The hinged electromagnetic pulse pincer on its right arm can clamp onto enemies, and a light-up brick behind the pilot sends power through a clear cable to the six-barreled laser cannon on its left arm.

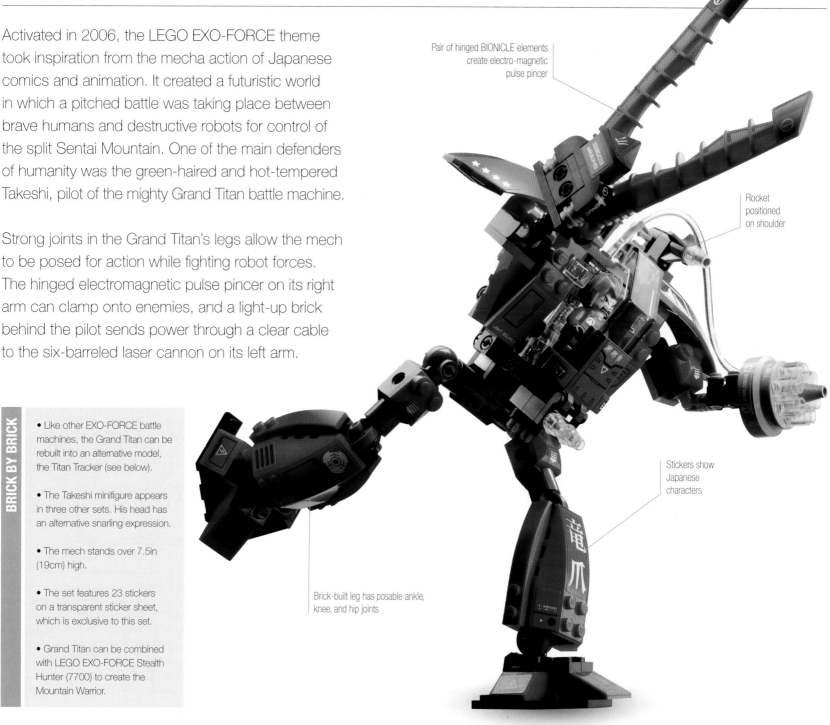

Pair of hinged BIONICLE elements create electro-magnetic pulse pincer

Rocket positioned on shoulder

Stickers show Japanese characters

Brick-built leg has posable ankle, knee, and hip joints

BRICK BY BRICK

• Like other EXO-FORCE battle machines, the Grand Titan can be rebuilt into an alternative model, the Titan Tracker (see below).

• The Takeshi minifigure appears in three other sets. His head has an alternative snarling expression.

• The mech stands over 7.5in (19cm) high.

• The set features 23 stickers on a transparent sticker sheet, which is exclusive to this set.

• Grand Titan can be combined with LEGO EXO-FORCE Stealth Hunter (7700) to create the Mountain Warrior.

Guided Tour

KEY

∧ **LASER CANNON**
The illuminating, spinning laser cannon is made up of six trans-neon green 1x1 round bricks, and is lit via the fiber-optic cable.

< **COCKPIT** A narrow windshield swings up to form Takeshi's cockpit. The minifigure stands in front of the light brick. Pressing a lever on the mech's back activates the light brick to "power up" the laser.

> **HINGED BODY** The mech has joints in the arms, hips, and ankles, allowing it to be posed in many different ways, as seen in the set's Titan Tracker alternative model.

Axonn

2006 • BIONICLE® • #8733 • Pieces: 196

The popular BIONICLE line, launched in 2001, features a universe of bio-mechanical heroes, villains, and creatures in the form of buildable action figures. These figures are made from LEGO Technic parts, ball-jointed pieces for movement, and decorative armor and weapon elements, including the theme's signature collectible masks of power. Part of the 2006 story, the mighty titan Axonn was a champion of justice whose origins lay in the legendary saga's distant past.

It isn't hard to see where Axonn got his name—it comes from his massive ax, the giant blades of which can only be found in one other set. On his face he wears the Kanohi Rode, the deception-piercing Mask of Truth.

- This set can be combined with BIONICLE Brutaka (8734) and Vezon and Fenrakk (8764) to create Vezon and Kardas (10204)—a new version of the Vezon figure and a dragon figure.

- This was the last set to contain the BIONICLE chest armor in the pearl-light-gray color.

- Axonn's Kanohi Rode mask was new in 2006. It featured in three BIONICLE sets that year.

- The double-headed ax is made up of two identical BIONICLE elements. The element also appeared in Race for the Mask of Life (8624) in 2006, where it formed part of a gateway.

Mask is a single piece

Eye visible through mask is trans-neon-green element

Identical BIONICLE pieces are fixed at either end of the ax—the element first appeared in 2003

Base of foot is formed with two black LEGO Technic beams

Guided Tour

KEY

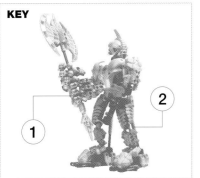

1

2

1

∧ **PREHENSILE GRIP** Axonn's huge hands were a new design. Ball joints act as fingertips and the fingers and thumb can be posed to enable him to grip his weapon.

2

∧ **PISTON LEGS** Ball joints connect the front and back of the leg to the foot. A piston on the back of the leg moves in and out when the leg is articulated, and aids stability.

Monster Dino

2007 • LEGO® Creator • #4958 • Pieces: 792

In 2007, the LEGO Creator line introduced Power Functions, a series of lights, motors, and infrared remote-control transmitters and receivers that could be built into LEGO sets to give them movement and special effects. One of the first sets to feature Power Functions parts was Monster Dino, a three-in-one model that combined standard bricks with LEGO® Technic parts and glow-in-the-dark detail elements to create any one of a trio of ferocious-looking predatory creatures.

At the press of a button, this monster of a dinosaur can walk forward or backward while swinging his tail, thrash his arms, and open his jaws to roar with the help of a sound brick inside his toothy mouth. The included instructions show how to use the same collection of parts to build a scuttling spider or a crawling crocodile.

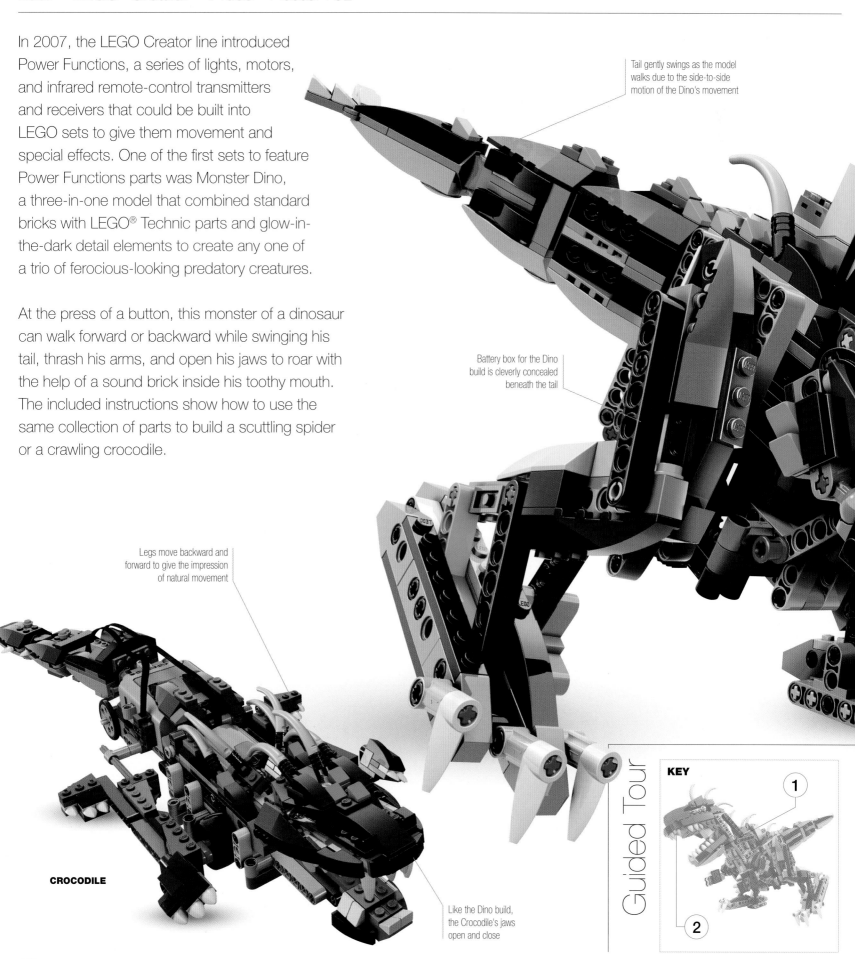

Tail gently swings as the model walks due to the side-to-side motion of the Dino's movement

Battery box for the Dino build is cleverly concealed beneath the tail

Legs move backward and forward to give the impression of natural movement

CROCODILE

Like the Dino build, the Crocodile's jaws open and close

Guided Tour

KEY

1

2

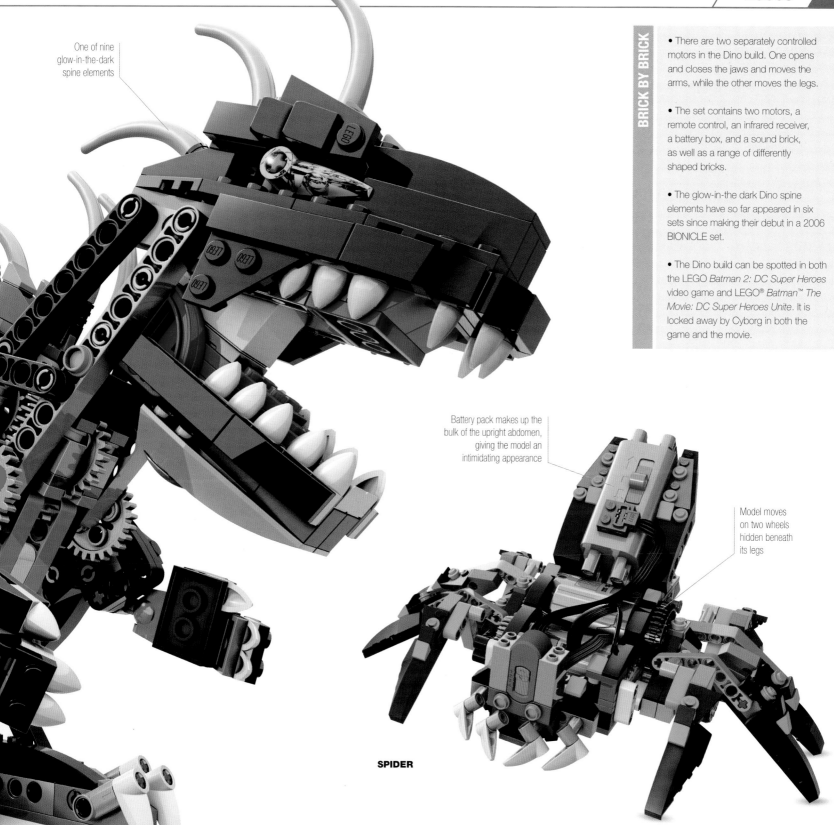

One of nine glow-in-the-dark spine elements

• There are two separately controlled motors in the Dino build. One opens and closes the jaws and moves the arms, while the other moves the legs.

• The set contains two motors, a remote control, an infrared receiver, a battery box, and a sound brick, as well as a range of differently shaped bricks.

• The glow-in-the-dark Dino spine elements have so far appeared in six sets since making their debut in a 2006 BIONICLE set.

• The Dino build can be spotted in both the LEGO *Batman 2: DC Super Heroes* video game and LEGO® *Batman*™ *The Movie: DC Super Heroes Unite*. It is locked away by Cyborg in both the game and the movie.

Battery pack makes up the bulk of the upright abdomen, giving the model an intimidating appearance

Model moves on two wheels hidden beneath its legs

SPIDER

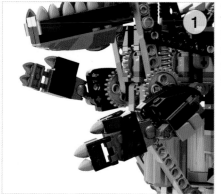

< JUST LIKE CLOCKWORK
The LEGO Technic gear system inside the model's chest allows a single motor to control the movement of the arms and the opening and closing of the jaw.

> CAUSING UPROAR The gray soundbox, hidden within the model's mouth, is unique to this set. It plays a terrifying roar when triggered by the motion of the jaw.

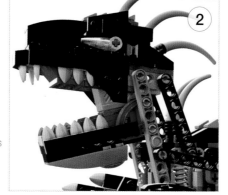

∧ **DUAL CONTROL** The remote control connects to the set's infrared receiver. It is able to control the two motors individually.

143

Fire Station

2007 • LEGO® City • #7945 • Pieces: 600 • Minifigures: 4

After a brief period as LEGO City in 1999–2003, and then LEGO World City, the classic LEGO Town play theme took on its modern name of LEGO City in 2005. The name reflected the theme's focus on life in the big city—and where would a big city be without a modern fire department to keep it safe? The 2007 Fire Station was designed for ease of assembly by younger builders, with numbered instruction books and parts bags so that it could be put together one section or vehicle at a time.

The Fire Station includes a fire truck and a Fire Chief's car, each with its own garage. The garages and the main building are built individually and then snapped together with LEGO Technic pins, making it simple to separate and even rearrange them.

BRICK BY BRICK

• LEGO City sets nearly always include coffee mugs. Henrik Andersen, who designed Fire Station, likes to put coffee machines in his LEGO City sets whenever possible, too.

• The fire truck's license plate sticker features the designer's initials—"HA" for Henrik Andersen—followed by the LEGO set number.

• The fire truck's crane extends to 15in (39cm) and contains rare LEGO Technic pieces.

• The inclusion of the vehicle cleaning area was inspired by the LEGO City team's trip to a real fire station. They also visited a fire academy where they dressed up in firefighting gear and put out fires.

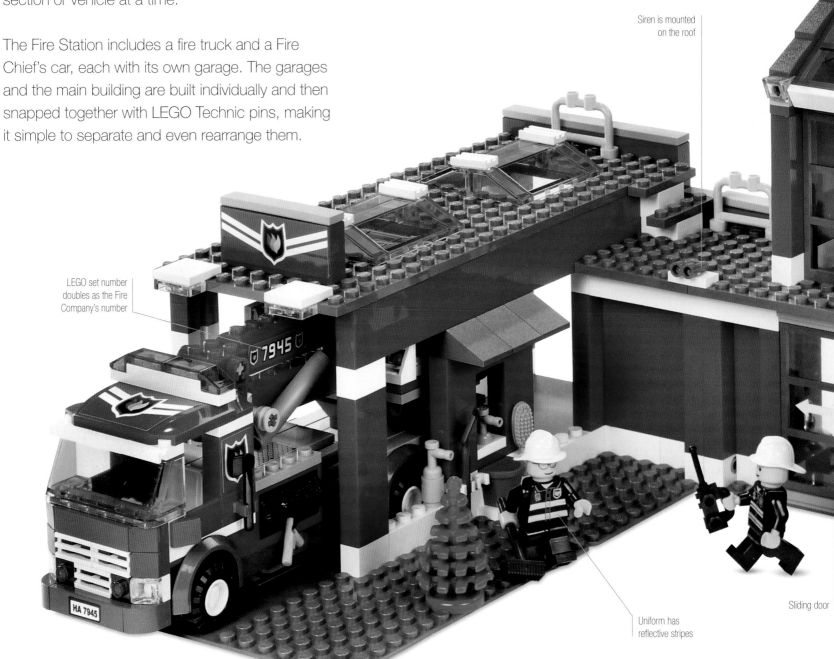

Siren is mounted on the roof

LEGO set number doubles as the Fire Company's number

Uniform has reflective stripes

Sliding door

KEY

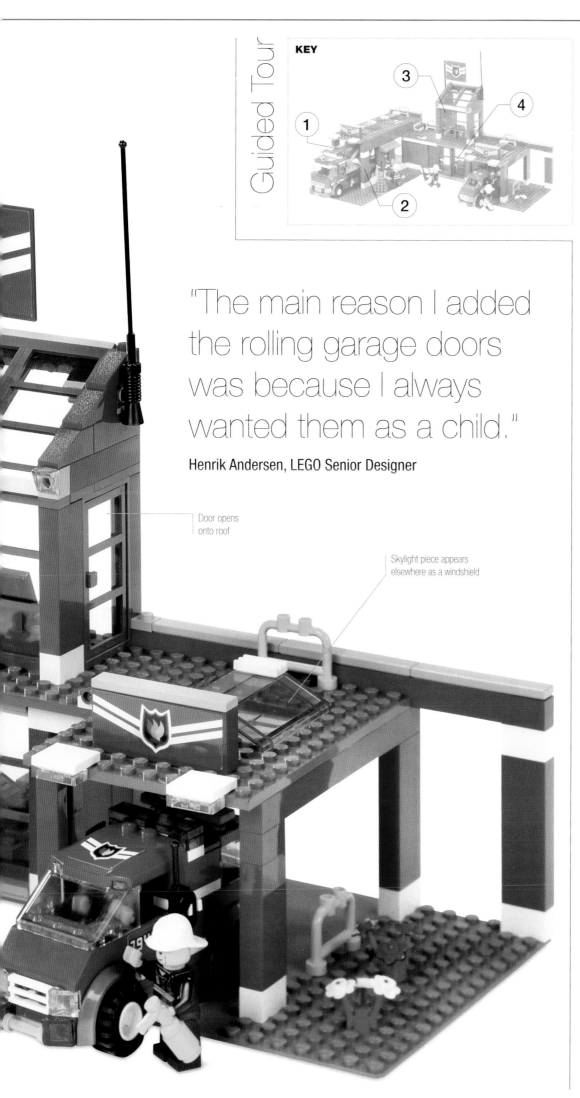

"The main reason I added the rolling garage doors was because I always wanted them as a child."

Henrik Andersen, LEGO Senior Designer

Door opens onto roof

Skylight piece appears elsewhere as a windshield

1

∧ **TO THE RESCUE!** The truck's crane has a basket at the end for reaching the city's tallest buildings. A minifigure can operate the boom from a seat on the side of the truck. The hose reaches up to the top of the ladder.

2

∧ **TWIN GARAGES**
The garages have functioning doors that roll up and down. This feature had been discontinued, but was reintroduced in City Airport (10159) in 2004, before being used again in this set.

3

> **CONTROL ROOM**
The Chief sits in the top-floor control room. His silver-colored helmet has appeared in around 30 sets.

4

∧ **ALARM ROOM** The firefighters' modern office is equipped with a state-of-the-art computer, as well as a coffee machine for early-morning emergencies.

Aquabase Invasion

2007 • LEGO® Aqua Raiders • #7775 • Pieces: 840 • Minifigures: 4, plus skeleton

Although the Aquazone play theme ended in 1999, a successor surfaced in 2007 with the arrival of the dauntless LEGO Aqua Raiders. Combining the undersea action of the older sets with the look of 21st-century submarine technology, the new theme pitted treasure-hunting divers and their vehicles against huge beasts from the ocean depths. The Aqua Raiders' greatest fight was in the Aquabase Invasion set, when their base came under attack by a ravenous giant squid.

With glow-in-the-dark eyes and tentacles, and a skeleton in its transparent belly, that squid means serious business. Fortunately, the Aquabase is armed with harpoon cannons and a rubber-tipped torpedo to drive off its multi-armed attacker. If the exploration pod needs reinforcements, a mini-sub can drop through the tube and into battle.

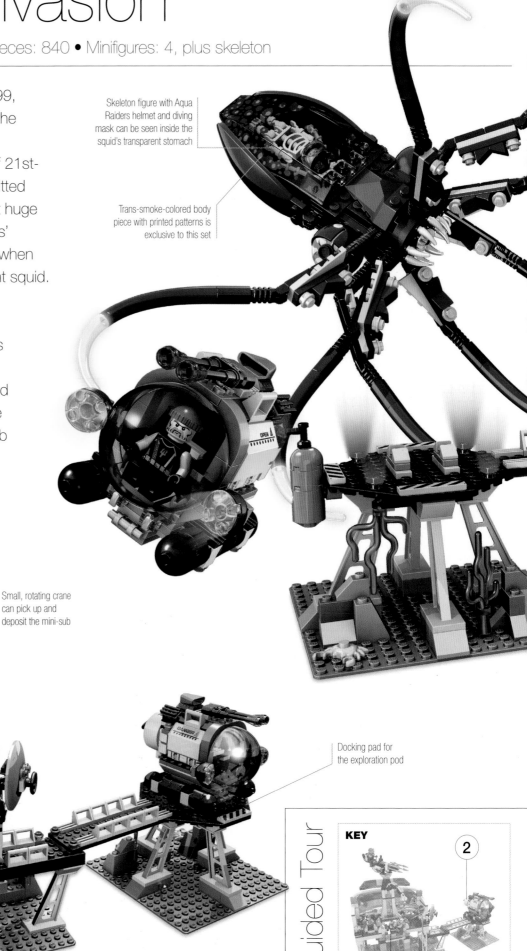

Skeleton figure with Aqua Raiders helmet and diving mask can be seen inside the squid's transparent stomach

Trans-smoke-colored body piece with printed patterns is exclusive to this set

Small, rotating crane can pick up and deposit the mini-sub

Docking pad for the exploration pod

REAR VIEW

Guided Tour

KEY

①

②

Manned harpoon turret with spring-loaded firing aqua-rocket and storage for flippers at the back

Control room's viewing gallery has a large window element, which is unique to this set in trans-light-blue

Mini-sub launching ramp

- The ends of the squid's tentacles are glow-in-the-dark pieces that first appeared a year earlier in BIONICLE Piraka Stronghold (8894).

- The squid's red and white eyeball was new for this set. The following year it appeared as a fruit bowl in LEGO BELVILLE Sunshine Home (7586).

- The sticker sheet in this set is identical to the sticker sheet in LEGO Aqua Raiders Crab Crusher (7774). Each set uses some but not all of the stickers on the sheet.

- This is the biggest of the seven Aqua Raiders sets released.

- Three of the four Aqua Raider minifigures are unique to this set. All the minifigures have printing on the front and backs of their torsos and helmets.

1 < **ACTION STATIONS** The main control room features a computer, weapons, and oxygen tanks. A minifigure puts on his helmet before heading outside. The gray ramp is pushed up to launch his mini-sub down through the tube.

> **EXPLORATION POD** There is space for one minifigure to pilot the pod. Two central hatches can open to reveal a cargo bay where a crate, containing coins and gems, can be stowed.

2

Inter-City Passenger Train Set
• 1980 • LEGO Trains • #7740

ALL ABOARD

LEGO® trains through the years

The earliest electric LEGO trains were produced in the mid-1960s and featured 4.5-volt battery-powered engines and thin blue rails. The 1980s introduced gray rails, glowing lights, and remote-controlled options for switching tracks, regulating speed, and even more functions. Many modern train sets are part of the LEGO® City theme and can be operated by LEGO Power Functions controls and motorized components, while other loco-notable models include chunky and child-safe LEGO® DUPLO® trains, miniature LEGO Creator trains, and the haunted ghost train battled by the LEGO Monster Fighters.

Steam Cargo Train Set
• 1985 • LEGO Trains • #7722

Emerald Express
• 2014 • LEGO® Creator • #31015

Maersk Train
• 2011 • LEGO® Advanced Models • #10219

Christmas Train
• 2012 • LEGO Seasonal • #40034

Cargo Train
• 2010 • LEGO® City • #7939

The Ghost Train
• 2012 • LEGO Monster Fighters • #9467

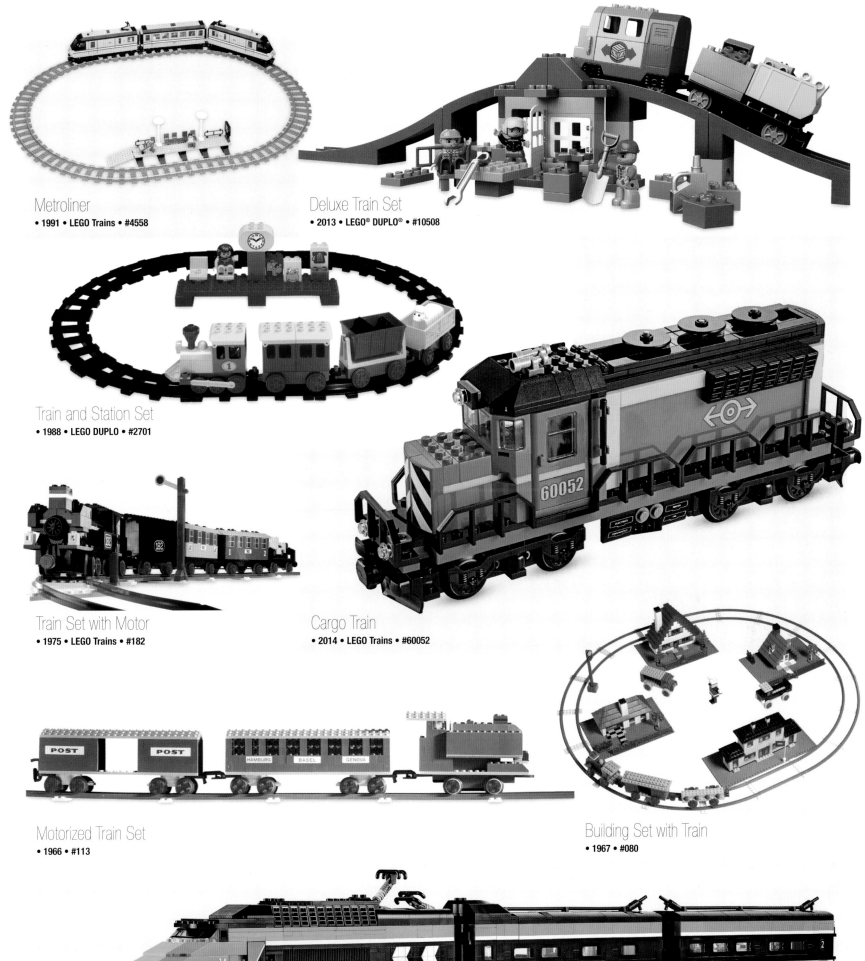

Metroliner
- 1991 • LEGO Trains • #4558

Deluxe Train Set
- 2013 • LEGO® DUPLO® • #10508

Train and Station Set
- 1988 • LEGO DUPLO • #2701

Train Set with Motor
- 1975 • LEGO Trains • #182

Cargo Train
- 2014 • LEGO Trains • #60052

Motorized Train Set
- 1966 • #113

Building Set with Train
- 1967 • #080

Horizon Express
- 2013 • LEGO® Creator Expert • #10233

Hobby Trains

2007 • LEGO® Factory • #10183 • Pieces: 1060

Starting in 2005, LEGO Factory let fans create and purchase their own custom sets using 3D building software and the LEGO online store. Some fans even worked with the LEGO model designers to make officially produced sets, including 2007's Hobby Trains. The set came with steps for constructing the main "Crocodile" engine model, and instructions for a whopping 29 more could be downloaded from the LEGO Factory website!

An expert-level set for builders 16 and over, Hobby Trains was made as a fond farewell to the 9-volt LEGO train system, which had recently been replaced by a new radio-controlled electric motor. The main model is based on a Swiss electric locomotive with articulated noses at both ends for traveling around curved tracks. It does not come with a motor, but has directions for installing one from the builder's own collection.

Printed envelope tile was first introduced in LEGO BELVILLE in 1999

1x1 trans-clear round plate has appeared in more than 500 sets

The old-style magnet piece on the buffer was discontinued after this year

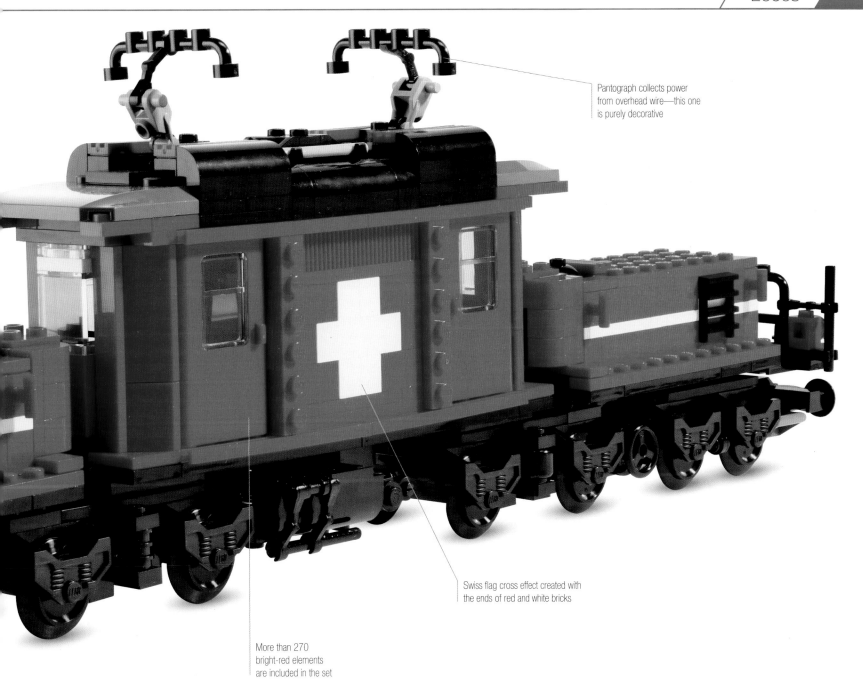

Pantograph collects power from overhead wire—this one is purely decorative

Swiss flag cross effect created with the ends of red and white bricks

More than 270 bright-red elements are included in the set

CREATIVE CHALLENGE Ten LEGO train fans from across the world were each given the same bag of 1,080 bricks to create models for this train builder set. Thirty favorites were chosen for the set, including steam trains, trolley cars, cabooses, and gondolas.

Ultimate Collector's *Millennium Falcon*®

2007 • LEGO® *Star Wars*® • #10179 • Pieces: 5195 • Minifigures: 5

What's 33in (84cm) long, 22in (56cm) wide, and can make the Kessel Run in less than 12 parsecs? It's the Ultimate Collector's *Millennium Falcon*, and in 2007, it was the biggest LEGO set ever made! Released as part of the Ultimate Collector Series, the gigantic model was hailed by fans as one of the best LEGO sets of all time.

There are multiple LEGO models of Han Solo's beloved smuggling starship, but at more than 5,000 pieces, this is by far the largest and most movie-accurate one. From its side-mounted cockpit to the quad-laser turrets on the top and bottom, it is built in a close scale to its minifigure pilots and passengers. It has a framework of LEGO® Technic elements hidden inside to make it sturdy, too.

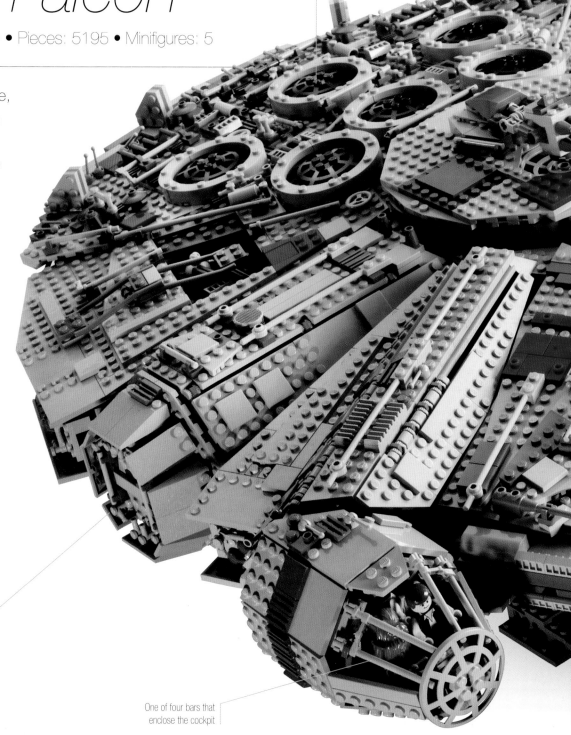

Heat exhaust vent

Starboard docking ring and boarding ramp

One of four bars that enclose the cockpit

Guided Tour

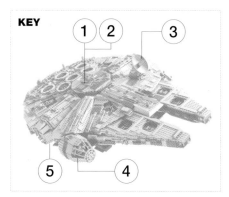

KEY

1 2 3

5 4

< **UPPER QUAD LASER CANNON**
The cannon can rotate 360 degrees for precise aiming and firing. The laser cannon underneath the model can also rotate.

> **GUNNER'S SEAT**
Luke Skywalker's minifigure faces upward in the gunner's seat to fire the upper quad laser cannon.

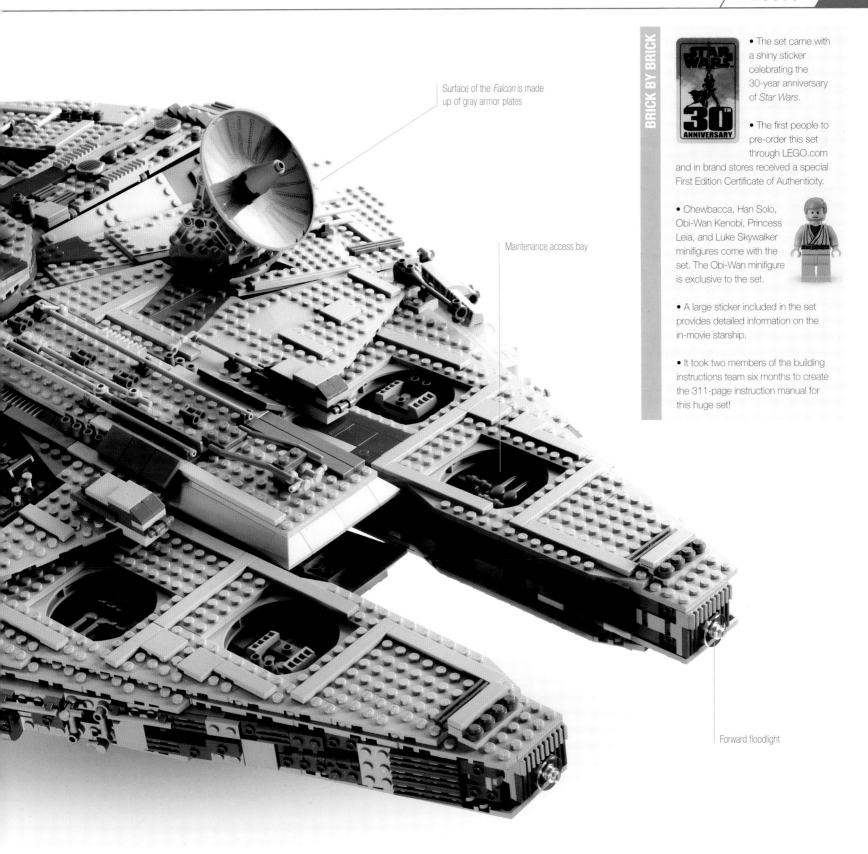

Surface of the *Falcon* is made up of gray armor plates

Maintenance access bay

Forward floodlight

BRICK BY BRICK

- The set came with a shiny sticker celebrating the 30-year anniversary of *Star Wars*.

- The first people to pre-order this set through LEGO.com and in brand stores received a special First Edition Certificate of Authenticity.

- Chewbacca, Han Solo, Obi-Wan Kenobi, Princess Leia, and Luke Skywalker minifigures come with the set. The Obi-Wan minifigure is exclusive to the set.

- A large sticker included in the set provides detailed information on the in-movie starship.

- It took two members of the building instructions team six months to create the 311-page instruction manual for this huge set!

3

△ **RADAR DISH** A 10x10 dish with spokes pattern printing is exclusive to this set. It is mounted on top of the craft and can rotate 360 degrees and move up and down.

4

< **CONICAL COCKPIT** The roof of the cockpit lifts off, and there is space for four minifigures. Three stickers make up the display panels. The two T-shaped steering control pieces made their debut in 1984.

> **BOARDING RAMP** Behind the starboard docking ring, a hinged ramp can descend from the base of the *Falcon*. It provides swift access for the minifigure crew!

5

Taj Mahal

2008 • LEGO® Advanced Models • #10189 • Pieces: 5922

The LEGO® *Star Wars® Millennium Falcon* (10179) may be the largest LEGO model in terms of size, but its record for having the most pieces was beaten just a year after its release. A fantastic replica of India's famous seventeenth century marble mausoleum, the Taj Mahal set is built from nearly 6,000 LEGO elements, setting a record that it still holds today. How can it have the most elements, but not be the biggest? Simple—in order to create its intricate details, many of its pieces are extremely small!

Designed for display rather than play (no minifigures here!), the Taj Mahal is an advanced LEGO builder's dream. It features rare element shapes and colors, and uses unusual building techniques in the construction of its elegant minarets, arches, and spired central dome.

"It's strange—I went to a fan event in New Zealand. One fan asked me to sign her completed Taj Mahal and another asked me to sign the unopened box."

Henrik Andersen, LEGO Senior Designer

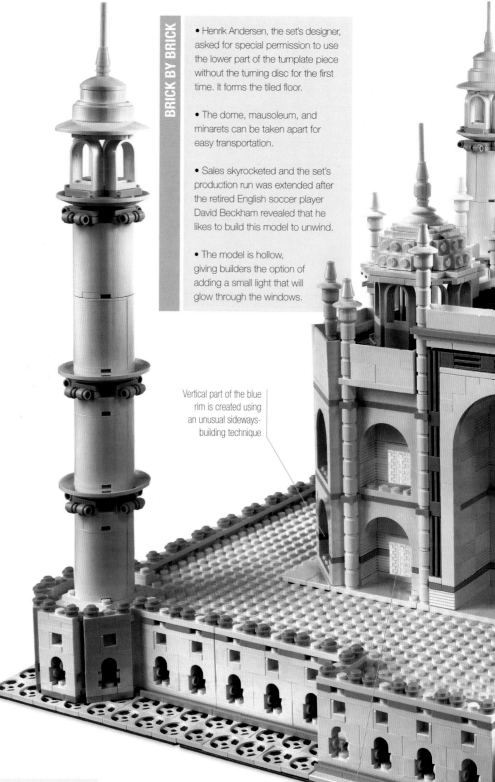

• Henrik Andersen, the set's designer, asked for special permission to use the lower part of the turnplate piece without the turning disc for the first time. It forms the tiled floor.

• The dome, mausoleum, and minarets can be taken apart for easy transportation.

• Sales skyrocketed and the set's production run was extended after the retired English soccer player David Beckham revealed that he likes to build this model to unwind.

• The model is hollow, giving builders the option of adding a small light that will glow through the windows.

Vertical part of the blue rim is created using an unusual sideways-building technique

Each small window is made up of 12 clear 1x1 plates

Henrik Andersen | LEGO Senior Designer

Henrik has worked for the LEGO Group since 1998, first on LEGO Model Team (a vehicle line), and then LEGO *Star Wars*. He designed the Ultimate Collector Series X-wing Fighter (7721) and TIE Interceptor (7181). Vehicles have always been his favorite sets to create, and Henrik now works primarily on LEGO City, although he also takes on enormous side projects, such as the Taj Mahal and Sopwith Camel (10226). When he completed the Taj Mahal, Henrik rang the designer of the Ultimate Collector's *Millennium Falcon* (10179) to joke about the fact that he had beaten his record-breaking piece count!

Bright yellow minifigure head piece makes up part of the dome's finial

Large onion-shaped dome is formed by stacked plate pieces

104 "lamp holder" pieces (named after their most-common use) decorate the model

200 white lower turnplate pieces and six blue base plates create an elegant tiled floor effect

Guided Tour

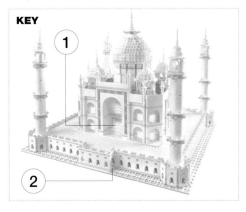

KEY

1

2

1

∧ **BEAUTIFUL DECORATION** The model features windows made with patterns of clear and solid plates. The mid-blue tiles around the lower windows represent the stone inlay designs of the original building.

2

∧ **MAUSOLEUM PLATFORM** Arched and square-shaped recesses decorate the entire square platform. As with the real building, there are stairwells along one side of the platform.

∧ **OVERHEAD VIEW** A view from above shows the model's perfectly symmetrical design. Its designer, Henrik Andersen, studied the top of the building using Google Maps.

Green Grocer

2008 • LEGO® Advanced Models • #10185 • Pieces: 2352 • Minifigures: 4

The 2008 Green Grocer set was part of the still-ongoing Modular Buildings subtheme, a line of exclusive models for older builders. Each set could be assembled to create a complete minifigure-scaled building on a section of city sidewalk. By connecting several sets together, builders could make an entire neighborhood. Like the other Modular Buildings, the Green Grocer uses special LEGO elements in surprising ways to create its impressively realistic architecture.

The Green Grocer is designed to look charming and a little bit old-timey. On the first floor is a grocery, with fruits and vegetables on display outside. Next door is a lobby for the set of apartments up above. Inside are cleverly built details, such as mailboxes, tiled floors, and even a sneaky rat with a pilfered slice of cheese.

Finial is made from a feather element that was first created for LEGO Western in 1997

Hammer element is used as part of railings

Rare "Rune Stone" flat tiles were originally created for LEGO Vikings sets in 2006

All four minifigures are exclusive to the set

BRICK BY BRICK

• A grandfather clock was originally built to conceal an unattractive part of wall. The designer, Jamie Berard, decided not to use the detail that created the ugly part, but he included a grandfather clock in the final design as he liked it so much.

• This was one of the first LEGO sets to include standard LEGO bricks in a sand-green color.

• LEGO Space skeleton arms are used in the mechanism for the foldable fire escape.

• The white lamp originally appeared in LEGO FABULAND sets. When Jamie Berard heard that the piece was going to be retired, he made a gentleman's agreement that he would use it within a year. He used it in Café Corner (10182) in 2007, and it has featured in every Modular Building since.

• A 1x2x3 train window in white was used in the bay window because the 1x2x3 standard window had not yet been created.

• The set stands 14in (35cm) tall and is 10in (25.5cm) wide.

"Originally, it was all about the building experience. But we slowly learned people want the interiors, details, and stories as well."

Jamie Berard, LEGO Design Manager Specialist

Guided Tour

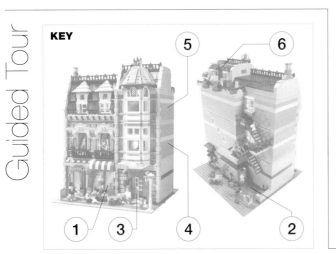

KEY

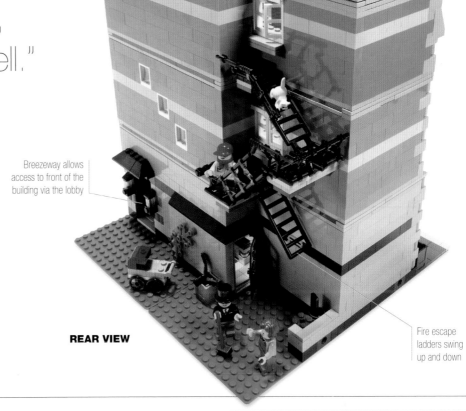

Breezeway allows access to front of the building via the lobby

REAR VIEW

Fire escape ladders swing up and down

∧ **FRESH FRUIT** The shop interior includes a stunning tiled floor, a serving counter complete with cash register, a large display fridge crammed with tins and cartons, and shelves of produce, including lots of fruit and vegetables and croissants.

∧ **COURTYARD** The yard can be reached via a door at the back of the shop or another at the back of the lobby. There are two trash cans and a box containing various tools, a shovel, and a broom.

∧ **LOBBY** The four mailboxes, each containing a letter, add to the realistic feel of this area. Stairs lead up from here to the apartment on the upper floors. There is even a rat hole for builders to discover under the stairs. Eek!

∧ **SECOND FLOOR** The interior has a unique, glowing fireplace, windows framed by heavy red drapes, a table, and more flowers. There are two ornate Juliet balconies and a spot for the cat to hide behind the stairs.

∧ **THIRD FLOOR** Among the detailed features on the top floor of the apartment are a grandfather clock, radiator, colorful rug, and flowering plant. A flight of stairs from the back of this floor leads out onto the roof terrace.

∧ **ROOF TERRACE** A stairway from the back of the third floor leads up to a roof terrace, which is furnished with chairs and a table with a parasol. There is also a grill and some potted plants.

Police Headquarters

2008 • LEGO® City • #7744 • Pieces: 953 • Minifigures: 7

A shiny new Police Headquarters arrived in 2008. While most earlier LEGO police stations were built primarily from black, white, and gray pieces, this set brightened things up with a touch of blue. The result was a modern, hi-tech headquarters for the brave officers of the LEGO City Police Department. Much to the dismay of the locked-up crooks, there was a brand-new handcuffs element as well. On the bright side, at least the prison cells came equipped with toilets!

The Police Headquarters set is full of possibilities for play. It is built in two sections that can be repositioned to create different station layouts. Builders can even stage prison breaks thanks to a pair of dangling keys and a break-away jail cell wall.

"I put two jail cells in the set. The children can choose to have the two crooks plan an escape. They can put all the cops in the cells and take the police car."

Raphaël Pierre Roger Pretesacque,
LEGO Senior Designer

Radar dish swivels around in all directions

Cell door was a new piece for 2008

Barriers can be raised and lowered

Searchlight can be
turned through
360 degrees

Skylight opens
upward

Guided Tour

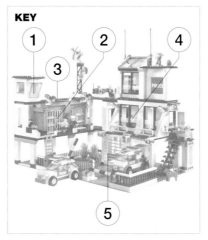

∧ **INSIDE THE WATCHTOWER** A turn plate allows the guard's chair to swivel, so he can survey the station from all angles.

∧ **BEHIND BARS** The cells contain a bed, toilet, and mug. Keys hang outside the cell door. If only there was a way to escape...

∧ **FREEDOM!** Flip the lever behind each cell and the back wall falls away, setting the crook free! A sticker with chalk scribbles is on the wall.

"Wanted" poster on white tile—it looks like the cops have got the right man!

WANTED

∧ **INTERROGATION ROOM** A small interview room on the third floor features recording equipment and a board with "Wanted" posters.

∧ **ROLL-UP GARAGE DOORS** The two garage doors slide up to reveal space for the police van, car, and motorcycle.

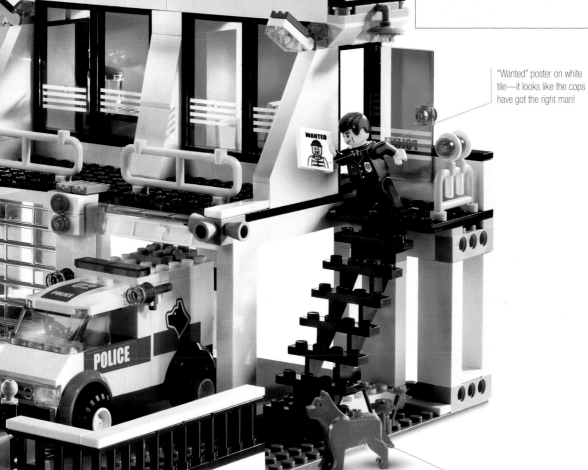

POLICE

POLICE

The dog figure was first introduced in this color in 2005

Life Guard
• 2007 • LEGO® City • #4937

The Brick Bounty
• 2015 • LEGO® Pirates • #70413

Motor Boat with Walter Walrus
• 1986 • LEGO FABULAND • #3633

Naida's Epic Adventure Ship
• 2015 • LEGO® Elves • #41073

Paravane
• 1996 • LEGO Aquazone • #1748

Ferry Boat
• 1968 • LEGO Model Maker • #343

Boat with Armor
• 1996 • LEGO Castle • #1752

Cragger's Command Ship
• 2013 • LEGO® Legends of Chima™ • #70006

Glade Runner
• 1993 • LEGO Town • #6513

Dolphin Cruiser
• 2013 • LEGO® Friends • #41015

Cargo Ship
• 1973 • LEGOLAND • #312

Diving Expedition Explorer
• 1997 • LEGO Town • #6560

Maersk Line Triple-E
• 2014 • LEGO® Creator Expert • #10241

MAKING WAVES

LEGO® boats through the years

From ferries with hinged hulls to boats that really float on water, the oceans, lakes, and seas of the LEGO® world are full of ships of all shapes and sizes. LEGO sets have included rowboats, speedboats, boats steered by knights, and boats captained by walruses. There have been whole themes built around them, like the rafts and sailing ships of LEGO Pirates and the submarines of LEGO Aquazone. Their crews include Vikings, treasure-hunters, and metal-bearded movie stars. When it comes to LEGO boats, there's always something happening above— and below—the waves!

Neptune Carrier
• 2010 • LEGO Atlantis • #8075

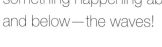

Bath-Toy Boat
• 1978 • LEGO DUPLO • #534

MetalBeard's Sea Cow
• 2014 • THE LEGO® MOVIE™ • #70810

Kraken Attackin'
• 2009 • LEGO Pirates • #6240

Mobile Command Center

2008 • LEGO® Agents • #8635 • Pieces: 1154 • Minifigures: 7

The LEGO Agents theme premiered in 2008 and continued in 2009 as Agents 2.0. It starred a team of hi-tech secret agents who protected the world from the schemes of the evil super-genius Dr. Inferno and his henchmen, a motley crew of cyborg criminals. Distinct in silver, gray, and blue, the Agents' vehicles had built-in surprises—such as the Mobile Command Center truck, which opens up into an entire super-spy headquarters.

"There's so much going on in this set. Seven years later it's still a favorite of mine. I don't think I'll ever top it!"

Mark John Stafford, LEGO Senior Designer

The Mobile Command Center stores five small Agents vehicles for missions on sea, air, or land, along with a loading crane, a high-security jail, a light-up mission briefing projector, and an arsenal of hidden weapons. The Agents will probably need them all when Dr. Inferno drops by with his own dangerous task force of villains...

Image of Dr. Inferno projected onto mission briefing screen on back wall of trailer

Gold Tooth pilots Dr. Inferno's jet

Cabin opens up to seat two minifigures

Buggy is equipped with small rockets

NAB-1183577

- The light-up brick shines light onto unique trans-clear tiles, printed with images of Dr. Inferno and his sharks. These images are then projected onto the briefing screen in the trailer.

- Three of the Agent minifigures have reversible head pieces with not-so-happy expressions on the other side.

- These versions of Gold Tooth and six-legged Spy Clops are exclusive to the set.

- Inspiration for including smaller vehicles that break away from the main truck came from the separating parts of 1980's LEGOLAND Space Galaxy Commander (6980).

- Designer Mark Stafford included his internet LEGO community name, NABII, on the truck's license plate (NAB-1183677).

Guided Tour

KEY

Equipment stored in the trailer includes tools and diving gear

Wings of the Agents' jet fold out when in flight mode

High-security jail for locking up villains

< **UNDER THE HOOD** The grille on the front of the truck cab opens downward, allowing the red missiles that are hidden beneath to be fired. The license plate, Agents logo, and detailing on the side of the engine are all stickers.

∧ **READY FOR LAUNCH** The front section of the trailer folds out, acting as a launch ramp for the jet inside. A command center, with printed computer screen tiles, is found in this section, too.

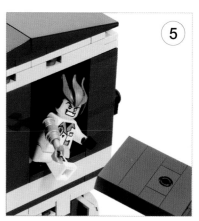

∧ **OVER LAND AND SEA** The sides of the lower section of the middle of the trailer open, allowing the car and jet-boat to emerge. The swiveling crane can hook onto the buggy and lift it onto the trailer bed.

∧ **SKIMMING THE SURFACE** Removing a section of the wall at the back of the trailer reveals yet another Agents vehicle hidden inside: a little Jet Ski, which can be detached from the wall piece.

∧ **BREAKOUT** Turning a lever on the back of the trailer causes a section of the rear wall to break away and allow Dr. Inferno to escape from his cell. His distinctive striped hair piece is unique to his minifigure.

MT-201 Ultra-Drill Walker

2008 • LEGO® Space • #7649 • Pieces: 759 • Minifigures: 2, plus 1 Alien Commander

Following a six-year break, LEGO Space sets made their triumphant return with the Mars Mission theme, in which an astronaut expedition seeking those ever-popular energy crystals encountered a force of hostile glow-in-the-dark aliens from the Red Planet's core. Like other vehicles from the theme's second year, the 2008 MT-201 Ultra-Drill Walker is designed with moving (and removable) parts that let it convert between multiple modes.

In one configuration, the Ultra-Drill Walker is a four-legged mech-like vehicle that strides over Martian terrain, using its powerful back-mounted cannon to fend off alien attacks. But when it discovers a cache of crystals, the cockpit can detach as an observation shuttle, and the cannon rotates down to become a gear-powered mining drill.

Boxes store trans-neon-green crystal pieces

Each leg can move forward and back

Hinged trans-orange shield lifts to allow access to the cockpit—it is exclusive to this set in this color

> "This was my first Space set. I was told to design a four-legged drilling machine. I built a walking tank with a cannon that doubles as a drill."
>
> **Mark John Stafford, LEGO Senior Designer**

BRICK BY BRICK

• A sticker on the side of the model features a graphic of designer Mark Stafford's dog, an English Bull Terrier named Bandit (RIP, Bandit).

• Fans had complained about the lack of backpacks in the Mars Mission subtheme, so Mark Stafford gave the astronauts white backpack pieces to wear in this set.

• When the Walker is in vehicle mode, the cannon mounted on top can rotate 360 degrees.

• The two Mars Mission astronaut minifigures are exclusive to this set. The alien has appeared in three other sets.

• Stickers of the classic LEGO Space logo are placed on the observation shuttle's fins.

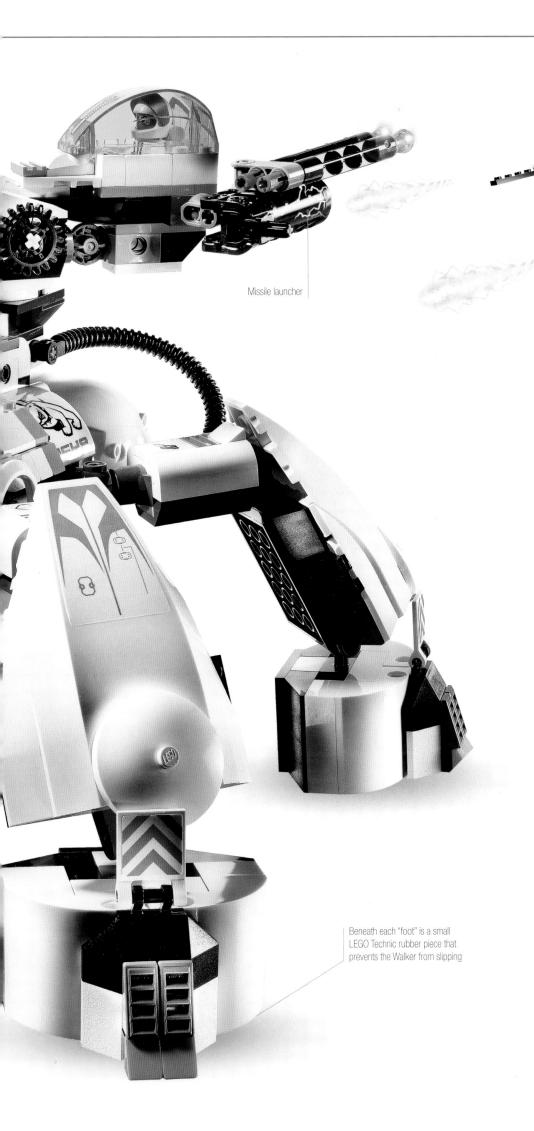

Missile launcher

Beneath each "foot" is a small
LEGO Technic rubber piece that
prevents the Walker from slipping

Alien commander figure was
new for Mars Mission in 2008

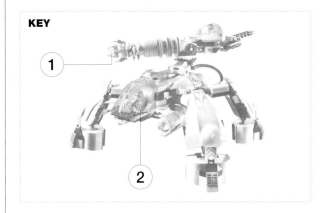

Guided Tour

KEY

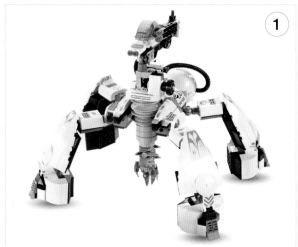

1

2

△ **DRILL IN POSITION** When the observation shuttle detaches from
the walker, the main drill section can be rotated 90 degrees down
for drilling. Turning the black gear on the side spins the drill.

2

△ **CRAFT WITHIN A CRAFT** In homage to the LEGO spaceships
of the 1970s and 1980s, an even smaller craft comes out of the
back of the detached observation shuttle.

Temple Escape

2008 • LEGO® _Indiana Jones_™ • #7623 • Pieces: 554 • Minifigures: 4, plus 2 skeletons

The LEGO Adventurers may have been influenced by the famous film escapades of a certain hat-wearing, whip-cracking archaeologist, but 2008 saw the much-anticipated minifigure debut of the real thing. Over a two-year span, the LEGO® _Indiana Jones_™ theme produced heroes, villains, vehicles, and locations from all four exciting movies. The action-packed Temple Escape set hailed from the memorable opening scene of the very first installment in the series, _Raiders of the Lost Ark_.

Deep in the jungle of Peru, Indiana Jones seeks to recover a legendary golden idol from an ancient and overgrown temple. But to get it back to the museum, he'll have to run a booby-trapped gauntlet of collapsing walls, flick-firing arrows, swinging sword blades, and a giant rolling boulder. Even if he makes it out in one piece, he'll still face evil rival archaeologist Belloq… not to mention a seaplane with a surprise snake inside. Indy hates snakes!

"We met with Steven Spielberg to discuss the films. I kept thinking, 'I'm in the same room as Spielberg. I have to pay attention!'"

Matthew James Ashton, LEGO Vice President

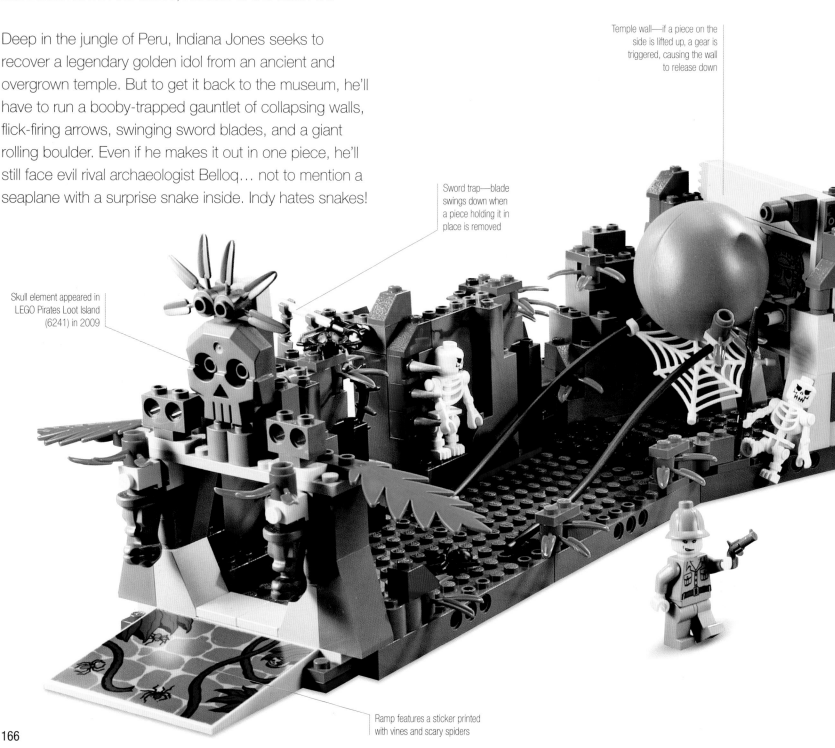

Temple wall—if a piece on the side is lifted up, a gear is triggered, causing the wall to release down

Sword trap—blade swings down when a piece holding it in place is removed

Skull element appeared in LEGO Pirates Loot Island (6241) in 2009

Ramp features a sticker printed with vines and scary spiders

• The side of the plane has a sticker with "OB-CPO"—short for Obi-Wan Kenobi and C-3PO, which is a reference to *Star Wars*, the other famous movie series that actor Harrison Ford appears in.

• The whip element appeared twice in LEGO Harry Potter Diagon Alley (10217) in 2011, but was not used as a whip—the two pieces form the top of an ornate bookcase in Olivander's wand shop.

• The Joker minifigure also sports Indy's hat in dark purple in two LEGO Batman sets, and the Bandit from LEGO Minifigures Series 6 has it in black.

• The Satipo minifigure shares his tousled black hair piece with Harry Potter's minifigure.

• The set contains more than 50 green bricks and elements, giving the temple its organic, overgrown look.

Guided Tour

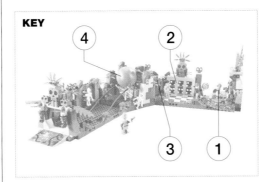

KEY

One of four white plates that form the seaplane's wings

The object of Indy's quest, the golden idol, is exclusive to this set

∧ **LOOK OUT BELOW** When the golden idol is removed, the statue tips forward, causing an avalanche of rocks to fall onto Indiana Jones below.

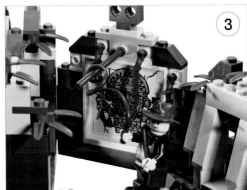

∧ **SHOOTING ARROWS** Poison arrows, belonging to the hostile Hovitos tribe, are pushed through the holes in the wall, forming a deadly booby trap.

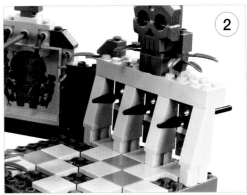

∧ **WHIP SMART** Indy's flexible rubber whip can uncoil and wrap around this pole. Now Indy can swing across the perilous pit unharmed.

∧ **BOULDER DASH** There is a final trap on the way out of the temple—as the wall lowers, it nudges the boulder, causing it to roll down the tracks after Indy.

Matthew James Ashton | Vice President
Matthew Ashton remembers sitting on the floor playing with LEGO bricks and thinking he wanted to be a toy designer when he grew up. A chance meeting with LEGO headhunters at his graduate fashion show led to his childhood dream becoming a reality. Matthew started with the LEGO CLIKITS line of buildable jewelry. Now, as Vice President, he oversees half the play themes—those relating to TV shows and movies, as well as LEGO City and the LEGO Minifigures series. He was an executive producer on THE LEGO MOVIE and co-created the Unikitty character. *Indiana Jones* was his dream license because he got to create toys he "would have done anything for as a child."

Death Star

2008 • LEGO® _Star Wars_® • #10188 • Pieces: 3803 • Minifigures: 18, plus 6 droids

Two mighty Imperial battle stations were combined into one ultimate LEGO _Star Wars_ set with 2008's Death Star, which incorporated characters and scenes from the first Death Star in the original _Star Wars_ movie and the rebuilt Death Star II from _Return of the Jedi_. Although an Ultimate Collector Series display model of the second Death Star had been released in 2005, this one took builders beneath the spherical station's moon-sized shell and let them play inside.

The mind-blowing Death Star model comes with 24 minifigures and droids, and lets fans reenact almost every scene that took place aboard each station. Among its many rooms are the tractor beam generator chamber, detention block, and trash compactor (with hungry Dianoga beast) from the first Death Star, and the Emperor's sinister throne room from the Death Star II.

> "You have to take chances when you can. You have to create the best model possible. Who knows if or when there will be another LEGO Death Star model?"

Bjarke Lykke Madsen, LEGO Design Master

Knob twists to rotate, elevate, and lower the superlaser, which is operated by a Death Star trooper

Rotating cannon fires using its pull-back mechanism

Pushing the LEGO Technic axle causes the trash compactor walls to close in—a feature added after a challenge set by the project's creative lead

The trash compactor contains the tentacled Dianoga (or garbage creature)—the rear door slides open for minifigures to escape

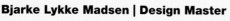

Bjarke Lykke Madsen | Design Master

With a background in engineering, Bjarke joined the LEGO Group in 1997. He has worked across multiple themes including LEGO Castle, LEGO _Star Wars_, and LEGO _The Lord of the Rings_. Bjarke now mostly works on larger LEGO sets, such as Hogwarts Castle (4842) and The Tower of Orthanc™ (10237). Over the years, Bjarke has mentored many designers, including Bas Brederode, who co-designed the Death Star. Bjarke enjoyed working as a pair on the set because they were both so passionate about the subject and constantly challenged each other.

Darth Vader sits in the Imperial conference chamber with Grand Moff Tarkin

Minifigures can drop down through a hole in the floor of the prison block into the trash compactor below

Obi-Wan must disengage the tractor beam by pulling the levers

Guided Tour

KEY

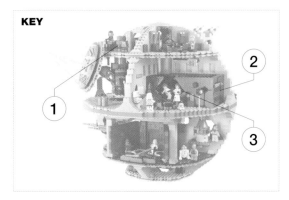

⋀ **SUPERLASER CONTROL ROOM** The commander of the Death Star I, Grand Moff Tarkin, stands beside a tracking screen—a brick with a sticker of the planet Alderaan. Slide the brick out and turn it over to see Yavin 4 moving into firing range.

⋀ **DETENTION CELL** The cell door is opened by turning a LEGO Technic cog on the outside, revealing Princess Leia being interrogated by Darth Vader and a droid. There is a removable panel at the end of the cell for easy access, too.

⋀ **DETENTION BLOCK** A clever combination of a sticker on the back wall, bricks gradually being placed closer together, and the ceiling height reducing create an optical illusion of a long, narrowing corridor.

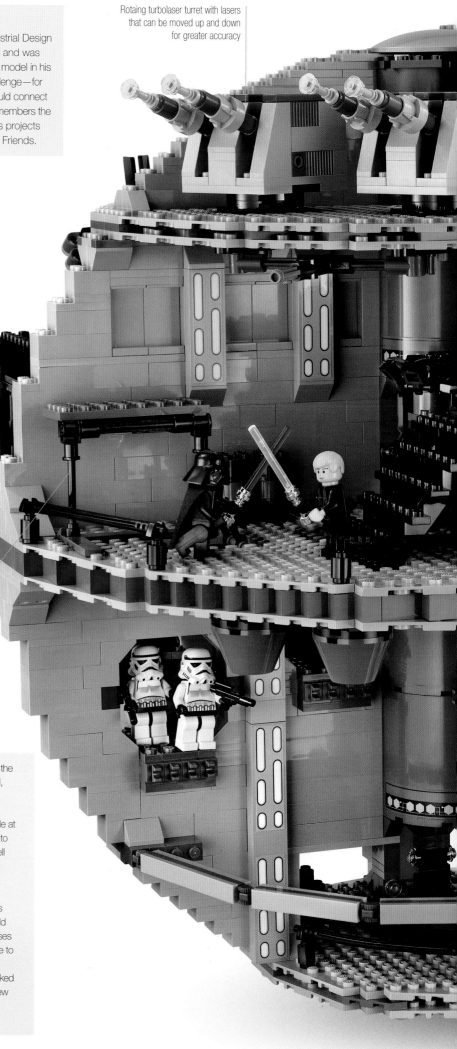

Bas Brederode | Senior Designer

Bas's love of LEGO bricks as a child inspired him to study Industrial Design Engineering. He joined the LEGO Group as a designer in 2006 and was soon assigned the Death Star alongside Bjarke. It was his dream model in his dream theme in his dream job! Although the set was a huge challenge—for example, working out how all the different rooms and scenes would connect together (there were sticky notes everywhere!)—he especially remembers the great collaboration. After the Death Star, Bas worked on various projects including LEGO Games, and is now a Senior Designer for LEGO Friends.

Rotaing turbolaser turret with lasers that can be moved up and down for greater accuracy

"We've heard that children have saved up for years to buy the set, and when they get it, it actually exceeds their expectations. That's what you want to achieve with a model."

Bas Brederode, LEGO Senior Designer

Walkway collapses as it does during the final battle between Luke and Darth Vader in Episode VI

• Designers Bjarke and Bas wanted fans to be able to play out every Death Star scene. They watched the movies again and again and recreated all the Death Star scenes in LEGO bricks.

• Due to Lucasfilm feedback, extra figures and the TIE Advanced model were added toward the end of the design process. These last-minute details increased the piece count by another 700 pieces and took the number of figures from 17 to 24.

• Bas tried to sneak in a scene with stormtroopers taking a bath at the base of the model after seeing a similar, humorous scene in a LEGO Star Wars video game. Although the idea was dropped, the LEGO Star Wars team kept the sketch model.

• Four of the characters are exclusive to the set: Obi-Wan Kenobi, the assassin droid, interrogator droid, and protocol droid.

• Bas and Bjarke originally included a hole at the bottom of the model to make it easy to collect LEGO bricks and elements that fell down the central shaft (which happened often!). The turbolift was added later.

• For the initial production run, the pieces were not put in numbered bags. The build begins with the interrogation droid that uses a silver 1x1 round plate that builders have to find in a volume of 3,803 mostly gray elements, which seems mean. When asked about it, Bjarke and Bas replied, "We knew it was an evil thing to do, but hey, it's the Galactic Empire!"

Knob controls the central turbolift—it pulls a platform up and down via a piece of string

A protocol droid is repaired in the droid repair bay—Bjarke and Bas used this droid's very brief appearance in Episode IV as a reference

Crank handle raises and lowers the pilot elevator

One of three Luke minifigures in the set—he also appears in his black Jedi Knight robes and stormtrooper outfit

Guided Tour

KEY

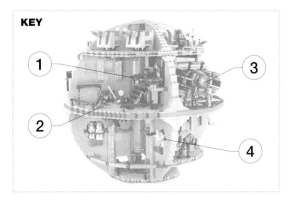

1
2
3
4

∧ **EMPEROR'S THRONE ROOM** Darth Vader presents Luke to Emperor Palpatine, who sits atop his throne as his red Imperial Guards look on. Bjarke had previously designed Emperor Palpatine's throne for Final Duel I (7200) in 2002.

∧ **FINAL MOMENTS** Darth Vader's helmet is removed after his battle with Luke to reveal his gray, scarred face. Behind him, in the throne room, is the reactor shaft through which Emperor Palpatine's minifigure can be thrown to his doom.

> **HOLD ON TIGHT!**
Builders can recreate the famous scene in Episode IV where Luke and Leia swing across the air shaft chasm while stormtroopers fire at them.

∧ **TIE ADVANCED** The unique, mini TIE Advanced hangs on a moving launch rack in the hangar bay. The TIE Advanced can be removed from the main set and the cockpit viewscreen opens to seat Darth Vader's minifigure (without his cloak).

Town Plan

2008 • LEGO® Advanced Models • #10184 • Pieces: 1981 • Minifigures: 8

In 2008, the LEGO Group celebrated 50 years of the modern LEGO brick by releasing a completely new and updated version of the classic Town Plan set 700/1 from 1958. The model made use of all of the advancements in pieces, colors, and building techniques developed in the decades since the 1958 set.

The all-new Town Plan still let builders make a 1950s-style town, complete with a movie theater, service station, and town hall. Yet, unlike the original 1950s and '60s Town Plan sets with their pre-assembled miniature replicas, this set includes minifigure townsfolk and buildable vehicles. The fountain displays three gold-colored bricks to honor the golden 50th anniversary.

Service station and shop are connected via a hinge, so they can be moved apart, too

Red gas truck is similar to the one in the original set

Detailed movie poster graphics on stickers show upcoming attractions

Rare metallic-gold 2x2 bricks were first introduced in this anniversary set

KEY

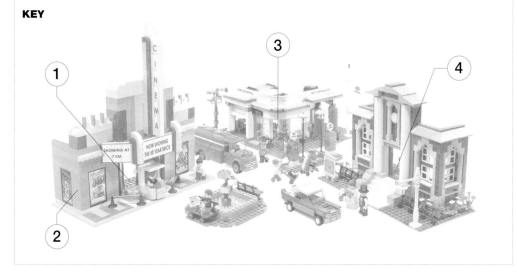

△ **POPCORN COUNTER** The popcorn seller stands in the movie theater lobby. The 12 bright yellow-colored 1x1 round plates make some tasty-looking popcorn.

"It was wonderful to work with two rock star designers of the LEGO world, and to then recreate the original box, too!"

Jamie Berard, LEGO Design Manager Specialist

- As in the 1958 version of Town Plan (700/1), the box features Kjeld Kirk Kristiansen, the grandson of the founder of the LEGO Group, and now the company's vice-chairman, playing with the set.

- The team were unable to completely recreate the image on the front of the box, because they could not track down the girl, who was a professional model.

- Three designers designed the model: Jamie Berard laid it all out and designed the cinema, and he called in help from veteran designers (and his idols!), Steen Sig Andersen and Jørn Thomsen, to complete the town hall, garage, and vehicles.

- Kjeld Sørensen and Simon Kent designed the graphics, including the movie posters, movie screen, and signs.

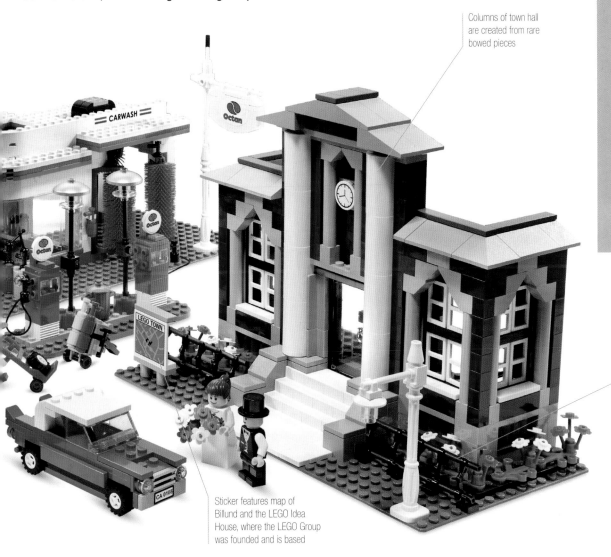

Columns of town hall are created from rare bowed pieces

Railings are made from pieces usually used as LEGO *Star Wars* Battle Droid arms

Sticker features map of Billund and the LEGO Idea House, where the LEGO Group was founded and is based

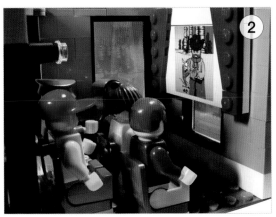

∧ **MOVIE THEATER** The minifigure audience enjoys the movie. The dark-red curtain pieces appeared as part of a tank in LEGO *Star Wars* Republic Fighter Tank (7679), also in 2008.

∧ **FOOD AND FUEL** As well as filling up their vehicles, customers can buy drinks and food, such as a banana, croissant, or apple, from the service station shop.

∧ **I DO!** Inside the Town Hall are two happy newlyweds. The bunch of flowers clips into the bride's hand. Since its debut in 1980, the groom's top hat has appeared in more than 60 sets.

Original Horse
- 1984 • LEGOLAND Castle • #6021

Elephant
- 2003 • LEGO Adventurers • #7418

Creative Animals
- 2014 • LEGO® DUPLO® • #10573

Snow the Foal
- 2013 • LEGO Friends • #41003

Monkey
- 1989 • LEGOLAND Pirates • #6285

CREATIVE CREATURES

LEGO® animals through the years

Whether it squawks, squeaks, barks, or brays, if it's an animal, then you can build it with LEGO® bricks. The LEGO creature collection has included everything from single-piece birds to many-jointed fantasy dragons and fully buildable (and rebuildable) LEGO Creator models. In between is an entire plastic menagerie of forest animals, farm animals, prehistoric predators, and deep-sea denizens. Minifigures can ride them, battle them, befriend them, and take care of them. Just don't get too close to that T. rex!

Zebra
- 2009 • LEGO DUPLO • #5635

Enki the Panther Cub
- 2015 • LEGO® Elves • #41075

Goldie the Bird
- 2012 • LEGO® Friends • #3065

Octopus
- 1996 • LEGO Aquazone • #6104

Fafnir Dragon
- 2005 • LEGO Vikings • #7019

Husky Dog
• 2014 • LEGO® City • #60062

Crocodile
• 2015 • LEGO City • #60070

"I really try to make the animals work together so that they can all be played with side by side— no matter when they were first created."

Gitte Thorsen, LEGO Design Master

T. rex
• 2012 • LEGO® Dino • #5887

Cow
• 2009 • LEGO Castle • #10193

Gitte Thorsen | Design Master

Gitte joined the LEGO Group in 1981, and has worked on almost every part of the LEGO design process in her 30+ year career. Gitte has spent much of her career sculpting elements. She sculpted one of the first minifigure female hair pieces and pots and pans for LEGO Homemaker (some of them are still in use). As well as innumerable wigs, she has made LEGO animals, including dragons, bears, dogs, a horse, a crocodile, and many more. Having grown up on a farm, Gitte finds that animal shapes come relatively easily to her, but maintaining the recognizable shape while making it fit to the LEGO stud grid can be a challenge!

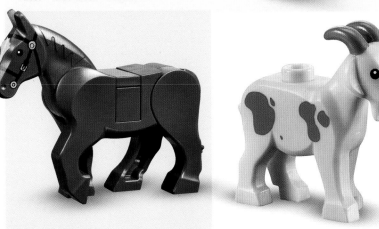

New Horse
• 2012 • LEGO® The Lord of the Rings™ • #9469

Goat
• 2011 • LEGO® Kingdoms • #7189

Bear
• 2012 • LEGO City • #4438

Thunder Driller

2009 • LEGO® Power Miners • #8960 • Pieces: 235 • Minifigures: 2, plus 1 rock monster figure

Like LEGO Rock Raiders ten years earlier, the 2009 LEGO Power Miners theme starred a rough, tough crew of hi-tech miners. This time the action was set on Earth, where the heroes had dug beneath the surface to investigate a series of ground-shaking tremors. When the cause turned out to be frenzied rock monsters gorging on energy crystals, the Power Miners set out to stop their rampage with the rugged Thunder Driller and their other mining gear.

The Thunder Driller was the Power Miners' main mode of transportation. An internal system of gears makes the front and back sections of its massive planetary drill turn in opposite directions as it rolls. In a handy re-use of parts, its huge spiked wheels are the same new LEGO element as the base portion of its drill.

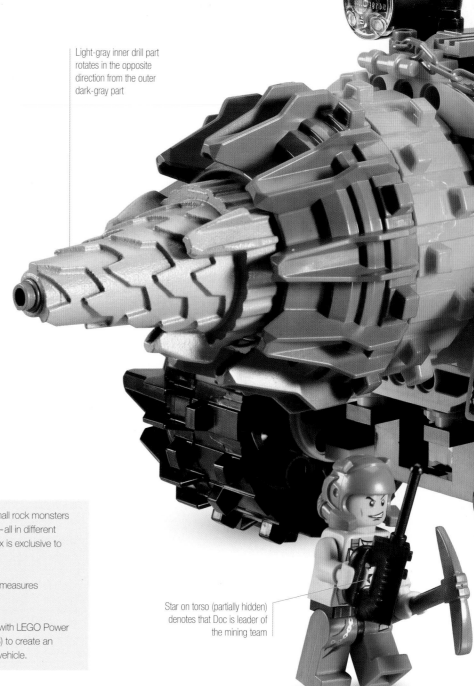

Light-gray inner drill part rotates in the opposite direction from the outer dark-gray part

Star on torso (partially hidden) denotes that Doc is leader of the mining team

BRICK BY BRICK

- This version of Duke (the miner with gray soot on his face) appears in two other sets, and this version of Doc (the Power Miners team leader) appears in one other set, but with a removable visor clipped to his helmet. Both minifigures have frightened expressions on the other sides of their faces.

- The dynamite element was new for 2009. Previously, it was printed on a tile. It has now appeared in more than 50 sets.

- There were five types of small rock monsters in the first year of the theme—all in different colors. The trans-orange Firox is exclusive to this set.

- The Thunder Driller vehicle measures 8in (20cm) in length.

- This set can be combined with LEGO Power Miners Granite Grinder (8958) to create an aircraft and armored ground vehicle.

Guided Tour

KEY

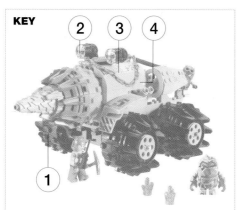

◁ POWERFUL WHEELS
The four wheels with studs and spikes can trample over almost anything in the Driller's path. Glow-in-the-dark stickers decorate the mudguards.

▷ ON TOP The roof features a pair of large headlights, stickers, and a chain. To the rear is a black roll cage that pulls down to protect the driver.

Stickers give a
dirt-splattered effect

"We went to a mining museum and down an old mineshaft to get inspiration. So many ideas for Power Miners were driven from that visit."

Mark John Stafford, LEGO Senior Designer

Bright-green wheel piece
first appeared in 2006
LEGO EXO-FORCE sets

Rock monsters have
stony exteriors with
crystal-like markings

Trans-neon-orange crystal—one
of the new crystal colors launched
by the Power Miners theme

< **STORAGE SPACE** Energy crystals are stored in the mid-section. The top lifts off to display the gear system that causes the planetary drill to rotate as the vehicle's wheels move.

> **CONTROL PLATFORM** At the rear, the miners use levers and the tunnel-mapping display to control the driller. They also store dynamite here, and top up the vehicle's magma core engine with fuel.

Medieval Market Village

2009 • LEGO® Castle • #10193 • Pieces: 1601 • Minifigures: 8

In the spirit of 1984's Blacksmith Shop (6040) and 1986's Guarded Inn (6067), the epic Medieval Market Village set emphasized the common folk of the LEGO Castle world rather than the usual knights and nobility. It was extremely well-received by LEGO Castle fans, who welcomed the set's use of rare and classic pieces, as well as the opportunity to build its well-designed buildings and colorful marketplace.

The Medieval Market Village set isn't just for show; it's full of great details and functions, too. Both buildings can be opened on hinges, revealing their interiors and making the village look twice as large. A waterwheel drives the blacksmith's hammer, and a menagerie of animals includes brick-built chickens and a duck. There are even soldiers to collect the taxes!

BRICK BY BRICK

- The new cow element made its debut in this set—the two brown cows have udders, and heads that move up and down.

- Pieces usually seen as black vehicle mudguards are used as arched window features on the tan-colored building.

- The sticker sheet includes portraits and signs for the blacksmith's workshop and the stables.

- The hexagonal piece used in the waterwheel was new in 2009. It is also used as part of a rotary thresher in LEGO City Combine Harvester (7636).

- The shiny knights' helmets have appeared in more than 30 sets.

- There is even horse poop in this set! It comes in the form of two dark-brown carrot pieces.

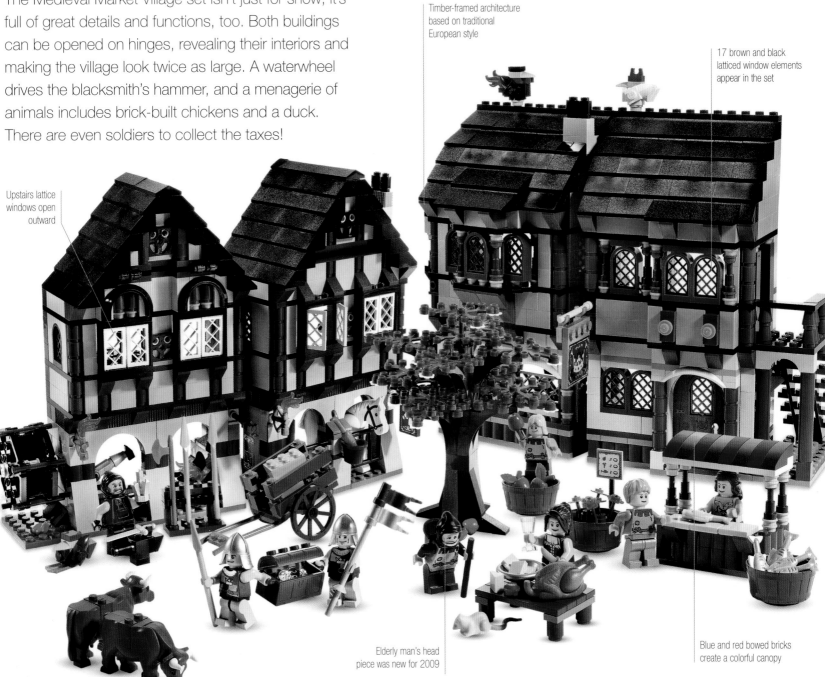

Timber-framed architecture based on traditional European style

17 brown and black latticed window elements appear in the set

Upstairs lattice windows open outward

Elderly man's head piece was new for 2009

Blue and red bowed bricks create a colorful canopy

Bedroom features brick-built fireplace, checkered quilt on the bed, perfume bottle, hairbrush, and a pesky rat!

Upstairs kitchen has a stove that can be lit with a flame element

INSIDE VIEW

Waterwheel connects to the blacksmith's workshop

Guided Tour

KEY

> **MARKETPLACE FEAST**
The turkey element first appeared in LEGO SCALA sets in 1997. Its drumsticks can be removed.

< **HIDEY-HOLE** Above the blacksmith's workshop, this young man takes a break. If he lifts off the table top, he may be lucky enough to find gold coins hidden inside the barrel!

> **BLACKSMITH'S WORKSHOP** The blacksmith works in his forge. As the waterwheel rotates, it triggers a hammer, which bangs against a sword on the anvil.

Emerald Night

2009 • LEGO® Advanced Models • #10194 • Pieces: 1065 • Minifigures: 3

Released in 2009, the special-edition Emerald Night train set was only available directly through the company's brand stores and website. Its locomotive, striking in dark green and black bricks with gold trim, was based on the Class A3 Super Pacific engine of the late 1920s and '30s. It was the first set to have a new large-sized LEGO train wheel that used LEGO Technic parts to replicate the piston movement of a real locomotive.

Along with its engine and a matching tender to carry fuel, the Emerald Night has a passenger car that can be decorated with stickers reading "First," "Second," or "Third," letting builders expand their trains by buying additional sets. The locomotive can be motorized to drive on tracks by installing a LEGO Power Functions motor, infrared receiver, and lights.

> "We tried to create a train that would really connect with LEGO train fans."
>
> Jamie Berard, LEGO Design Manager Specialist

Smoke deflector

Light—seven levels of intensity can be controlled remotely when Power Functions lights and motor are attached to the set

• The engineer's head piece first appeared in LEGO Adventurers Scorpion Palace (7418) in 2003.

• The letters "LRTS" on the side of the tender car stand for LEGO Railway Train System.

• The set was originally called Emerald Knight, but the "K" was dropped as the LEGO designers felt it evoked more mystery.

• Ten fan builders were flown to the LEGO head office in Billund, Denmark to meet with the LEGO designers to discuss what they wanted from a new LEGO train set.

• A new large wheel piece and elements in dark green and tan were included as a result of the LEGO fan feedback.

• The firebox can be removed and replaced with a motor.

Jamie Berard | Design Manager Specialist

A huge LEGO fan from a young age, Jamie landed his dream job as a designer for the LEGO Creator line in 2006. Jamie is now responsible for all the Creator Expert models—brainstorming new ideas, overseeing a team of designers, and building sets himself, too. Always brimming with new ideas, Jamie keeps a parking lot of build ideas at the end of his desk. Jamie is a true LEGO superfan, and loves to include surprises for fans—whether that's introducing elements in rare colors (such as dark-green bricks in Emerald Night), finding a new and unusual use for an existing element, or adding something unexpected, such as the rat hole and rat with cheese in Green Grocer (10185), which builders don't discover until partway through the build.

Guided Tour

KEY

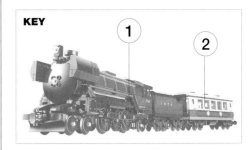

Unique tan window included in response to LEGO fan builders' request

SIDE VIEW

New large train wheel

∧ **FIREBOX** In the engine's cab, the firebox opens to reveal a flame piece. A coal shovel can clip to the side of the firebox, and there is standing room for the engineer.

∧ **TICKETS PLEASE!** The ticket collector passes down the train car. There are two sets of chairs where minifigures can relax with a drink. Their luggage can be stowed beside the drawers.

Dark-green piece with gold trim is exclusive to the set

Removable roof for extra playability

Winter Toy Shop

2009 • LEGO® Advanced Models • #10199 • Pieces: 815 • Minifigures: 7

The LEGO Group has a long history of sets themed for the seasons, with Christmastime as a particular favorite. The Winter Toy Shop, produced near the end of 2009, was the first in a series of annual releases taking place in a snow-covered town during the holidays. The festive scene made a wonderful surprise gift under the tree, or a home decoration that the whole family could build and enjoy together.

From its trimmed Christmas tree to its rosy-cheeked carolers, the Winter Toy Shop set has a charming timelessness that could exist any time in the last hundred years or so. A light-up brick gives the old toymaker's upstairs workshop a heart-warming glow during chilly winter nights.

• The designer, Jamie Berard, based the tree-trimming minifigure on his mother because she loves the festive season.

• The rosy-cheeked caroler minifigure heads are exclusive to this set, although their torsos have appeared elsewhere.

• Originally, the transparent globe piece was created solely as Sandy's helmet in the LEGO® SpongeBob SquarePants™ line. Jamie Berard saw another use for it—as part of the streetlamp in this set. It was used as a streetlamp again in 2013 in Winter Village Market (10235).

• A mini blue robot and red train are the enticing toys on display in the shop window.

• The Christmas tree uses dark green 2x4 plates with three holes. This was the first set to include this element in the dark-green color.

Star first appeared in LEGO BELVILLE sets in 2002 in trans-medium-blue—it made its debut in trans-yellow in this set

Brick-built snowman with plain white minifigure head

"It's a fun challenge to take a piece that people think has only one use and to find a new use for it."

Jamie Berard, LEGO Design Manager Specialist

White plates form the snow-covered roof

Snowballs are white 1x1 round plates

Two capes are layered to create red lining effect

Purple ski pole appears in LEGO *Star Wars* sets as Mace Windu's lightsaber blade

Guided Tour

KEY

> **DETAILED BRICKWORK**
To create the chimney, light-gray tiles are placed over dark-gray bricks, giving a textured finish and a ramshackle, old-fashioned look.

△ **UPSTAIRS WORKSHOP** The toymaker's workshop is small but functional, and warmly lit by a light-up LED brick. A tool rack is attached to the desk and a turn plate allows the chair to swivel.

△ **COZY SHOP FLOOR** The shop's interior features an open fireplace. Two trans-orange flame pieces, first featured in LEGO *Indiana Jones*, form the roaring fire that keeps the minifigures toasty.

△ **BEHIND THE COUNTER** The shop's cash register is a printed gray sloped brick that sits atop a small brick-built counter. The toymaker's inquisitive cat heads toward the toy robot on display.

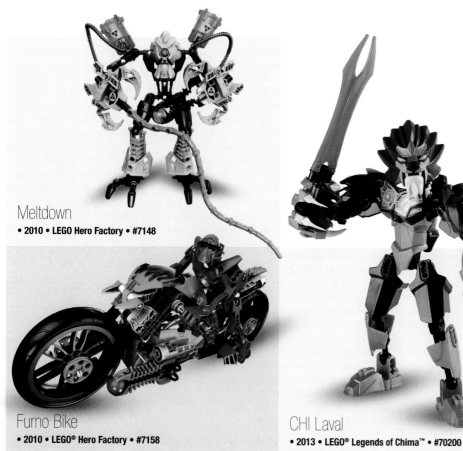

Meltdown
- 2010 • LEGO Hero Factory • #7148

Furno Bike
- 2010 • LEGO® Hero Factory • #7158

CHI Laval
- 2013 • LEGO® Legends of Chima™ • #70200

Rahkshi Guurahk
- 2003 • BIONICLE® • #8590

Cerim Manovi | Senior Design Manager

It was always robots that inspired Cerim's creativity—he even created buildable porcelain robots as part of his industrial design degree. Cerim was discovered by a LEGO employee at a Christmas market in Munich, and joined the company in 2008. He began designing for LEGO® Ben 10™: Alien Force, before helping to develop the "constraction" building system that was first introduced in LEGO Hero Factory and LEGO Legends of Chima. Cerim enjoys leading a team of super-talented people, and loves having the opportunity to conceptualize the models and create new elements, as well as building the models themselves.

Lord of Skull Spiders
- 2015 • LEGO® BIONICLE® • #70790

Raanu
- 2009 • BIONICLE • #8973

Vladek
- 2004 • LEGO Castle – Knights' Kingdom II • #8774

Gorast
- 2015 • LEGO BIONICLE • #8695

Thulox
- 2007 • BIONICLE • #8931

Kopaka – Master of Ice
• 2015 • LEGO BIONICLE • #70788

Swamp
• 2000 • LEGO Technic – RoboRiders • #8509

Tahu
• 2001 • BIONICLE • #8534

Granite
• 1999 • LEGO® Technic – Slizer • #8506

Lehvak
• 2002 • BIONICLE • #8564

INTO ACTION!

LEGO® buildable action figures through the years

Not all LEGO characters are minifigures—and not all sets are made of bricks. Starting with the Slizers (a.k.a. Throwbots) series in 1999, the company has produced a number of themes featuring constructible action figures, nicknamed "constraction figures." Many of these large-scale heroes and villains are built around a core of LEGO® Technic beams and pins, with ball-jointed limbs for movement. The most famous is LEGO® BIONICLE®, while others include LEGO Hero Factory and LEGO® Legends of Chima™, along with licensed themes such as LEGO® Ben 10™: Alien Force and both LEGO® Marvel Super Heroes and LEGO® DC Comics™ Super Heroes.

Batman™
• 2012 • LEGO DC Super Heroes • #4526

Reidak
• 2006 • BIONICLE • #8900

EVO XL Machine
• 2014 • LEGO Hero Factory • #44022

Galactic Enforcer

2009 • LEGO® Space • #5974 • Pieces: 825 • Minifigures: 6 plus 1 droid

In 2009, a classic LEGO Space subtheme returned with a sleek and futuristic new look. The Space Police now patrolled the universe in pursuit of the alien Black Hole Gang. The mighty Galactic Enforcer was the flagship of the new Space Police fleet, carrying multiple prison pods with blast-apart break-out functions, and an interrogation room and forensic lab inside.

The Galactic Enforcer can split apart into four smaller ships for special missions. For many adult fans, it brought back memories of the much-loved modular LEGO spaceships of their childhoods, in particular 1983's Galaxy Commander (6980), which has the same blue and white color scheme.

> "Everything I loved about LEGO Space sets as a child, I squeezed into this set."
>
> Mark John Stafford, LEGO Senior Designer

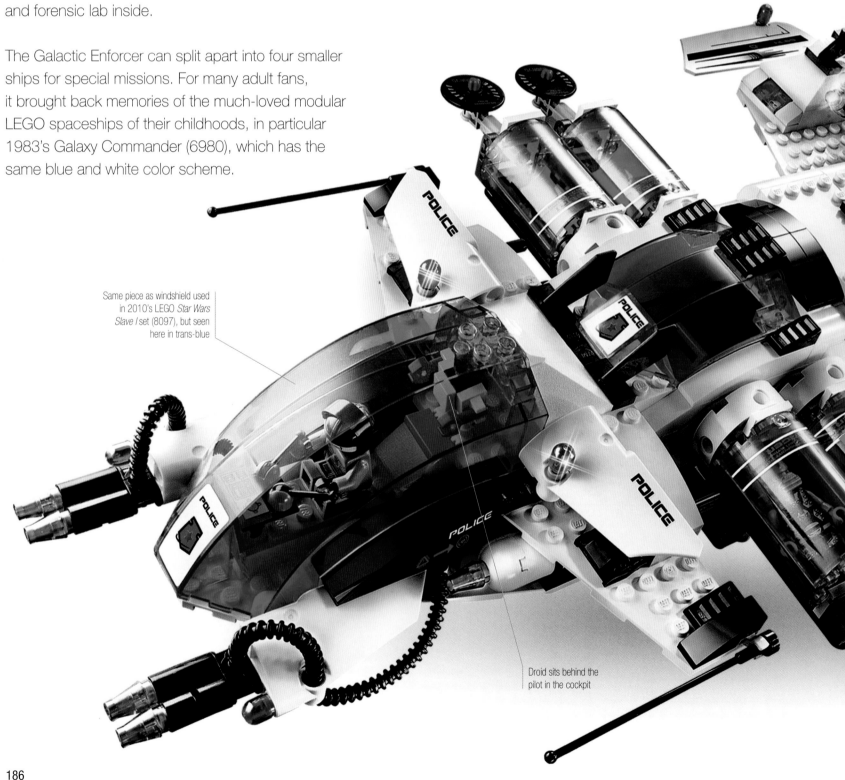

Same piece as windshield used in 2010's LEGO *Star Wars Slave I* set (8097), but seen here in trans-blue

Droid sits behind the pilot in the cockpit

- A statue of the first LEGO spaceman features in the set. The statue's Latin text is a close translation of "Thirty years of construction in the infinite heavens" to mark the 30th anniversary of LEGO Space.

- One female and two male Space Police minifigures protect the galaxy in this set.

- The set number appears on the spaceship's wing.

- The set's alien space-crook minifigures are named Kranxx (the orange leader of the gang) and Slizer. They have stolen the statue of the LEGO spaceman.

- The alien strikecraft features a "Spyrius Rules" sticker, which is a reference to the 1990s LEGO Space Spyrius subtheme.

- The droid with a red light for a head is exclusive to this set.

Guided Tour

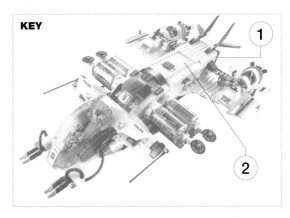

KEY

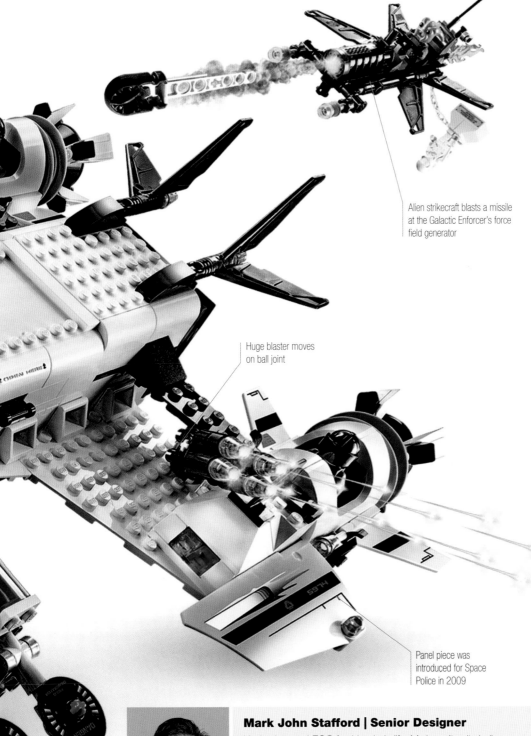

Alien strikecraft blasts a missile at the Galactic Enforcer's force field generator

Huge blaster moves on ball joint

Panel piece was introduced for Space Police in 2009

If the force field generator target is hit, the top of the blue prison pod pops off, releasing Slizer, the prisoner

Mark John Stafford | Senior Designer

Having been a LEGO fan his whole life, Mark can't quite believe that his hobby is now his job. He has worked at the LEGO Group for nine years on many themes, including LEGO Agents, LEGO Space, and LEGO Legends of Chima. Mark has a signature brick; he often builds 1x2 grille tiles into his models—although he wasn't aware he was doing it for years! Building a big LEGO spaceship, the Galactic Enforcer, was a dream come true for Mark. He had fun paying homage to his favorite LEGO spaceships in this set.

∧ **SPACE BUGGY** A ground vehicle can be released from the back—just like 1979's Space Cruiser and Moonbase (928). A black ramp swings down for exiting and boarding.

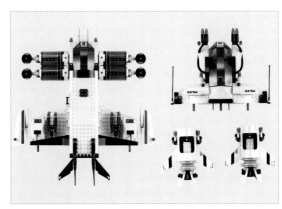

∧ **COMMAND CENTER** A hinged door opens to reveal a forensics lab and questioning area. The printed computer panel is a redesign of the one first used in LEGOLAND Space.

∧ **MODULAR BUILD** The spaceship can be reconfigured to create a super-fast spacecraft from the forward-cockpit section and two mini spaceships from the two main thrusters.

Grand Carousel

2009 • LEGO® Advanced Models • #10196 • Pieces: 3263 • Minifigures: 9

As children who grow up playing with LEGO bricks get older, they sometimes want a set that challenges them, but still captures the sense of fun and discovery that they remember from their early years of building. The Grand Carousel was just what those fans were looking for: a satisfyingly complex build made from over 3,000 pieces, resulting in a model that was a colorful, musical, whirling delight straight out of their childhoods.

Gold-colored elements, transparent jewels, and mirror-like decals give the Grand Carousel a dazzling appearance as it spins. Its horses and swing boats automatically go up and down with the help of hidden wheels and LEGO Technic pieces. A LEGO Power Functions motor provides the motion, while a sound brick plays a merry accompanying tune.

• The sound brick is located beneath the canopy. It plays music as the carousel turns.

• The eight canvas triangles that make up the carousel's canopy are exclusive to this set.

• Eight gold-colored dish pieces have metallic gold-effect stickers on them. The gold dish first appeared in 2006 in LEGO BELVILLE sets.

• The jester hat appears in four other sets, including LEGO Advanced Model Winter Toy Shop (10199) in 2009, where it is worn by a Jack-in-the-box.

• There are eight jester heads with four different facial expressions.

• The 48x48 base plate is currently the largest base plate in a dark-green color.

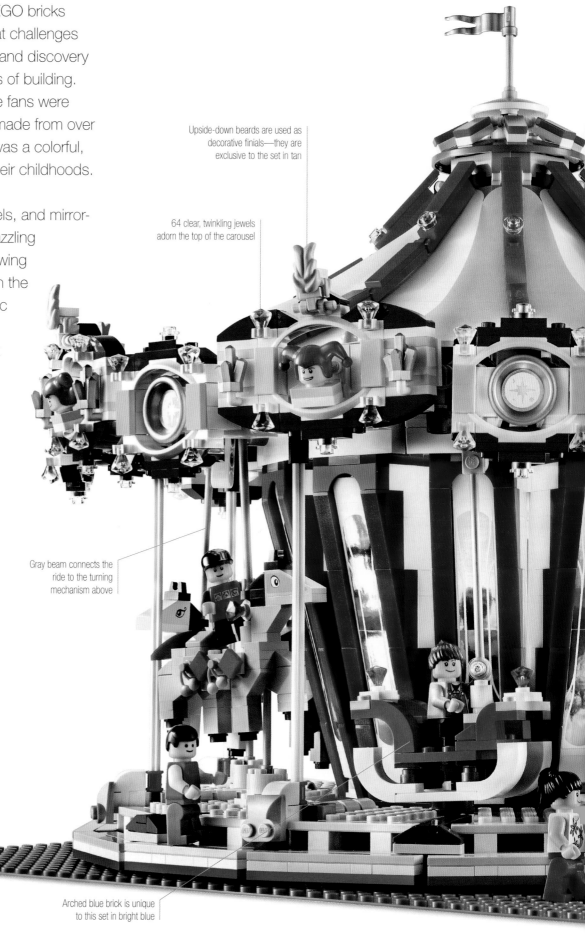

Upside-down beards are used as decorative finials—they are exclusive to the set in tan

64 clear, twinkling jewels adorn the top of the carousel

Gray beam connects the ride to the turning mechanism above

Arched blue brick is unique to this set in bright blue

INSIDE VIEW

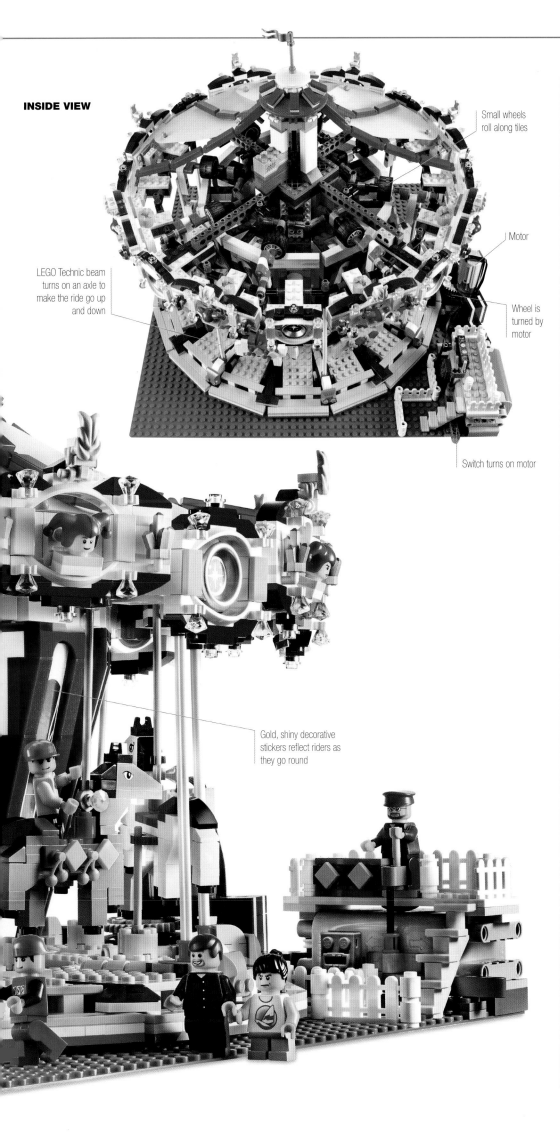

LEGO Technic beam turns on an axle to make the ride go up and down

Small wheels roll along tiles

Motor

Wheel is turned by motor

Switch turns on motor

Gold, shiny decorative stickers reflect riders as they go round

Guided Tour

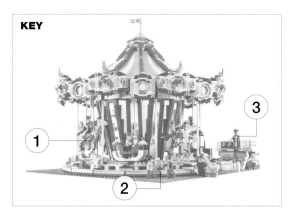

1
2
3

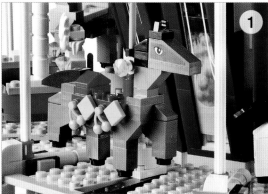

1

∧ **HORSING AROUND** The six brick-built horses have raised legs—making them look like they are galloping. Their eyes are stickers, and they are decorated with green cherry elements.

2

∧ **UNIQUE TWINS** Although these minifigures are exclusive to this set, the boy and girl's printed torsos have appeared in more than 30 LEGO City sets since their debut in 2006.

3

∧ **RIDE OPERATOR** Standing on his raised platform, this bearded minifigure clasps a lever, and appears to control the carousel. The lever connects to the battery box switch below.

2010s

In the 2010s, LEGO® models and minifigures came alive on screens around the globe, from the television adventures of elemental ninja and animal warriors to a blockbuster theatrical movie. New licensed themes let builders construct their own Middle-earth, Metropolis, and Springfield. Divers discovered long-lost Atlantis, astronauts battled space bugs, and one minifigure got a little ill on a fairground ride—and that was all just in the first half of the decade!

Imperial Shuttle

2010 • LEGO® *Star Wars®* **• #10212 •** Pieces: 2503 • Minifigures: 5

After a decade of LEGO® *Star Wars®* Ultimate Collector Series models, the first release for the line in 2010 was the Imperial Shuttle from *Return of the Jedi*. This LEGO version of the vehicle was also the first to be in correct minifigure scale. The size of the Empire's three-winged transport starship model is impressive: it reaches a towering 28in (71cm) when perched on its buildable display stand in flight mode.

Built-in LEGO® Technic beams reinforce the Imperial Shuttle's heavy wings, which fold up or down with the turn of removable crank-action keys below the engines in the back. Its four-seat cockpit can open to hold Imperial crew members and dignitaries—or sneaky Rebel spies—and its laser cannons rotate just like the ones in the movie.

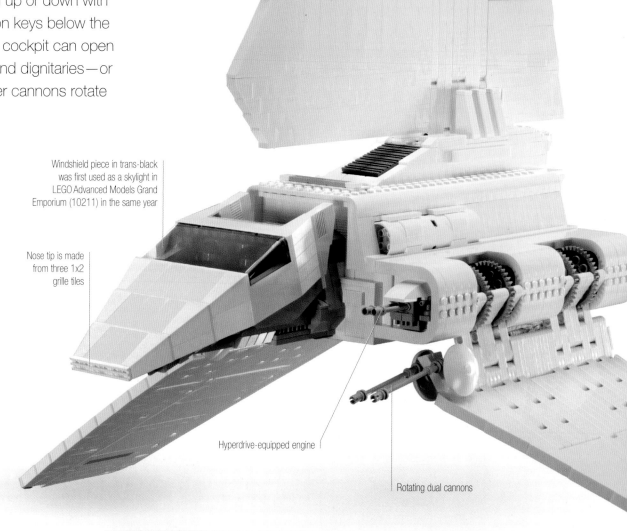

Windshield piece in trans-black was first used as a skylight in LEGO Advanced Models Grand Emporium (10211) in the same year

Nose tip is made from three 1x2 grille tiles

Hyperdrive-equipped engine

Rotating dual cannons

• The stormtrooper's blaster has appeared in more than 100 sets since it was introduced in 2007:

• These versions of the Imperial Pilot, Imperial Officer, and Luke Skywalker minifigures are exclusive to this set. Luke's minifigure is only slightly different to another variant—in this set, his eyes have printed pupils.

• The recommended age for building this set is 16+. In the same year, a smaller Imperial Shuttle set (20016) was released for builders aged 7+.

• With its wings deployed, the Imperial Shuttle measures 22in (57cm) wide.

• 1,361 white pieces are used to build this craft.

• During the design process, set designer Adam Grabowski watched *Return of the Jedi* again and again, and studied pictures of the original model of the Imperial Shuttle used in the movie. Adam also used a close friend's fan model as inspiration for parts of the set—with his permission, of course.

Adam Siegmund Grabowski | Senior Designer

Adam trained as an illustrator and was working at the LEGO Brand Store in Cologne, Germany in 2005 when he was invited to a recruitment workshop at the LEGO Group. He got the job, and started on LEGO Agents. Adam has since worked across a range of themes, including LEGO Monster Fighters, LEGO *Star Wars*, and LEGO Marvel and DC Comic Super Heroes. He has designed many huge models, such as Imperial Shuttle and Haunted House (10228), but he enjoys designing models with fewer than 200 pieces, too, because he can be very creative at a fast pace, and also many younger builders will own and play with the smaller sets.

Guided Tour

KEY

Navigation light

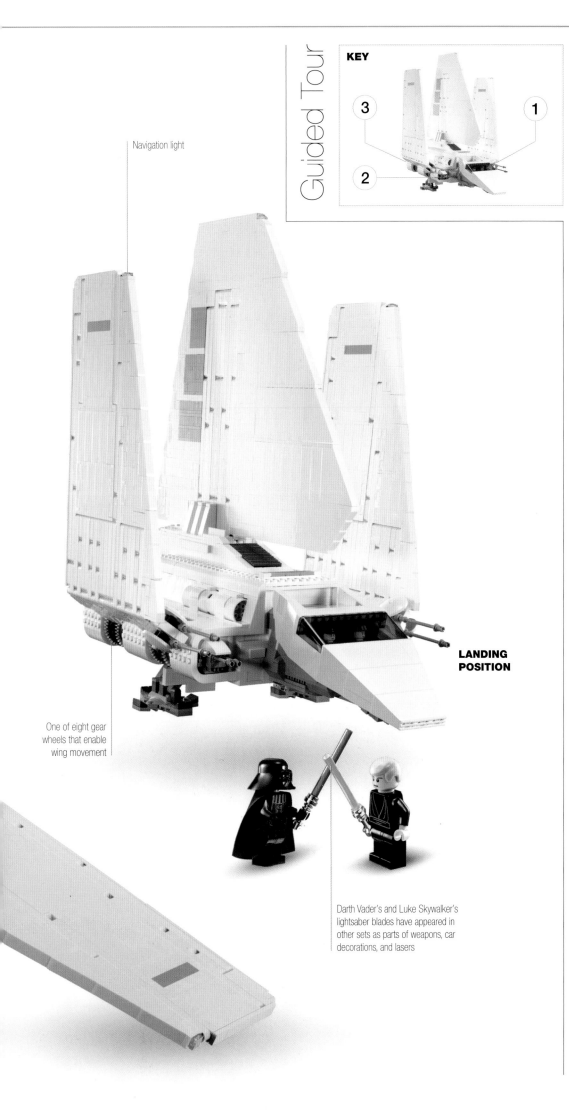

LANDING POSITION

One of eight gear wheels that enable wing movement

Darth Vader's and Luke Skywalker's lightsaber blades have appeared in other sets as parts of weapons, car decorations, and lasers

< **COCKPIT** The black-uniformed Imperial Pilot and gray-uniformed Imperial Officer sit in the front-opening cockpit. There is space for two passengers to sit behind.

> **BLAST AWAY**
At the front of the Imperial Shuttle are two sets of twin rotating long-range cannons and above them, a pair of offensive guns (in fixed position). There are two more guns at the rear.

< **ON DISPLAY** When built, the Imperial Shuttle can be displayed on a stand made from LEGO Technic pieces. A large sticker gives detailed information about the ship.

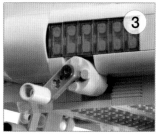

∧ **CRANK HANDLE** At the rear of the ship, below each blue engine, there is space to insert a crank key. Turn the key and the wing can be folded up or down.

∧ **MOVING WINGS** When it is preparing to land, the wings of the Imperial Shuttle are articulated upward. In this position, it can be secured to its brick-built landing gear base.

Imperial Flagship

2010 • LEGO® Pirates • #10210 • Pieces: 1664 • Minifigures: 9

From an Empire of starships to one of ocean vessels! The LEGO Pirates returned in 2009, 20 years after the swashbuckling play theme originally set sail. Up against new pirate leader Captain Brickbeard were his opponents, the classic Imperial Guard. Although the line was intended to last one year, it ended with an amazing final model: the Imperial Flagship, a square-rigged, three-masted, 30in-long (75cm) pirate-hunting juggernaut that in 2010 was the biggest LEGO ship set ever made.

The spectacular flagship carries four brick-firing cannons below-decks, accessible by removing the model's upper sections. A cook prepares dinner for the crew in the galley, and the captain can play the pipe organ or look through the telescope in his cabin while he counts the gold in his treasure chest—provided the cunning Captain Brickbeard hasn't already stolen it.

"I spent about a week reading and gathering information from LEGO fan sites to really understand what everyone loves about LEGO ships."

Raphaël Pierre Roger Pretesacque,
LEGO Senior Designer

Flag first used in LEGO Pirates Soldiers' Fort (6242) in 2009

Saw shark figurehead—this was included as a response to fan feedback on other LEGO ships

37 round 1x1 plates decorate the hull

Hinged grid piece opens to access cannon bays below

Guided Tour

KEY

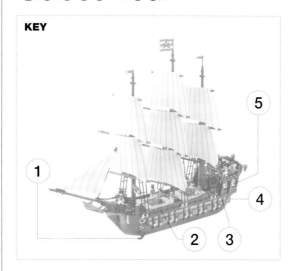

Textile mizzen sail—all sails were created exclusively for this set

Blue flap lifts up to reveal cannon

∧ **RAISING ANCHOR** The soldier minifigure turns the wheel to raise the ship's anchor on a vertical winch. The brig below is where prisoner minifigures can be held in shackles.

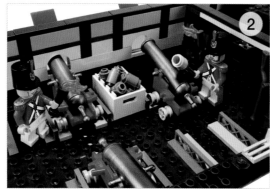

∧ **HEAVY FIREPOWER** Four firing cannons can be wheeled around the ship's eight cannon bays. Dark-gray round 1x1 bricks are used as cannonballs.

∧ **IN THE GALLEY** The ship's cook chops a carrot—a slice is an orange 1x1 round plate—while a turkey leg roasts on a rotating spit. Pans and utensils are secured to the walls.

∧ **MOVE ALONG** With a knife in his hand, the ship's cook is a long way from the galley. The rudder at the stern below is a movable piece that steers the ship to the left or right.

∧ **CAPTAIN'S QUARTERS** The ship's captain plays old sea shanties on the pipe organ. In his luxurious quarters, the map, poison bottle, and treasure chest are hidden from pirates.

• The anchor element was first created for 2002's LEGO Legends Black Seas Barracuda set (10040). The set was a reissue of the classic 1989 LEGOLAND Pirates set.

• A silhouette of this three-masted Imperial Flagship first appeared on the box of LEGO Pirates Brickbeard's Bounty (6243) in 2009.

• At the end of the design process, the designer, Raphaël Pierre Roger Pretesacque, added two extra pieces to take the final piece count up to 1,664. Raphaël is French, and couldn't resist referencing the French beer Kronenbourg 1664.

• The small red flags at the top of the masts have appeared in more than 120 sets.

Hogwarts™ Castle

2010 • LEGO® Harry Potter™ • #4842 • Pieces: 1290 • Minifigures: 10 plus 1 knight statue

The fourth version of the famous school of witchcraft and wizardry to be produced in the LEGO® Harry Potter™ theme, 2010's Hogwarts Castle set merged locations and artifacts from throughout the film series into one magical model full of hidden secrets and surprises. The four sections of the castle are connected by hinged panels so that they can be changed into different configurations, much like the real Hogwarts' ever-shifting stairs and corridors.

The set comes with 10 key hero, villain, and staff characters from the film saga, plus a knightly statue. Special items include the Sorting Hat™, the Marauder's Map, the Sword of Gryffindor™, Harry's invisibility cloak, and various animals, newspapers, and hidden notes.

Owlery features new owl element with three different designs—and owl droppings, too!

Chains (pieces usually used as handcuffs) can be removed to access the three books in the restricted area of the library

FRONT VIEW

Darker sand-colored bricks give the effect of walls in shadow

An identical Vanishing Cabinet appears in Borgin and Burke's shop in Diagon Alley (10217) in 2011

Hermione Granger™ minifigure sits at the dining table for a feast in the Great Hall

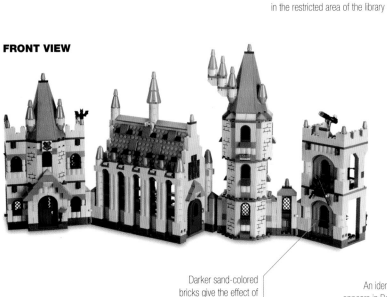

KEY

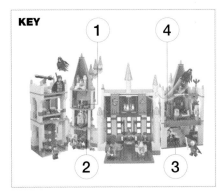

< **GRYFFINDOR COMMON ROOM**
The face of Sirius Black™ appears as a sticker on a red tile in the common room fire. The Marauder's Map is printed on a 2x2 tile.

> **SECRET DIARY** Twist around the knight statue and discover a diary belonging to Tom Riddle™ hidden in the stonework. This rare black book piece can be removed and opened.

"I thought it would be cool to include little details from all the movies."

Bjarke Lykke Madsen, LEGO Design Master

A Sorting Hat with printed details is unique to the set

- A rare textile piece is used for Harry Potter's invisibility cloak. It also appeared in Hogwarts Express (4841) in the same year.

- Mustachioed Professor Flitwick and miserable-looking Argus Filch make their one and only minifigure appearance in this set.

- These minifigure versions of Professor McGonagall™ (in her dark-green robe) and the shinier Gryffindor knight statue are also exclusive to this set.

- The conflict between Slytherin™ and Gryffindor is a key focus of the set. Their common rooms are featured, and the Great Hall is decorated with the two house banners.

- The large cake in the Great Hall was inspired by a scene in a LEGO Harry Potter videogame.

- This set connects to 2011's LEGO Harry Potter Hogwarts set (4867) to add even more rooms to the castle.

Parchment piece can be hidden inside the treasure chest

< HIDDEN STAIRCASE
Gray blocks open out to reveal a spiral staircase that leads to the office of Albus Dumbledore™. Behind Harry is a James Potter seeker award for Quidditch™.

> DUMBLEDORE'S OFFICE
The headmaster's office is packed with small details, including potions, a frog, the Quibbler magazine, and Gryffindor's Sword.

∧ STICKERS The set's stickers include symbols for the house banners and old portraits that feature the LEGO Harry Potter design team as different fictional historical characters.

Fire Temple

2011 • LEGO® NINJAGO™ • #2507 • Pieces: 1173 • Minifigures: 7

"Ninja... GO!" That was the battle cry with which LEGO® NINJAGO™ spun into action in 2011. Featuring function-filled building sets, a competitive game played with trading cards and top-like Spinjitzu spinners, and a computer-animated TV series to tell its story, the tale of element-powered ninja heroes versus skeleton warriors quickly became one of the company's biggest play themes ever. The cornerstone set of its first year was the Fire Temple, a large and elegant model inspired by the architecture of feudal Japan.

The Fire Temple set is based around the battle for control of the golden Sword of Fire. Kai, the red Ninja of Fire, must obtain the legendary weapon to save the world of Ninjago from the evil Lord Garmadon and his four-armed skeleton lieutenant, Samukai. Pulling up on the sword makes the entire Fire Temple set split in two, revealing its protector: a giant fireball-spitting dragon that Kai can befriend and ride into battle.

BRICK BY BRICK

- The dark-green dragon statue was introduced in 2010. It appeared as Norbert the baby dragon in LEGO Harry Potter Hagrid's Hut (4738) in 2010.

- This set features all four of the Golden Weapons of Spinjitzu.

- The pearl-gold colored minifigure Sword of Fire first appeared in 2011.

- The window panels with gold dragon design printing are exclusive to this set.

- The red-garbed Nya minifigure has an alternate face with a red battle mask printed across her mouth.

- Samukai, the Skeleton Army warrior, has a head that is in two parts. It is hinged at the back and can open up.

Japanese cherry blossom tree

Lord Garmadon's minifigure blasts an evil magic bolt at Sensei Wu

Guided Tour

Feather element is exclusive to the set in this color—it appears (in other colors) as a helicopter blade in LEGO City sets

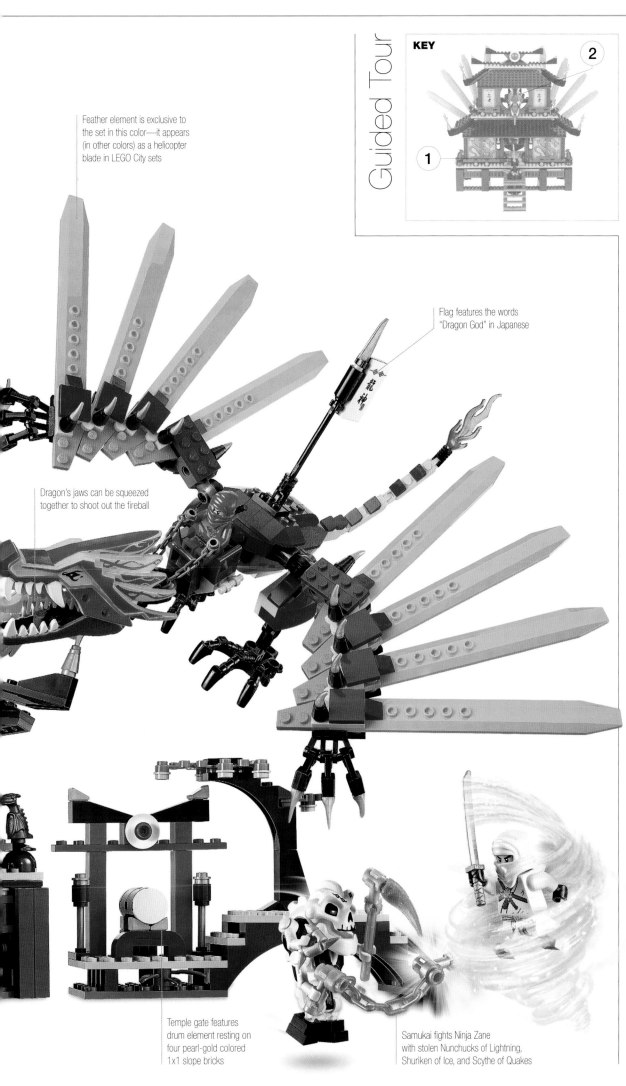

Flag features the words "Dragon God" in Japanese

Dragon's jaws can be squeezed together to shoot out the fireball

Temple gate features drum element resting on four pearl-gold colored 1x1 slope bricks

Samukai fights Ninja Zane with stolen Nunchucks of Lightning, Shuriken of Ice, and Scythe of Quakes

KEY

Guided Tour

∧ **SWORD OF FIRE** The weapon is displayed on a rotating pedestal in front of the temple. Panels printed with gold dragons flank the entrance.

∧ **DRAGON HEAD** The Fire Dragon pokes through the top floor. Japanese-inspired printed screens decorate the temple windows on each side.

∧ **REAR VIEW** The Fire Dragon can perch on a platform at the back of the temple. Its eight wing feathers are posable, as is its tail.

∧ **SPLIT TEMPLE** Pull up the Sword of Fire, and the temple splits open, releasing the mighty Fire Dragon and adding even more playability.

Volkswagen T1 Camper Van

2011 • LEGO® Advanced Models • #10220 • Pieces: 1332

Peace, love, and LEGO bricks… that's what the Volkswagen T1 Camper Van set is all about. A miniature—but still quite hefty at nearly a foot (30 cm) long—licensed replica of the classic VW van from 1962, it includes all of the memorable details of the vehicle loved around the world, from the V-shaped design and divided "splittie" windshield at the front to the air-cooled flat-four-cylinder boxer engine in back. Its Sixties-style interior too is fully fitted out and ready for a cross-country drive.

The Camper Van's designer, John-Henry Harris, wanted to make the model as authentic as possible, both inside and out. He used curved bricks to give the exterior its gently rounded shape. The doors, windshield, and engine hatch open, the rear bench seat and dinette table fold down, and the pop-up roof has a fabric curtain. He even snuck his initials into the painting inside!

Roof rack for storing luggage and surfboards

Bright-red ladder piece is used as an air vent

Rare, curved, white brick is used for the fender

- A T-shirt hangs in the side window. Its design is a nod to the flower power age of the 1960s.

- Six plaid-print textile curtains, exclusive to this set, create an authentic 1960s vibe.

- On the front of the vehicle is a metallic sticker of the VW logo.

- The orange textile used on the roof is unique to the set. It accordions down when the roof is closed.

- Two flexible hoses are curved to form the characteristic "V" shape at the front of the Camper.

- This model is based on the 1962 Volkswagen "splittie," so-called because of its split front windshield with safari-style windows.

Rare metallic-silver colored hubcap also appeared as an examination light in LEGO Friends Heartlake Vet (3188) in 2012

Brick-built pop-up roof is raised by a criss-cross scissor mechanism that uses four LEGO Technic beams

Guided Tour

KEY

License plate features the year this model of Camper Van was first manufactured

H-VW 1962

∧ **ENGINE SPACE** Lift up the rear flap and the engine is in the back, between the wheels. The real vehicle's distinctive engine is recreated in intricate detail.

∧ **RELAX, MAN** Passengers can enjoy a drink as they chill out in the Camper Van's dinette. The artwork features a sticker with the LEGO designer's initials just visible on the surfboard.

∧ **TIME FOR BED** Fold away the table, lay down the rear bench seat, and settle back and watch the lava lamp in the corner (a cup element with trans-neon green cone piece). Psychedelic!

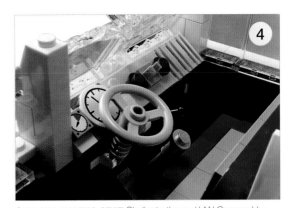

∧ **IN THE DRIVING SEAT** Similar to the real VW Camper Van, the stick shift comes up from the floor and there is a bench seat. The large speedometer is used as a clock face in other sets.

Crooks' Hideout
• 2015 • LEGO® City • #60068

Helicopter Pursuit
• 2015 • LEGO City • #60067

Doctor's Car
• 2006 • LEGO City • #7902

ALWAYS ON DUTY

LEGO® emergency services through the years

For over forty years, there have been LEGO® sets of fire stations, police departments, hospitals, and other essential emergency services. On land, sea, and air, these dedicated civil servants chase down crooks, lend aid to stranded sailors, and rescue kittens from trees. They work in the cities and towns, the forests and swamps, and anywhere else that there are crimes being committed, recycling bins on fire, and citizens in need of help. So let's have three cheers for these hardworking LEGO heroes!

Coast Guard Patrol
• 2013 • LEGO City • #60014

Fire Station
• 2013 • LEGO City • #60004

4x4 Fire Truck
• 2012 • LEGO City • #4208

ATV Patrol
• 2015 • LEGO City • #60065

Police Heliport
• 1972 • LEGOLAND • #354

Hospital
- 1978 • LEGO Homemaker • #231

Police Station
- 2008 • LEGO® DUPLO® – Town • #5602

Fire Motorcycle
- 2013 • LEGO® City • #60000

Coast Guard Helicopter and Life Raft
- 2008 • LEGO City • #7738

Police 4x4
- 1992 • LEGO Town • #6533

Fire Station with Mini Cars
- 1970 • LEGO Model Maker • #347

Ambulance
- 1994 • LEGO Town • #6666

Coast Guard Kayak
- 2008 • LEGO City • #5621

Armored Car Action
- 2003 • LEGO® World City • #7033

Police Boat
- 2006 • LEGO City • #7899

Harley-Davidson® 1000cc
- 1976 • LEGO Hobby Set • #394

Earth Defense HQ

2011 • LEGO® Space • #7066 • Pieces: 879 • Minifigures: 5, plus Alien Clinger

Aliens invaded Earth for the first time in Alien Conquest, a new LEGO Space subtheme that was inspired by both the classic alien invasion movies of the 1950s and futuristic sci-fi video games and movies. The theme followed the Alien Defense Unit (ADU), who protected Earth's civilians from a bunch of eerie alien intruders. Fortunately for the earthlings, the ADU had an impressive Earth Defense HQ—the biggest set in the one-year subtheme.

The ADU's Mobile Launch Station has a trailer that can be unhooked for high-speed pursuits, an interceptor shuttle to fight off the aliens' UFO, and two missile launchers that can each fire four flick missiles at once. Inside the station, there is a lab for studying the outer-space intruders and a prison pod for locking them up. It's probably best to not take any chances—that brain-sucking Alien Clinger has its eye on a minifigure's head!

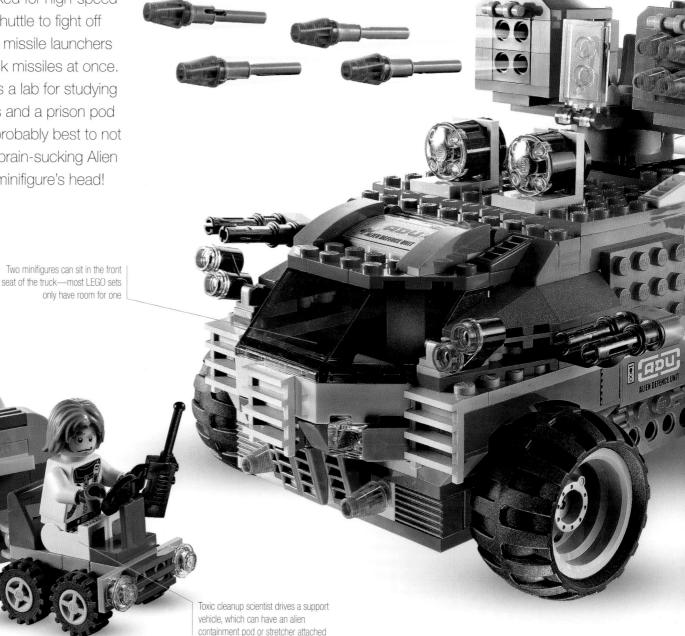

Transparent dome on the aliens' UFO has since been used as a helicopter windshield in a LEGO Friends set

Two minifigures can sit in the front seat of the truck—most LEGO sets only have room for one

Toxic cleanup scientist drives a support vehicle, which can have an alien containment pod or stretcher attached

• The aliens' laser guns first appeared in 2010 in the LEGO Minifigures line. The ADU soldiers needed a weapon that could stand up against it, so a new two-barreled gun was created for them.

• The set uses the classic blue, gray, and yellow color scheme of LEGOLAND Space sets of the 1970s and '80s. It includes pieces that were created in bright blue for the first time.

• The interceptor shuttle features two stickers as a tribute to the late Nate Nielsen, who went by the internet name "nnenn." He was a talented and prolific LEGO fan builder, known for his spaceship builds.

• The toxic cleanup scientist minifigure looks familiar. Could it be based on the set's designer, Mark Stafford?

Guided Tour

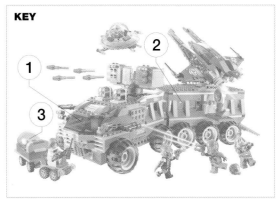

KEY

1

2

3

Interceptor shuttle can be elevated and rotated into position for takeoff

Ramp for loading support vehicle with trailer

Alien Android has a metal peg-leg, mechanical arm with barb, and a new head mold with semi-transparent brain

∧ **ANALYSIS AREA** Computer screens and a swivel chair fit behind the driver's cab. The cab and trailer can be separated, or tightly connected as a single, long multi-axle vehicle, or loosely connected as an articulated cab and trailer.

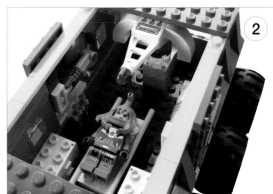

∧ **RESEARCH BAY** The lab is fitted with a scanner and other medical equipment. An Alien Clinger has attached itself to an ADU soldier's head. Quick, someone help her!

∧ **PRISON POD** The Alien Android is secured inside an ADU containment pod. The pod's light-blue windshield has appeared in six other sets.

City of Atlantis

2011 • LEGO® Atlantis • #7985 • Pieces: 686 • Minifigures: 5

In a new underwater play theme, launched in 2010, LEGO Atlantis took a crew of deep-sea salvage divers on a journey to the ocean floor as they searched for the lost treasures of sunken Atlantis. They collected ancient keys and battled guardian sea creatures and fish-headed warriors, and in the theme's second—and final—year, at last discovered the legendary City of Atlantis itself.

Modeled on the marble temples of historical Greece, the City of Atlantis set depicts the crumbling ruins of a once-proud civilization. Turning a key in the special lock piece causes the city's noble ruler, the Golden King, to rise up through a door in the floor of the temple.

"Functions are very important to fantasy play themes. We often work on the function, like the king popping up, from the very beginning of the set design."

Mark John Stafford, LEGO Senior Designer

Harpoon gun carried by Atlantis diver Ace Speedman

Giant Crab Guardian has working pincers

This plant piece first appeared in BIONICLE sets in 2007, but it was new in dark green for this set

Guided Tour

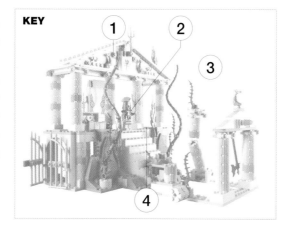

KEY
1
2
3
4

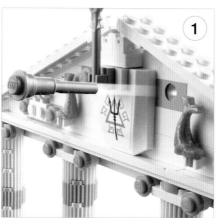

1

< **ON TARGET** Don't be fooled by the circular gold decorations on the front of the temple. They are actually gold-tipped flick-fire missiles that can be fired from behind.

2

> **GOLDEN SURPRISE**
Turning a key in the gray lock piece at the foot of the stairs causes the Golden King to rise into view. He carries a trident and wears a detailed breastplate and helmet.

Atlantis diver Samantha Rhodes pilots the sub

The trans-violet and gold key piece used for raising the Golden King is exclusive to this set

Ax swings down across the entrance when the gold cone piece at the top is pushed in

- The Golden King minifigure has a double-sided head piece. As well as his gold-colored statue face, he has a yellow "real" face with a gray beard.

- The design team deliberately didn't provide a detailed story with the set to let builders decide for themselves whether the King is alive, magical, or a statue.

- Behind the King is a sticker printed with a drawing of merman guards.

- The torso of the Lobster Guardian is printed with teeth. Its red rubbery head piece and claws are detachable.

- The green, fanged Atlantis Barracuda Guardian also appeared in LEGO Atlantis Angler Attack (7978) in the same year.

- The classical columns are built from round 2x2 bricks with grille in white and brick-yellow—these were both new for 2011.

< **PILLAR THRILLER**
This particular pillar is hinged onto a special base, enabling it to lean and appear to tumble onto an unsuspecting explorer.

> **DOOR IN THE FLOOR** Pull out the Technic axle and a trapdoor is released, sending a surprised diver down into the depths of the underwater city. Mind your step!

Mercedes-Benz Unimog U 400

2011 • LEGO® Technic • #8110 • Pieces: 2048

At 2,048 pieces and 22in (56cm) in length, the Mercedes-Benz Unimog U 400 was the largest LEGO® Technic set ever made when it came out in 2011. Modeled after the popular multipurpose truck, it was just as rugged and useful as its namesake. And if builders ever got tired of driving it around and picking things up with its working grabber arm, they could rebuild it into an alternate version of the Unimog equipped with a monster-sized snowplow!

Like the real truck, the Unimog model is built with four-wheel drive, functional steering, independent suspension systems, and a gear block for extra ground clearance when driving off-road. A LEGO Power Functions motor controls the pneumatic pistons and its articulated crane and claw, as well as the recovery winch in front of its cab.

"With LEGO Technic, we want to keep up with the latest technology, so we evolve a lot. We recreate authentic designs of today."

Markus Kossmann, LEGO Senior Designer

Knob rotates to change direction of wheels

Mercedes-Benz logo sticker

Recovery winch is connected to the Power Functions motor—it can move up or down with the flick of a lever

BRICK BY BRICK

• There was a contest at Mercedes-Benz for how to celebrate the Unimog's 60th anniversary—and the winning suggestion was a LEGO Technic set of the vehicle.

• The vehicle is one-twelfth of the size of the real vehicle. It is 12in (30cm) high.

• This is the first LEGO vehicle to have full suspension.

• Many new pieces were made to recreate the model's iconic look, for example the elements used to lift the vehicle's axles off the ground for higher ground clearance.

• The panel and beam pieces used in the cab were produced in orange for the very first time for this set.

• The articulated crane and stabilizers can also attach to the front of the Unimog, and the winch can be moved to the rear.

• The set features over 12ft (almost 4m) of pneumatic piping.

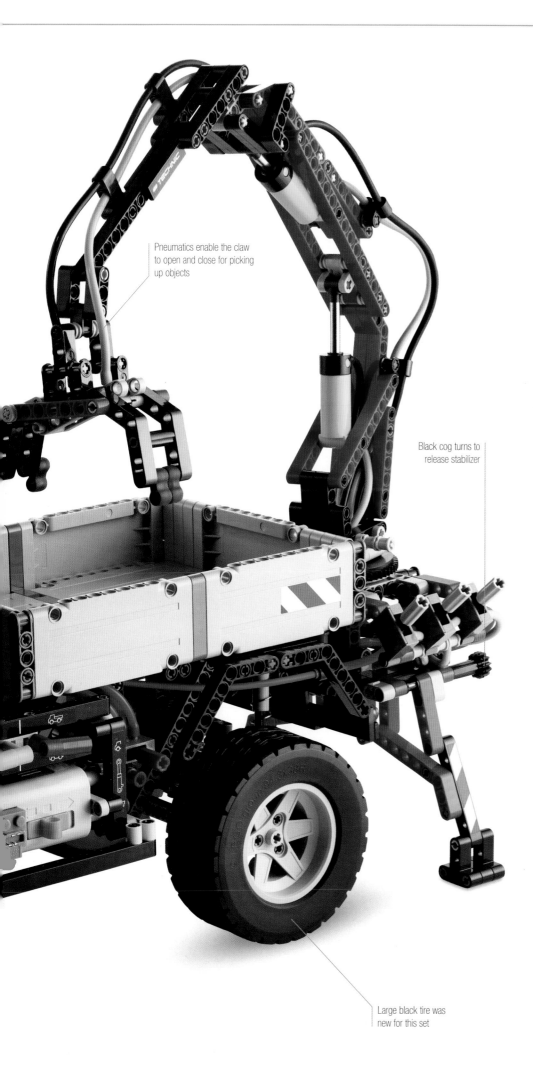

Pneumatics enable the claw to open and close for picking up objects

Black cog turns to release stabilizer

Large black tire was new for this set

Guided Tour

KEY

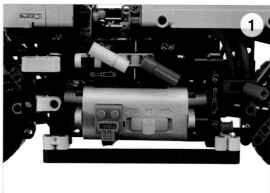

∧ **OPERATING PANEL** A Power Functions motor works in conjuction with pneumatic pumps to operate the crane and winch. A series of switches and levers controls their movement.

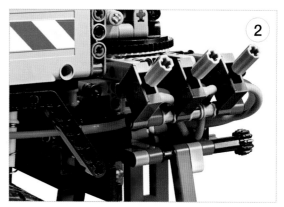

∧ **PNEUMATIC CONTROLS** Three levers, connected to the crane via pneumatic piping, raise and lower the crane's lower arm and upper arm, and open and close the crane's grabber.

∧ **ALTERNATE BUILD** The Unimog's crane and cargo bed can be rebuilt into a snowplow attachment. The snowplow can move up and down and it can be angled from left to right.

Olivia's House

2012 • LEGO® Friends • #3315 • Pieces: 681 • Mini-dolls: 3

The 2012 LEGO® Friends theme welcomed builders to Heartlake City, the home of BFFs Andrea, Emma, Mia, Olivia, and Stephanie. Featuring a new mini-doll figure and many new parts and colors, the theme offered a detailed building experience with an everyday-life, character-focused twist. Olivia got the biggest set of the theme's first year: the two-story Olivia's House.

Along with Olivia herself, the set includes her parents (with dad Peter as the first male mini-doll in the line) and pet cat. The house is built to be modular, with rooms that can be taken apart and rearranged, encouraging builders to customize and decorate them however they want.

Sun lounger on terrace can swivel

Outdoor grill with closing lid

Olivia's mom pushes the brick-built lawnmower

Letter, with printed detail, in mailbox

"With LEGO Friends, it's great to be able to indulge in all the little details."

Fenella Blaize Charity, LEGO Design Manager

Guided Tour

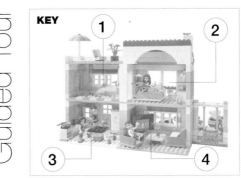

KEY 1 2 3 4

1

> **BEAUTIFUL BATHROOM** The bathroom has a shower with opening doors, sink, and a toilet—of course!

Fenella Blaize Charity | Design Manager

Fenella was spotted by LEGO scouts at the New Designers exhibition in London, UK in 2007. She picked up LEGO bricks for the first time in years for a two-day recruitment session, and got the job! Fenella joined a team of six designers with the task of making LEGO play even more relevant to girls. Years of focus testing and research resulted in LEGO Friends, for which she is now the creative lead. With two other designers, Olivia's House was the first set Fenella created. Like all LEGO products, the team develop the sets with input from children and parents around the world, but sometimes they draw on their own experiences, too. Fenella was organizing her wedding while designing 2014's Heartlake Shopping Mall (41058), so added a bridal shop!

- Peter and Anna, Olivia's parents, are exclusive to this set. Like all mini-dolls, their legs do not move independently and they are hinged at the waist.

- The house number, 30, is the house number of one of the set's designers.

- This is the only set to include Kitty, the cat.

- In the early days of LEGO Friends, the set designers sculpted lots of new elements themselves, such as hair accessories.

- The LEGO Friends designers always put toilets in sets with "house play." They joke about who can build one in a new way.

Trans-light blue shower door piece first appeared as part of a garage door in LEGO Town's Fire Control Center (6389) in 1990

Swing with space for one mini-doll

INSIDE VIEW

Three new types of flowers were introduced in this set

△ **OLIVIA'S BEDROOM** The vanity table in this colorful bedroom has a mirror (with metallic sticker) and space for perfume bottles. There is also a bedside table with lamp.

△ **STYLISH KITCHEN** The well-equipped kitchen includes a stove, blender, and fridge with printed milk carton inside. The carton was introduced in this set.

△ **SPACE TO RELAX** The living room is furnished with purple sofas (the curved bricks were new in this color) and a yellow coffee table. A sticker on the TV depicts an entertainment show.

Haunted House

2012 • LEGO® Monster Fighters • #10228 • Pieces: 2056 • Minifigures: 6

Inspired by the classic monsters of film and literature, the creature stars of the 2012 LEGO® Monster Fighters theme inhabited a scarily silly world of shrieks and shadows. Their biggest set was the Haunted House, a stately but ramshackle abode packed with details to make advanced builders scream with delight.

Boards across broken windows, a spiked iron gate, and zombie-headed columns warn visitors that this is no ordinary dwelling. A hinge built into the stone chimney lets the Haunted House split open to reveal six rooms full of spooky surprises.

The bat figure made its first appearance in LEGO Castle sets in 1997

"A haunted house in movies is always dusty and broken… To give that effect with new bricks wasn't easy."

Adam Siegmund Grabowski, LEGO Senior Designer

Sand-yellow bricks give the appearance of neglected brickwork

Shutter is attached with a single clip to make it appear broken

Side entrance leads to the kitchen

Zombie minifigure head

Separate brick-built front gate section

Guided Tour

KEY

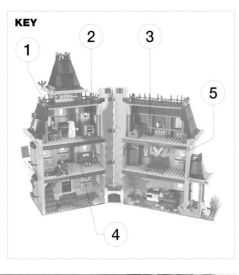

∧ **SPECIAL POTION** A ghost provides the ingredients for a bony brew in the top-floor potion room. The Vampyre Bride uses an old musket for stirring the creepy contents.

∧ **SECRET STAIRCASE** A lever in the chimney releases the drop-down, folding staircase for access to the even spookier top floor, which is filled with interesting pieces.

∧ **ATTIC ANTICS** A gramophone and records are stored in the attic, among other curiosities. The gramophone's horn is made from an element previously used as a pith helmet.

∧ **LORD VAMPYRE'S OFFICE** The master of the house writes letters using an old-fashioned quill and inkwell. The quill has been used as scissors and a feather headdress in other sets.

∧ **BEDROOM CLOSET** The Vampyre Bride hides a preserved heart in the closet. This printed piece has appeared in one other set: LEGO *Pirates of the Caribbean* The Mill (4183), in 2011.

BRICK BY BRICK

- The fireplace swings open to sit against the chimney. A ship in a bottle is displayed on the mantel.

- The glow-in-the-dark ghost minifigure was updated for the Monster Fighters theme. It has a more serious expression than its smiling predecessors.

- The Monster Butler and Zombie Chef minifigures have only ever appeared in this set.

- The Lord Vampyre and the Vampyre Bride minifigures have alternate, scarier faces.

- The pair of antlers above the bed in the bedroom is made from LEGO NINJAGO skeleton arms.

- The stickers featured include portraits, spider webs, and old curtains.

- The red-brown printed tiles that board up some of the windows first appeared in LEGO® *The Lord of the Rings*™ Uruk-Hai Army (9471) in 2012.

- This was the first house set that Senior Designer Adam Siegmund Grabowski designed. Parts of the front of the model were based on a sketch model he designed years earlier.

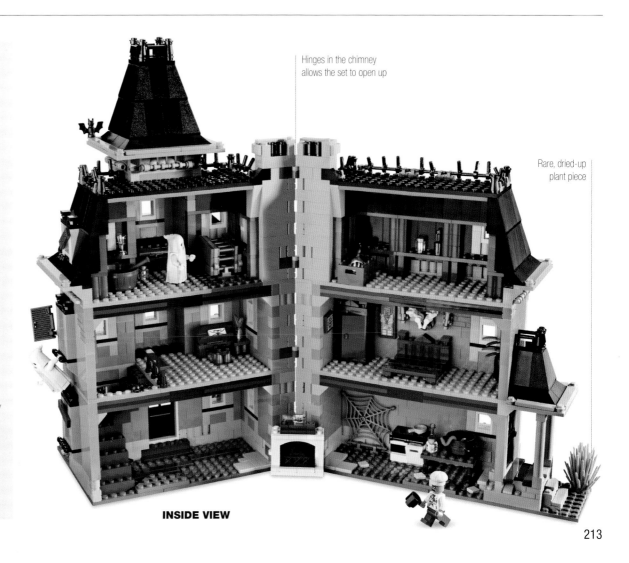

Hinges in the chimney allows the set to open up

Rare, dried-up plant piece

INSIDE VIEW

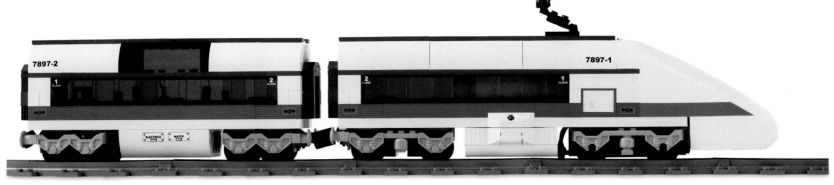

Passenger Train
• 2006 • LEGO® City • #7897

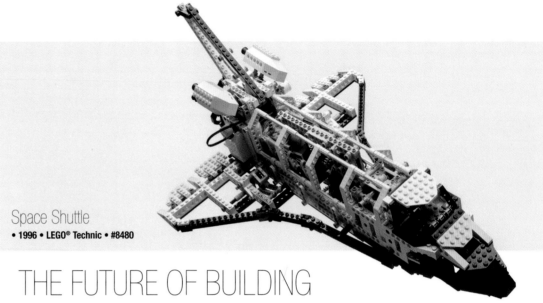

Space Shuttle
• 1996 • LEGO® Technic • #8480

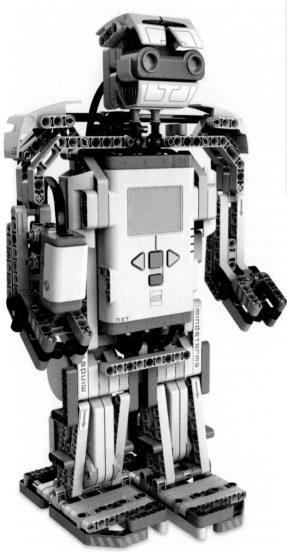

THE FUTURE OF BUILDING

Technology in LEGO® sets through the years

If you think that there isn't anything hi-tech about snapping plastic bricks together, then you haven't seen these sets! LEGO® models have been incorporating technology for decades, from electronic lights and sounds to air-powered pneumatic systems. As technology has advanced, LEGO sets have too, with movie cameras for making "brick films," programmable computer bricks connected to working motors and sensors, moving Power Functions models with infrared remote controls, and the latest sets that combine building with interactive apps for phones and other smart devices.

MINDSTORMS NXT 2.0
• 2009 • LEGO® MINDSTORMS™ • #8547

Life of George
• 2011 • LEGO® Life of George • #21200

Barcode Multi-set
• 1997 • LEGO Technic • #8479

Town Master
• 2014 • LEGO® Fusion • #21204

Cargo Plane
• 2013 • LEGO Technic • #42025

Excavator
• 1984 • LEGO Technic • #8851

Control Center
• 1990 • LEGO Technic • #8094

"We always try to use new technology.
We think, 'What can we do next?'"

Markus Kossmann, LEGO Senior Designer

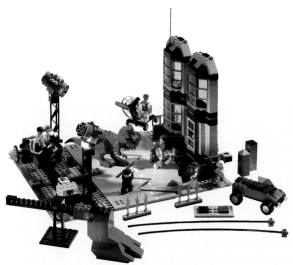

Steven Spielberg Moviemaker Set
• 2000 • LEGO Studios • #1349

Mobile Police Truck
• 1985 • LEGOLAND Town • #6450

Ferris Wheel
• 2007 • LEGO Creator • #4957

An Unexpected Gathering

2012 • LEGO® *The Hobbit*™ • #79003 • Pieces: 652 • Minifigures: 6

This richly detailed set depicts Bag End, where the epic adventure of *The Hobbit* begins. When the LEGO Group gained the license to make sets based on *The Hobbit* films, it was only to be expected that one of the first models would be of Bilbo Baggins' family home, where the wizard Gandalf arrives in search of a fourteenth member for his company of stalwart Dwarves.

The set lovingly recreates Bag End, a very civilized Hobbit-hole dug into the grassy hillside of Hobbiton. With its handsome round door and windows and its well-stocked dining room, it's easy to see why Bilbo so enjoys living in Bag End… and dreads the noisy chaos and clutter brought by his uninvited visitors.

> "We knew it was an absolute must to create round windows and doors as they are the visual icon of Bag End."
>
> Bjarke Lykke Madsen, LEGO Design Master

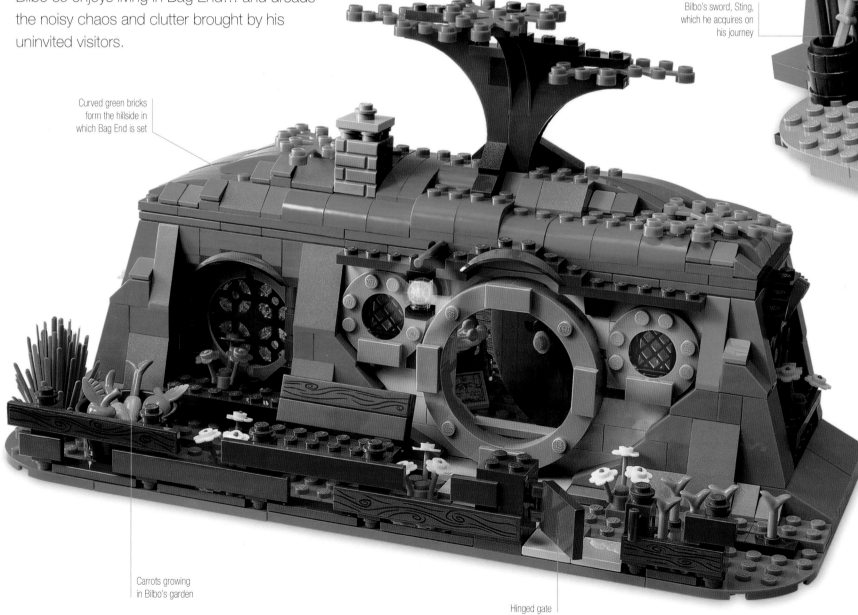

Bilbo's sword, Sting, which he acquires on his journey

Curved green bricks form the hillside in which Bag End is set

Carrots growing in Bilbo's garden

Hinged gate

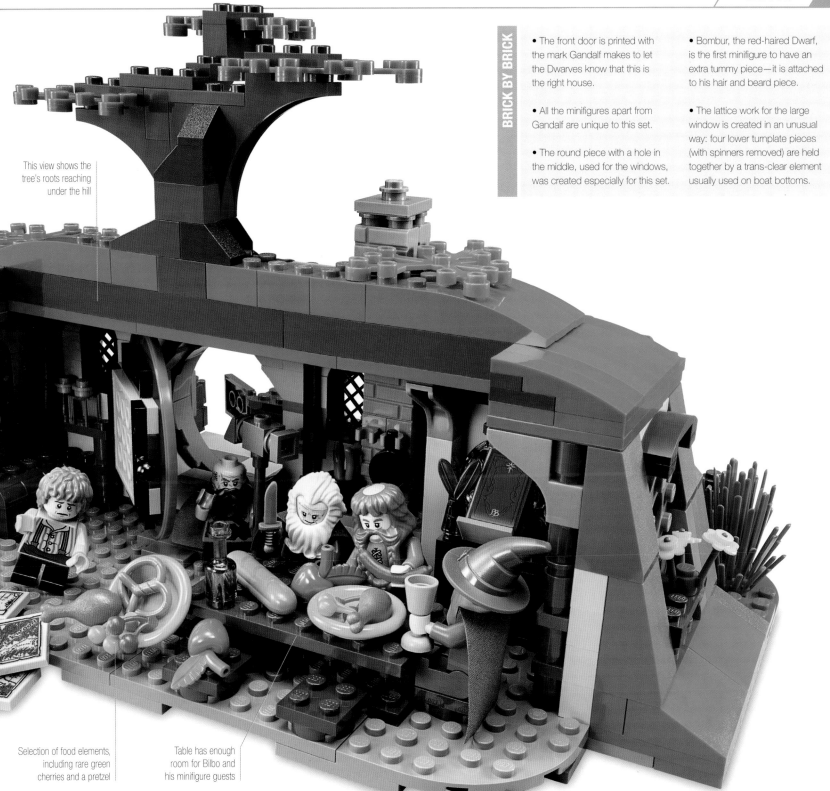

• The front door is printed with the mark Gandalf makes to let the Dwarves know that this is the right house.

• All the minifigures apart from Gandalf are unique to this set.

• The round piece with a hole in the middle, used for the windows, was created especially for this set.

• Bombur, the red-haired Dwarf, is the first minifigure to have an extra tummy piece—it is attached to his hair and beard piece.

• The lattice work for the large window is created in an unusual way: four lower tumplate pieces (with spinners removed) are held together by a trans-clear element usually used on boat bottoms.

This view shows the tree's roots reaching under the hill

Selection of food elements, including rare green cherries and a pretzel

Table has enough room for Bilbo and his minifigure guests

Guided Tour

KEY

1
2

1

∧ **KNOCK! KNOCK!** The entrance to Bag End is built using tan bricks and plates. Four brown bow pieces then fit over the outside to form the doorway's distinctive round shape.

2

∧ **A QUIET MOMENT** This well-lit corner is the perfect spot for Bilbo's desk. The three maps depict Bilbo and the Dwarves' route through the Shire and Mirkwood, to the Lonely Mountain.

Lion CHI Temple

2013 • LEGO® Legends of Chima™ • #70010 • Pieces: 1258 • Minifigures: 7

The LEGO Group created its own new fantasy world with 2013's LEGO Legends of Chima theme. Populated by animal tribes who race and battle aboard beast-shaped vehicles, the untamed realm of Chima is kept in balance by a magical energy called CHI. At the Lion CHI Temple, Prince Laval and his Lion and Eagle friends fight the power-hungry Crocodile Cragger and his Raven ally Razar, who are out to steal the temple's golden CHI for themselves.

At the top of the temple is a rare golden CHI orb... but to get it, the baddies will have to make it past the launching lion claw bikes and eagle drone, the missile-firing tower cannon, the booby-trapped drawbridge, and the chomping lion-head gate. It's no wonder the crocs switch to the good side in the theme's second year!

"I took my inspiration from the Yellow Castle, combined with concept art from the Chima TV show."

Mark John Stafford, LEGO Senior Designer

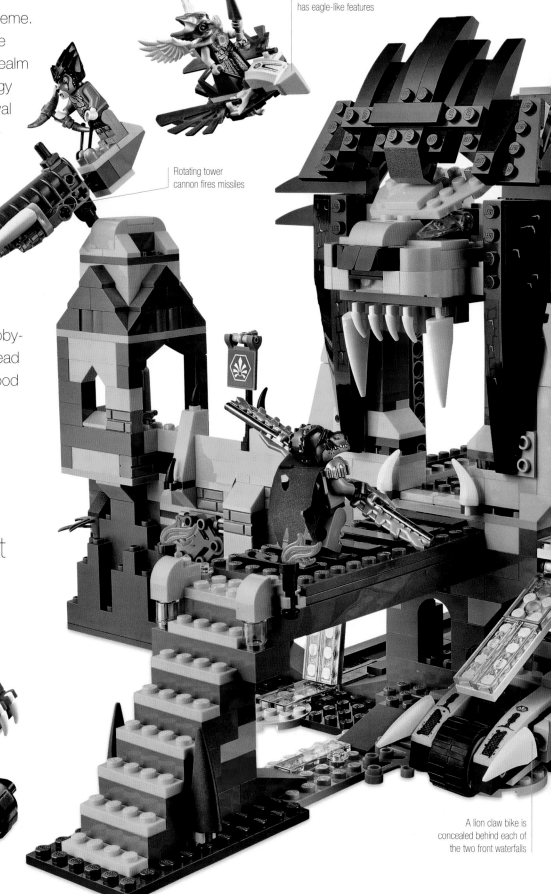

Ewald's drone fighter has eagle-like features

Rotating tower cannon fires missiles

A lion claw bike is concealed behind each of the two front waterfalls

Crawley's reptile raider moves on a single track, and has a biting mouth

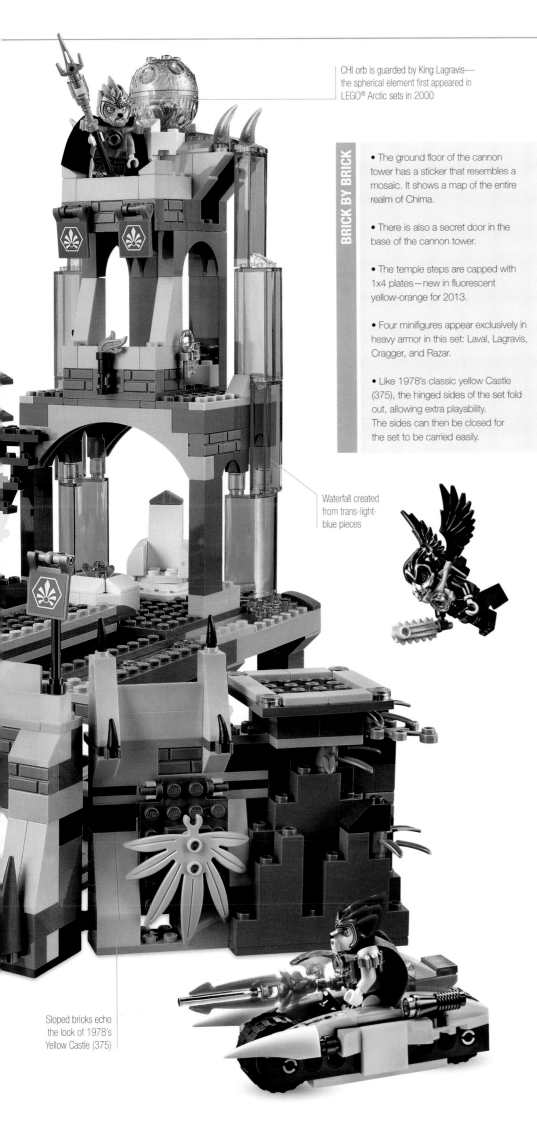

CHI orb is guarded by King Lagravis—the spherical element first appeared in LEGO® Arctic sets in 2000

• The ground floor of the cannon tower has a sticker that resembles a mosaic. It shows a map of the entire realm of Chima.

• There is also a secret door in the base of the cannon tower.

• The temple steps are capped with 1x4 plates—new in fluorescent yellow-orange for 2013.

• Four minifigures appear exclusively in heavy armor in this set: Laval, Lagravis, Cragger, and Razar.

• Like 1978's classic yellow Castle (375), the hinged sides of the set fold out, allowing extra playability. The sides can then be closed for the set to be carried easily.

Waterfall created from trans-light-blue pieces

Sloped bricks echo the look of 1978's Yellow Castle (375)

Guided Tour

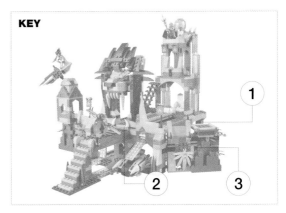

KEY

1

2   3

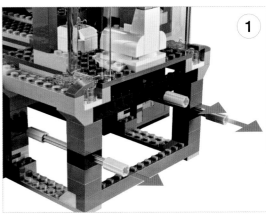

1

∧ **HIDDEN CONTROLS** The top LEGO Technic axles control the combined gate and drawbridge booby trap, and the bottom axles launch the lion claw bikes.

2

∧ **BOOBY TRAPS** The top jaw of the lion-head gate snaps down as the drawbridge slides behind the gate, causing sneaky intruders to get trapped in the jaws, or to fall into the pit below!

3

∧ **HIDDEN DOOR** Concealed behind greenery is the door to the tower prison. Longtooth, King Lagravis's loyal guard, locks the door behind a crocodile crook.

Tower of Orthanc

2013 • LEGO® *The Lord of the Rings*™ • #10237 • Pieces: 2359 • Minifigures: 5

When the LEGO *The Lord of the Rings* theme, based on the epic movie trilogy, was announced, most fans never imagined a set of Orthanc—one of the infamous two towers of Middle-earth—would be possible. Their surprise was matched only by their joy when the Tower of Orthanc was unveiled—a 28in (73cm) high, 2,359-piece, six-storied, spike-covered, incredibly detailed colossus of a LEGO model.

Three LEGO designers joined forces to recreate the dark fortress of the fallen wizard Saruman. Bjarke Lykke Madsen was in charge of the dungeon, entrance hall, and throne room (complete with Palantír to let Saruman communicate with his master, Lord Sauron); Hans Henrik Sidenius, the alchemy room and library; and Jordan Scott, the secret chamber and the Ent.

> "In the movie, you don't see much more than the throne room, so we had to figure out what else to put inside. Our creativity was really challenged."

Bjarke Lykke Madsen, LEGO Design Master

• Based on further reading into the Tolkien universe, as well as their own imaginations, the LEGO designers added many new areas to fill the space in the tower. Additions include the secret chamber at the tower's summit, as well as the trapdoor and dungeon.

• Saruman and Gandalf also appear together in LEGO *The Lord of the Rings* The Wizard Battle (79005). Their minifigures and the Palantír were updated for the Orthanc set.

• The Saruman minifigure comes with a printed sloped piece for his long robes and separate legs for sitting on his throne.

• The Gandalf, Wormtongue, Saruman, and Uruk-hai soldier minifigures all have alternate faces.

• The Ent model is fully posable due to its ball and socket joints, and has a swinging arm mechanism allowing it to throw items or minifigures gripped between its fingers.

Ent can grip the Orc minifigure due to its posable fingers

Eagle element was first developed for the LEGO *The Lord of the Rings* Battle at the Black Gate set (79007)

Grima Wormtongue minifigure is exclusive to the set

Studs-free building technique is used to create the iconic blades at the tower's summit

Barred windows are made with a hollow arch element first used in this theme

Saruman minifigure stands at the balcony to address his army of Urak-hai

Guided Tour

KEY

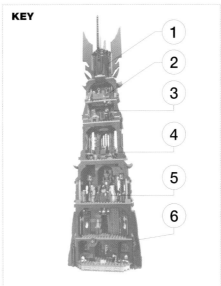

∧ **THE PINNACLE OF ORTHANC** Gandalf's minifigure is imprisoned on top of the tower. This minifigure also appeared in LEGO *The Hobbit* Dol Guldur Battle (79014) in the same year.

∧ **TERRIBLE TROPHIES** Saruman's minifigure keeps the staffs of defeated wizards and the keys to the two towers (Orthanc and Barad-dûr) in this secret chamber. It is accessed by a folding staircase.

∧ **SARUMAN'S LIBRARY** The library has books and scrolls for Saruman's minifigure to study dark magic. It also contains portraits of three wizards (printed on stickers).

∧ **ALCHEMY ROOM** The LEGO designers included an area for Wormtongue and the Uruk-Hai soldier minifigures to make weapons in preparation for the attack of Helm's Deep.

∧ **THRONE ROOM** Saruman's Palantír—or seeing stone—is represented by this unique ball. It is lit up by a light brick, which is activated by pushing up the chandelier in the entrance hall below.

> **TRAPDOOR** The LEGO designers added a trapdoor so that Saruman can dispose of unwanted guests. Evil creatures peer out of the darkness on a sticker in the dungeon below.

Batman™: Arkham Asylum Breakout

2013 • LEGO® DC Universe™ Super Heroes • #10937 • Pieces: 1619 • Minifigures: 8

Although the LEGO Batman™ line had ended in 2008, the Dark Knight returned in 2012 as part of the LEGO® DC Universe™ Super Heroes theme (later renamed DC Comics Super Heroes). Along with a number of never-before-made minifigures and models, the theme featured new versions of some old favorites, including a totally redesigned and very gothic Arkham Asylum—which wasn't quite upgraded enough to keep its super villain inmates from breaking back out again.

The asylum has cells to hold many of Batman's greatest foes, including custom cages for Poison Ivy and even Mr. Freeze if he happens to drop by. There's a comfy psychiatric examination chair for the Joker, too. So how do all of the villains keep escaping? Maybe it's an inside job—that doctor sure looks a lot like the Joker's hench-woman, Harley Quinn!

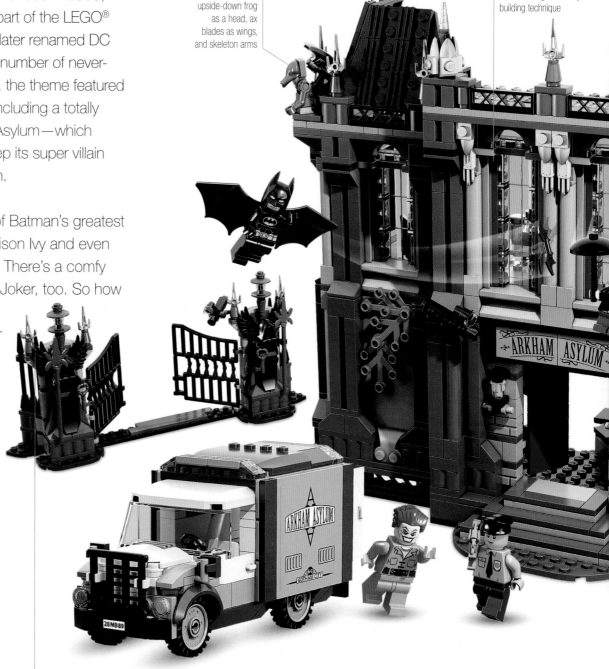

Gargoyle has an upside-down frog as a head, ax blades as wings, and skeleton arms

Window frames are created using a sideways building technique

Black angel statue uses wing pieces from LEGO Legends of Chima ravens

BRICK BY BRICK

• Set designer Marcos Bessa asked for the set number to include "0937" as it reads "LEGO" upside down, and it is the name of his LEGO fan community in his native country, Portugal.

• The van's license plate sticker, "28 MB 89," features Marcos Bessa's initials, his year of birth, and "28"—his grandfather's nickname.

• It is the first time Dr. Harleen Quinzel has appeared in a set. Her alter ego, Harley Quinn, appeared in sets in 2008, 2012, and 2015. Harley Quinn's hat is hidden at her secret changing table, and a hint of her black-and-red costume is just visible on her torso in this set.

• New versions of Batman, Robin, Scarecrow, The Penguin, and The Joker minifigures were created for this set.

• A LEGO DC Universe Super Heroes comic comes with the set.

• The building can split into three and its layout can be rearranged and secured using LEGO Technic pins.

Marcos Bessa | Senior Designer

Marcos works on licensed play themes, such as Marvel and DC Super Heroes, *Star Wars*, and THE LEGO MOVIE. He loves to push the building experience in his models—for example Arkham Asylum's windows use an unusual sideways building technique. As part of his training when he started at the LEGO Group in 2010, Marcos had to come up with an idea for a licensed project. He mocked up a car and figures for The Simpsons. Although unrelated, years later, he designed The Simpsons House (71006)—the car is very similar to his original build!

Window is made with a special trans-red plate with hole, which first appeared in this set

Sticker with temperature gauge for Mr. Freeze's cell

BACK VIEW

Trans-brown 1x1 slope piece looks like broken glass

"I try to inspire fans to use bricks in different ways. I used the frog piece as a head for the gargoyles, which fans really liked."

Marcos Bessa, LEGO Senior Designer

Guided Tour

KEY

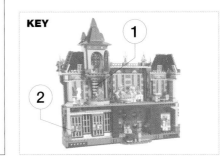

1
2

< **GLASS CELL** Poison Ivy languishes in a cell that was designed with a nod to the 2006 Arkham Asylum set (7785). In both sets, two hinged, trans-clear, curved doors open outward.

> **NAUGHTY NEIGHBORS**
The doors of the two cells containing Scarecrow and The Joker can slide open. Tiles with stickers of inmates' profiles are clipped on to the bars of each door.

∧ **RESTRAINING STRETCHER** Bars and elements that are usually used as LEGO *Star Wars* battle droid arms clip The Joker securely onto the gurney.

Sydney Opera House
• 2013 • LEGO® Creator Expert • #10234

Café Corner
• 2007 • LEGO® Advanced Models • #10182

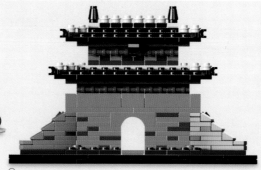

Sungnyemun
• 2012 • LEGO Architecture • #21016

Pet Shop
• 2011 • LEGO Advanced Models • #10218

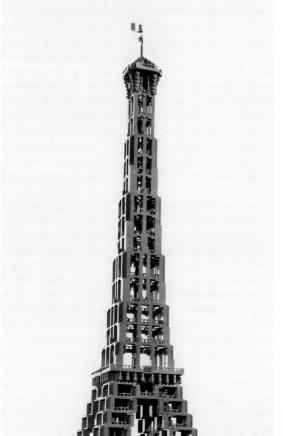

Eiffel Tower
• 2007 • LEGO Advanced Models • #10181

EXPERT BUILDERS ONLY!

Advanced LEGO® models through the years

Designed for expert builders, the largest and most elaborate LEGO® sets have included oversized sculptures, national landmarks, replicas of famous vehicles, and a fan-favorite series of modular buildings that fit together side-by-side to create an ever-growing city neighborhood. These advanced models make use of the LEGO design team's most clever building techniques and incorporate rare and unusual elements in even more unusual ways to produce incredibly detailed and lifelike brick creations.

Tower Bridge
• 2010 • LEGO Advanced Models • #10214

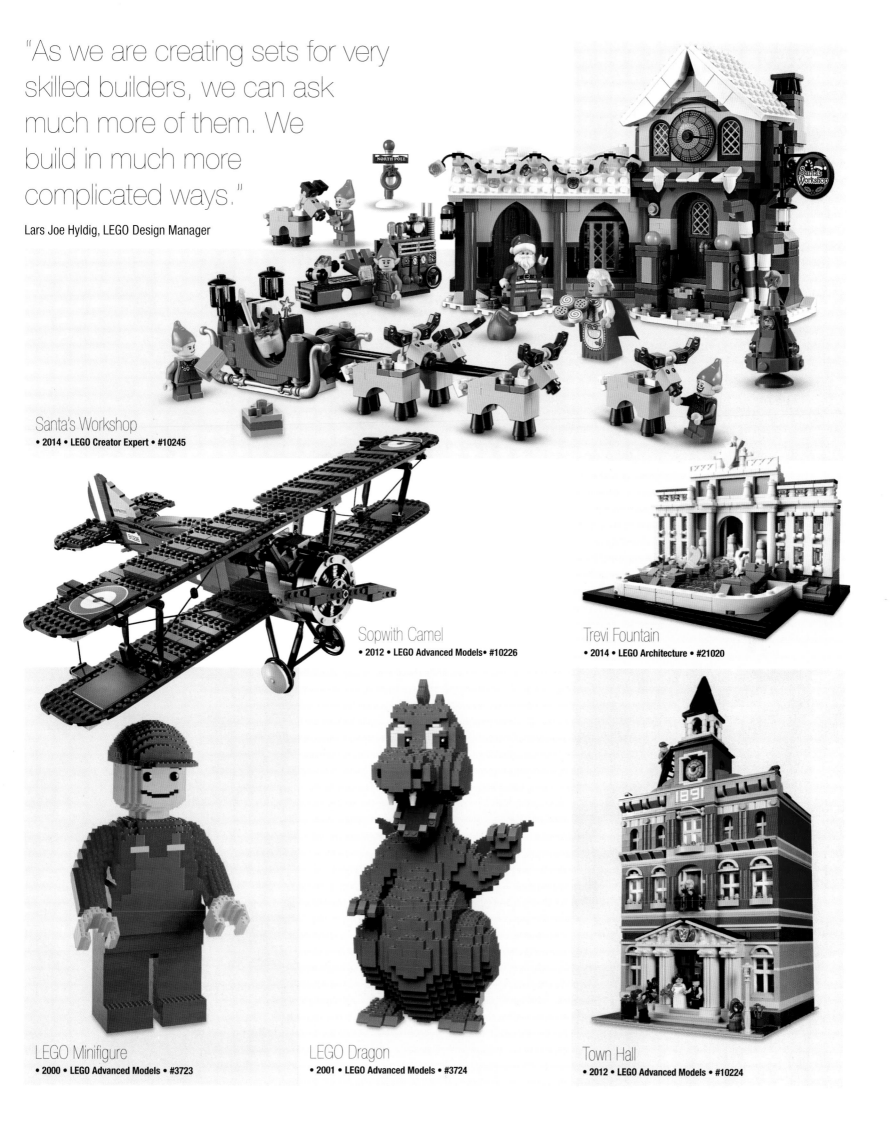

"As we are creating sets for very skilled builders, we can ask much more of them. We build in much more complicated ways."

Lars Joe Hyldig, LEGO Design Manager

Santa's Workshop
• 2014 • LEGO Creator Expert • #10245

Sopwith Camel
• 2012 • LEGO Advanced Models • #10226

Trevi Fountain
• 2014 • LEGO Architecture • #21020

LEGO Minifigure
• 2000 • LEGO Advanced Models • #3723

LEGO Dragon
• 2001 • LEGO Advanced Models • #3724

Town Hall
• 2012 • LEGO Advanced Models • #10224

United Nations Headquarters

2013 • LEGO® Architecture • #21018 • Pieces: 597

When the LEGO Architecture series began in 2008, its microscaled models of famous skyscrapers and other landmark buildings were aimed squarely at the office desks and mantelpieces of grown-ups. Subsequent releases were larger and more detailed, including 2013's 597-piece United Nations Headquarters. Like the others in the line, the set comes with a collector's booklet, which provides interesting facts about the real New York City building's history and construction.

Architects Le Corbusier and Oscar Niemeyer's modernist design is reflected in the LEGO model's smooth white surfaces and rows of transparent blue windows. When building micro-architecture, the key is to use parts inventively: a turntable base represents the Secretariat Building's circular fountain plaza, and a row of miniature antennas stands in for the flagpoles of the member states.

BRICK BY BRICK

- The set measures 8in (21cm) wide, 5in (14cm) high, and 6in (15cm) deep.

- LEGO Architecture designer Rok Zgalin Kobe faced the challenge of finding a scale that would work for the different sized buildings and recreating the buildings' curved facades. To create a smooth finish, Rok used a studs-free building technique with coatings of tiles and panels.

- The set features rare trans-light-blue bricks. It was the first set to use 1x2 plates in this color. There are 155 in the set in total.

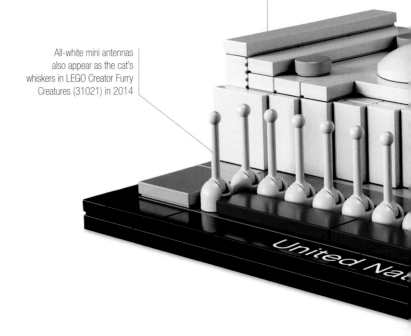

Stepped bricks give the effect of the curved roof of the original General Assembly Building

All-white mini antennas also appear as the cat's whiskers in LEGO Creator Furry Creatures (31021) in 2014

REAR VIEW

KEY

1

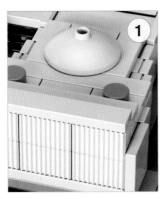

1

< GENERAL ASSEMBLY BUILDING
White 1x2 textured profile bricks are used for the ridged facade at the end of the General Assembly Building. The dome is a white radar dish piece.

> AERIAL VIEW The model stands on a gray 18x26 base plate. Two black tiles with the "United Nations Headquarters" printing are unique to this set.

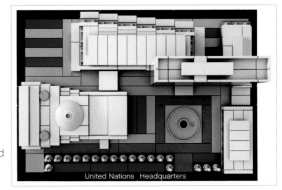

United Nations Headquarters

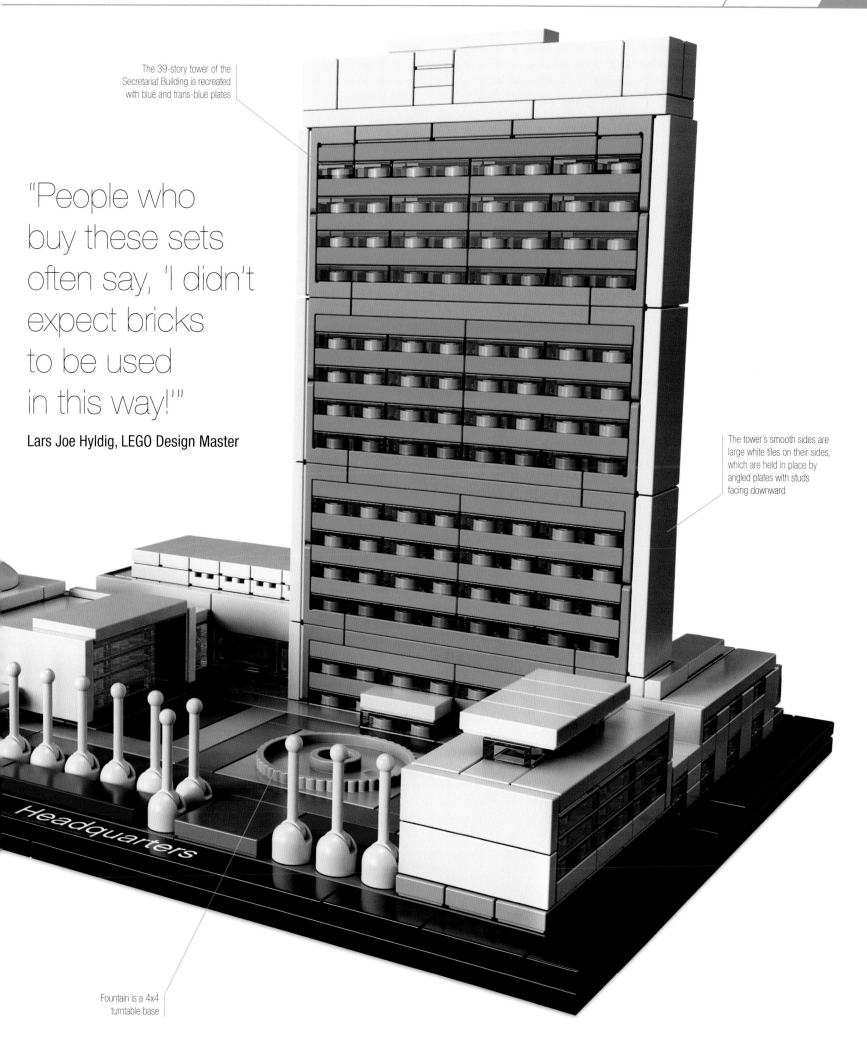

The 39-story tower of the Secretariat Building is recreated with blue and trans-blue plates

"People who buy these sets often say, 'I didn't expect bricks to be used in this way!'"

Lars Joe Hyldig, LEGO Design Master

The tower's smooth sides are large white tiles on their sides, which are held in place by angled plates with studs facing downward

Headquarters

Fountain is a 4x4 turntable base

MINDSTORMS EV3

2013 • LEGO® MINDSTORMS™ • #31313 • Pieces: 601

Following several upgrades over the years, the innovative Robotics Invention System evolved once more in 2013. With a new edgy, futuristic look, the MINDSTORMS EV3 set could be assembled as the mohawked EV3RSTORM, or rebuilt via downloadable instructions into the striking serpent R3PTAR, the hunter-seeker scorpion SPIK3R, and a multitude of other cutting-edge mechanized monsters and minions.

The set is made up of hundreds of multi-purpose Technic pieces. Its intelligent EV3 brick includes a USB connector and Micro SD port, and can be commanded by remote control or through an app for smart devices. A drag-and-drop interface lets users program motorized responses and sophisticated behaviors into their robotic creations… or just fire balls at anyone who comes into their rooms without permission.

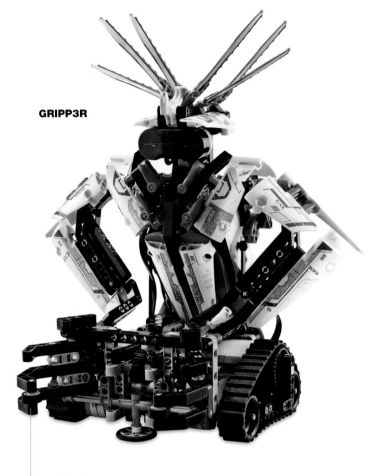

GRIPP3R

SPIK3R

SPIK3R has a crushing claw at the front, and its tail fires balls

Powerful grasping grippers allow GRIPP3R to pick up and drop objects

R3PTAR is programmed to open and close its jaw while rearing and lunging forward at nearby objects

R3PTAR

Lars Joe Hyldig | Design Manager

Lars originally joined the LEGO Group in 1992 and worked on LEGO DUPLO, LEGO SCALA, and LEGO Technic. After a break, he returned to the company in 2010, and now manages the LEGO MINDSTORMS and LEGO Architecture teams. Lars and his team spent three and a half years developing the very complex EV3 set. Lars finds creating LEGO MINDSTORMS robots an interesting challenge, and he enjoys developing the LEGO Architecture portfolio at the same time.

BRICK BY BRICK

- The LEGO MINDSTORMS team created instructions for five different EV3 robots. Twelve bonus models, which were created by a panel of expert fans, were also endorsed by the team, and were made available as free downloads.

- Infrared, touch, and color sensors allow EV3 robots to respond to a variety of stimuli. They can be programmed to produce sounds, too.

- The EV3 brick can connect to up to three other EV3 bricks, allowing for a robot with as many as 32 functional components.

- The LEGO MINDSTORMS website features videos and instructions for games that can be played with the robots.

- Hundreds of online videos show LEGO fans' robot creations, including a robot that can solve a Rubik's Cube!

EV3RSTORM

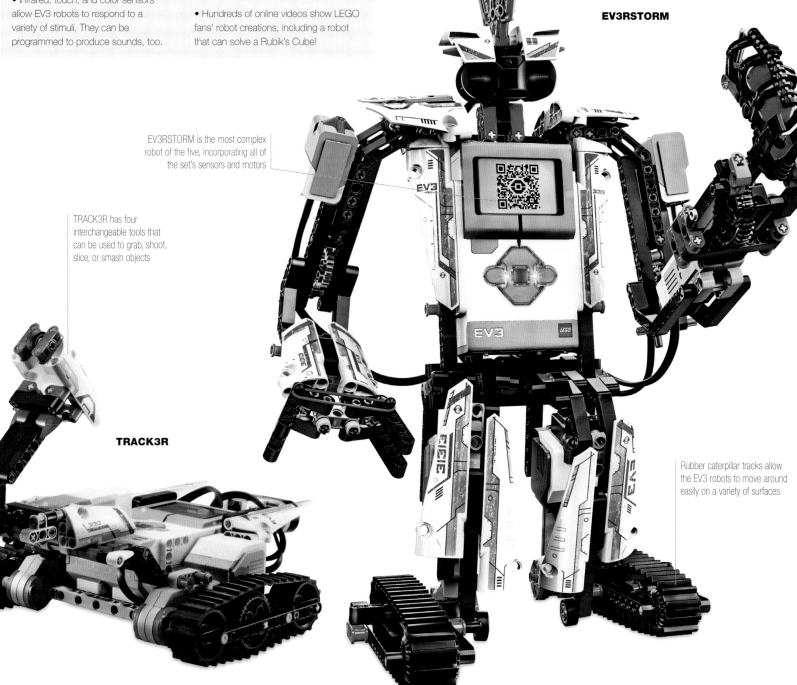

EV3RSTORM is the most complex robot of the five, incorporating all of the set's sensors and motors

TRACK3R has four interchangeable tools that can be used to grab, shoot, slice, or smash objects

TRACK3R

Rubber caterpillar tracks allow the EV3 robots to move around easily on a variety of surfaces

Guided Tour

KEY

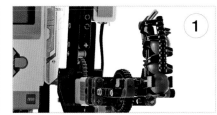

△ **LINE OF FIRE** A ball-firing bazooka can be built to fire at nearby targets. Instructions for programming a "Robo Shoot" game are featured on the LEGO MINDSTORMS website.

◁ **SENSITIVE VISION**
The eye element of the EV3 is an infrared sensor that receives transmissions from the remote control. It can be programmed as a proximity sensor, too.

▷ **INFRARED REMOTE**
As well as controlling the robot from afar, the remote control can be used as a tracking device.

Parisian Restaurant

2014 • LEGO® Creator Expert • #10243 • Pieces: 2469 • Minifigures: 5

The Modular Buildings release for 2014 was the Parisian Restaurant. Now branded as part of LEGO Creator, it let expert builders put together a fancy restaurant and upstairs apartments nestled in the heart of the romantic city of Paris, France. As usual for the line, sophisticated building techniques created unique architectural stylings, including a frieze of "v"-shaped feathers and roof decorations made with white seashells and, appropriately enough, pairs of croissants.

Within the restaurant model is a full kitchen where the chef prepares meals for the diners—one of whom is about to propose to his girlfriend with a shiny gold ring! Above, the cozy apartment has a folding bed that tucks into the wall. On the top floor is an artist's studio full of paintings built from LEGO tiles. Just for fans are a new red scooter, dark-blue roof slopes, and rare olive-green bricks to add to their collections.

> "It is one of the first Modular Buildings to really evolve the concept to a new level of storytelling and detailing."
>
> Jamie Berard, LEGO Design Manager Specialist

Rare bowed dark-blue bricks

Frieze made from 18 gray feather elements

Black gate piece doubles as a trellis

Four different types of bricks appeared in olive-green for the first time in 2014

The word "CHEZ" is spelled out with bricks on the ground—it gets covered up as the build progresses

Printed menu was created for this set

CHEZ ALBERT
RESTAURANT

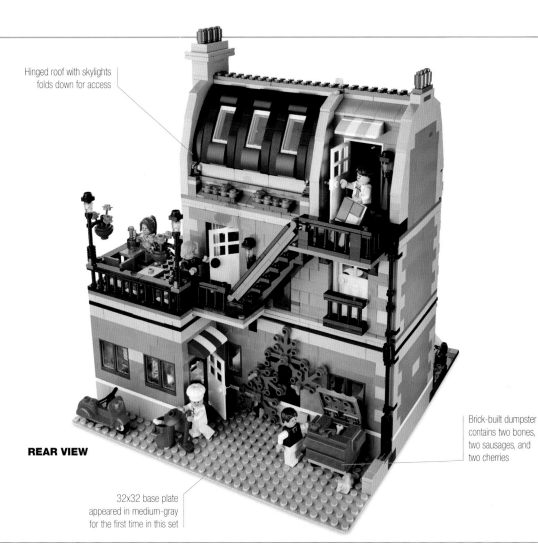

Hinged roof with skylights folds down for access

REAR VIEW

Brick-built dumpster contains two bones, two sausages, and two cherries

32x32 base plate appeared in medium-gray for the first time in this set

• Each masonry feature at the top of the building includes two croissants (that appeared in white for the first time in this set), a rare hinged shell element, and wheel arches.

• A new bowl piece appears in dark-red in this set as a plant pot, a lampshade, and the top part of a floor lamp.

• The scooter was originally developed by the LEGO Friends team. They worked with the LEGO Creator team to make it minifigure-compatible, too.

• Set designer Jamie Berard based the newly-engaged minifigure couple on his brother and his fiancée.

• The restaurant is named after Jamie's father, who owned a restaurant.

• The Modular Buildings series is the only LEGO theme that still features minifigures with classic smiley faces.

Guided Tour

KEY

5
4
1
3
2

∧ **INSIDE DINING** In front of the brick-built cabinet, a minifigure proposes to his girlfriend with a ring. The ring first appeared in a LEGO *The Lord of the Rings* set.

∧ **KITCHEN** The waiter busies himself in the kitchen. Behind him are knives and a rolling pin. A pie—first created for the LEGO Minifigures line—sits on the counter, ready to be served.

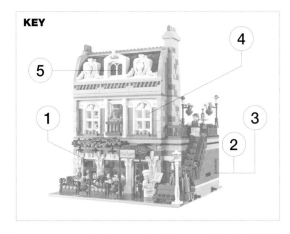

∧ **DINNER IS READY** The chef carves the turkey, which has removable legs. The fridge opens to reveal a milk carton (with printed decoration) and two blocks of cheese.

∧ **SECOND FLOOR APARTMENT** A minifigure pulls down a foldaway bed with checkered quilt. Behind him is a kitchenette, complete with microwave oven, and a table and stool.

∧ **ARTIST'S STUDIO** A hinged, dark-blue roof section is removed to reveal a studio where an artist paints modern art at her easel. Behind her is a pottery kiln.

The Simpsons™ House

2014 • LEGO® The Simpsons™ • #71006 • Pieces: 2523 • Minifigures: 6

To celebrate the milestone 25th anniversary of The Simpsons™, the LEGO Group collaborated with Twentieth Century Fox to produce a special episode of the TV series titled "Brick Like Me," a series of 16 collectible minifigure characters, and The Simpsons™ House, a buildable model of the animated family's suburban home. It was full of rooms and details that were instantly familiar to viewers of the show, and came with exclusive versions of all five Simpsons family members and neighbor Ned Flanders.

Fans will recognize Lisa and Bart's bedrooms, the dining room where the Simpsons eat their meals, and of course the family couch seen at the beginning of every episode. Stickers add extra gags and in-jokes, such as the graffiti on Bart's skateboard ramp and the "Property of Ned Flanders" labels on various objects that Homer has "borrowed."

OUTSIDE VIEW

Sloped bricks form a dent in the car hood

Bart's "El Barto" graffiti tag

BRICK BY BRICK

• Special head molds were created for The Simpsons characters. The minifigures in this set have different printing on their heads from those in The Simpsons LEGO Minifigures line.

• Maggie's torso and legs are a single piece, which is unique to her character.

• Bart's arms and legs and Homer's arms use a technique called "two-component molding," where two different colors of plastic are molded together.

• The LEGO design team worked closely with Twentieth Century Fox to include little details from the show, such as Lisa's A+ exam paper and Jazz Fest poster, *The Itchy & Scratchy Show* graphic on the TV screen, and a power drill for Maggie to play with!

TV antenna is made from four skeleton arms and two lightsaber blade elements—in black

Air conditioning unit—property of Ned Flanders!

Mixer and utensils were first introduced in LEGO Friends sets— they were new in yellow for this set

Guided Tour

KEY

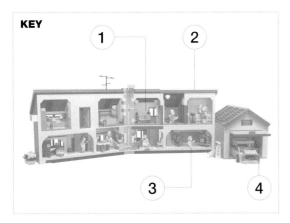

> "I included lots of mini builds across the house. I tried to make them exciting and unorthodox in the way bricks are used."

Marcos Bessa, LEGO Senior Designer

∧ **MAIN BEDROOM** Maggie's crib, in Homer and Marge's bedroom, is fixed to the floor with a single stud. Its sides are made from four ladder pieces, which were new in orange.

∧ **BART'S BEDROOM** Bart reads his favorite comic (printed on a tile). The pinboard and Krusty the Clown poster are stickers. His bedside lamp is built using a sausage element!

∧ **LIVING ROOM** The family settle down on the couch to watch *The Itchy & Scratchy Show*. Rare dark-orange colored bricks recreate the family's beloved couch.

∧ **GARAGE** The door swings up to reveal a workbench, tool rack, and Homer. It looks like Flanders has come to reclaim his wheelbarrow—which was new in lime-green in 2014.

Hinges open the house for greater playability, and the roof can lift off, too

Door to Bart's bedroom

The Simpsons' car includes bricks that were produced in pink for the first time

Radioactive bar from the nuclear power plant

Emmet's Construct-o-Mech

2014 • THE LEGO® MOVIE™ • #70814 • Pieces: 708 • Minifigures: 1, plus 2 Skeletrons and 1 Angry Kitty

Everything was awesome in 2014 when the blockbuster THE LEGO MOVIE hit the big screen, including the sets that tied into the film. Assembled during the big showdown in Bricksburg, Emmet's Construct-o-Mech was a hulking machine built out of the pieces of multiple construction vehicles. If the sight of that many yellow bricks wasn't enough to send Lord Business's Skeletron robots packing, then Emmet also had the adorable fury of Angry Kitty to back him up.

Emmet's mech carries a swinging wrecking ball on each shoulder, an excavator claw for one hand, and a steamroller for the other. Strong click-joints let it pose its massive limbs, and the rubber treads on its feet really work. But even more craved by collectors is the set's angry version of fan-favorite character Unikitty.

Girder element is unique to this set in bright yellow

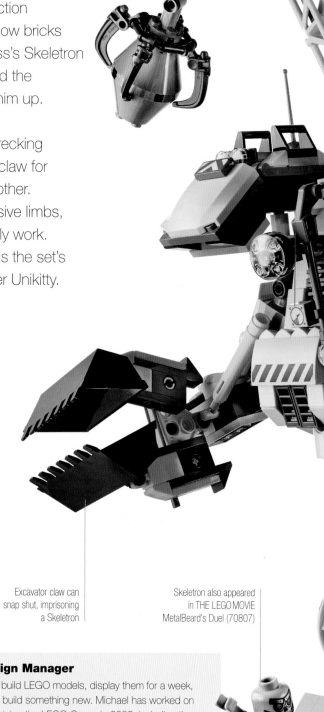

∧ **COCKPIT** The front part of the mech opens up for Emmet to stand at the controls. Emmet's minifigure has a double-sided head piece.

Excavator claw can snap shut, imprisoning a Skeletron

Skeletron also appeared in THE LEGO MOVIE MetalBeard's Duel (70807)

Michael Fuller | Design Manager

As a child, Michael loved to build LEGO models, display them for a week, and then smash them up to build something new. Michael has worked on a number of themes since joining the LEGO Group in 2009, including three years on THE LEGO MOVIE. He managed the product line, built many of the concept models, and worked with the animators to give them an understanding of what could be done with LEGO bricks. Although he never imagined he would be involved in a Hollywood movie, he is proud to be known in the company as a major driving force behind THE LEGO MOVIE.

Piece used to make wrecking ball has been used as rocket thrusters in other sets

"We had to make sure that everything you see on screen could actually be built with LEGO bricks."

Michael Fuller, LEGO Design Manager

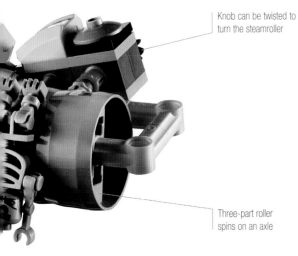

Knob can be twisted to turn the steamroller

Three-part roller spins on an axle

• The Construct-o-Mech is hinged at the hip, enabling the entire leg to be posed to look like it is walking.

• The Emmet and Angry Kitty figures are exclusive to this set, though Emmet's torso and legs have appeared in many other THE LEGO MOVIE sets. There have been eight different versions of Unikitty so far (plus two alternate expressions), including Astro Kitty, Queasy Kitty, and Biznis Kitty—which are all unique to the sets they appear in.

• At the front of the mech is a yellow 1x4 tile with a printed code (which is unique to each set) for unlocking parts of THE LEGO MOVIE video game.

Trash Chomper

2014 • THE LEGO® MOVIE™ • #70805 • Pieces: 389 • Minifigures: 3

Faced with an all-controlling scheme to glue their universe together, the citizens of the LEGO world fight back by taking ordinary objects and rebuilding them to be extraordinary. The movie line's "Creative Armada" sets allow LEGO builders to do the same, with two-in-one building steps that transform an everyday garbage truck into the flying, Micro Manager-munching Trash Chomper.

• Two garbage cans fit at the rear of the Trash Chomper to make jet boosters.

• A LEGO Technic knob on the side of the Trash Chomper can be turned so the "mouth" makes a chomping action.

• The arms of the Micro Manager are posable. Its "hands" can clasp objects and rotate.

• The Garbage Man Dan, Garbage Man Grant, and Chef Gordon Zola minifigures are all exclusive to this set.

• A broom and a shovel can be clipped onto the rear side of the Garbage Truck.

∧ **GARBAGE TRUCK** With the twist of a LEGO Technic knob, the rear part of the garbage truck can slide up and back, allowing trash to be thrown in.

Driver's cab has space for a single driver, who can enter via the open back or the removable roof

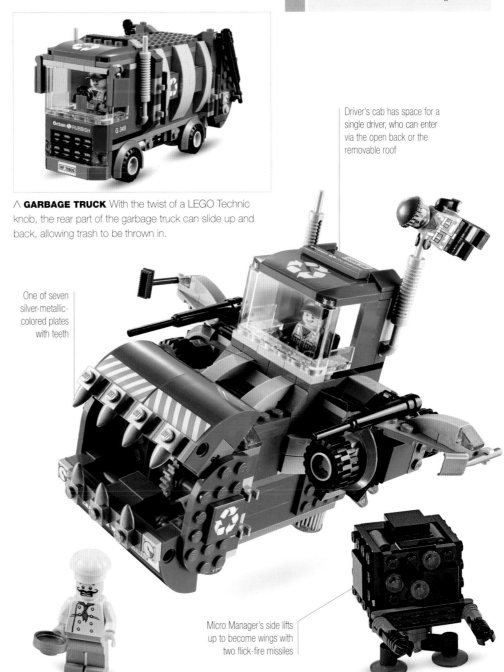

One of seven silver-metallic-colored plates with teeth

Micro Manager's side lifts up to become wings with two flick-fire missiles

Benny's Spaceship, Spaceship, SPACESHIP!

2014 • THE LEGO® MOVIE™ • #70816 • Pieces: 939 • Minifigures: 4, plus 2 Spacebots and Astro Kitty

With his cracked helmet, gravity-defying personality, and total obsession with building space vehicle models, Benny the 1980-something spaceman was definitely one of the breakout stars of THE LEGO MOVIE. One of the largest sets in the theme, the little blue astronaut's ultimate brick creation was named after his enthusiastically repeated catchphrase: the cosmically cool and righteously retro Benny's Spaceship, Spaceship, SPACESHIP!

Benny's spaceship may have been designed with modern functions that include extending wings, firing blasters, and detachable mini-flyers… but its look, pieces, and color scheme are a galaxy-sized tribute to the classic LEGO Space sets of the late 1970s and '80s. Even Benny himself is an homage to the old days, with his well-worn chest logo and broken chinstrap—a famous flaw in the original LEGO piece.

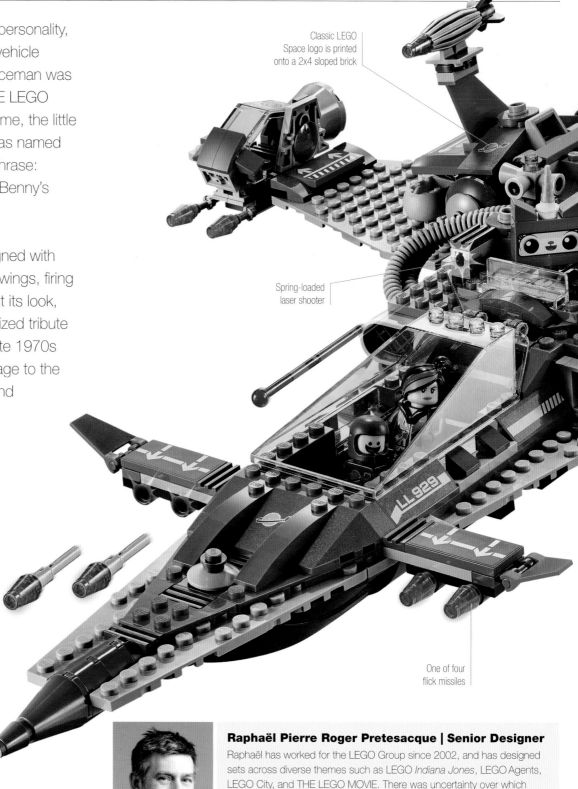

Classic LEGO Space logo is printed onto a 2x4 sloped brick

Spring-loaded laser shooter

One of four flick missiles

BRICK BY BRICK

• Five characters appear in the set: Benny, Robo Emmet, Space Wyldstyle, Astro Kitty, and Robo Pilot. Apart from Benny, they are all exclusive to the set.

• The spaceship's call sign "LL929" is a tribute to the set that inspired its design—Space Cruiser and Moonbase (928), also known as Galaxy Explorer (497) in the US, which had the call sign "LL928."

• The hinged cockpit was new in trans-yellow. It first appeared in trans-clear in the LEGO Star Wars Ultimate Collector Series Red Five X-wing Starfighter (10240) in 2013.

• Stickers featuring 1970s and '80s LEGOLAND Space computer screens are placed in the cockpit. There are two modern printed control panels at the front, too.

Raphaël Pierre Roger Pretesacque | Senior Designer

Raphaël has worked for the LEGO Group since 2002, and has designed sets across diverse themes such as LEGO *Indiana Jones*, LEGO Agents, LEGO City, and THE LEGO MOVIE. There was uncertainty over which direction to go with the movie's spaceship model, but when Vice President Matthew Ashton suggested a 1980s spaceship, Raphaël based it on his childhood favorite: Space Cruiser with Moonbase (928). Raphaël likes to add humor to his sets, whether that's including a frog (a nod to his nationality) or a portable toilet in a LEGO City set.

Rocket boosters are made from wheel elements that were introduced in 2008

Detachable flyer has heads-up display and two shooters

Special brick with positioning rockets was first created for LEGOLAND Space in 1979

Octan logo recreated as a space logo for Robo Police Interceptor

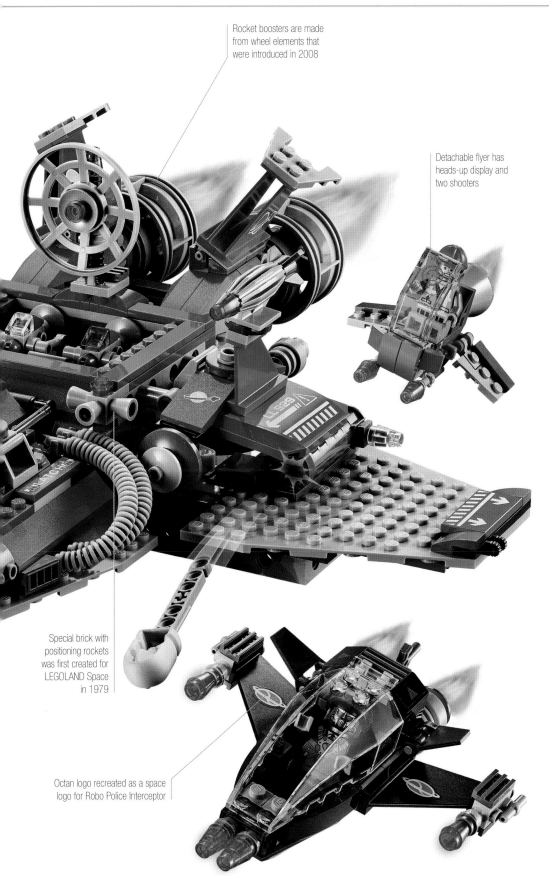

"It's good to think about how excited children get as you design. Even if I gave you £10 million, it wouldn't blow your mind like Benny's spaceship will do for a child."

Michael Thomas Fuller, LEGO Design Manager

Guided Tour

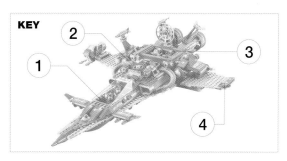

KEY

∧ **COCKPIT** The roof can be raised to allow access into the cockpit, which seats three minifigures. Astro Kitty sits in a trench behind the cockpit—her tail is secured with a gray latch piece.

∧ **CONTROL ROOM** Astro Kitty's octagonal platform can be lifted up to reveal a bay with printed computer screens and tools. Behind Benny is an engine with trans-yellow diamond elements.

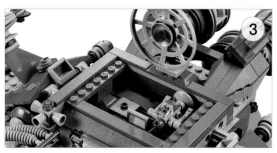

∧ **SPACEBOTS** Beneath the hinged radar dish is an area where two 1980s-style robots can be stored. The radar dish is reminiscent of the dish on 1983's Galaxy Commander (6980).

∧ **AWESOME WINGS** The wings can be extended by pushing in the lower exhaust at the rear, unleashing a spring-loaded space cannon on each side! Detachable flyers attach to each wing tip.

Fairground Mixer

2014 • LEGO® Creator Expert • #10244 • Pieces: 1746 • Minifigures: 12

The carnival came to town in 2014 with the special-edition LEGO Creator set Fairground Mixer. What starts as a pair of trucks can then be lifted, unfolded, and snapped together to create a whole traveling fairground with a colorful mixer ride in the middle. Other attractions include a ticket booth, a test-your-strength machine, a stilt-walking juggler, and a dunk tank. After sunset, the fairground comes alive with glow-in-the-dark elements.

Turning the crank makes the mixer and its seats spin, or a separate Power Functions battery box and motor can be hooked up to automate them. The LEGO designers thought of everything: snacks and prizes for the visitors, and a driver's truck-top sleeping compartment with a bed and TV. There's also a brand-new face print for one rider who's gone on the mixer a few too many times...

"My bosses let me go a little bit wild. I was told to make it fun."

Jamie Berard, LEGO Design Manager Specialist

Crank handle turns the large gear that connects to a long, white LEGO Technic axle and causes the ride to spin

Rare teddy bear first appeared with the Sleepyhead minifigure in 2013 as part of the collectible LEGO Minifigures line

- One visitor's happy face can be turned around to show a queasy expression on the other side!

- All 12 minifigures (eight adults and four children) are new and unique to this set.

- When he is not performing, the juggler minifigure can wear a small, gray hat. His stilts can be removed, too.

- Two mallets come with the test-your-strength machine—one for minifigures and one for humans!

- The steps leading up to the mixer can pivot to line up with each individual pod.

- It became a long-running joke that designer Jamie Berard would suggest a carnival set at every brainstorming session. He finally got to design it!

Guided Tour

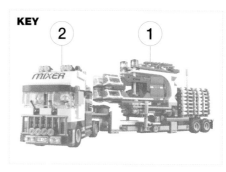

KEY **2** **1**

Club clips to juggler's hat to give the impression he is really juggling

Bell is a metallic-gold-colored dish element, which is exclusive to this set—the piece appears in chrome-gold in other sets

Glow-in-the-dark 1x1 round tile is unique to this set

Pods rotate individually as the mixer spins

DUNK TANK

If the ball successfully hits the red-and-white target, the trapdoor opens, and the female minifigure gets a dunking!

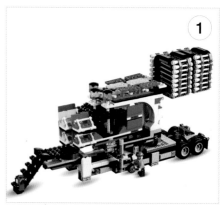

1

∧ **FOLDAWAY FAIRGOUND** All the parts of the mixer ride, as well as the fence, can be packed onto the white truck. With the cab removed, the arms of the mixer easily fold out to become a fully-operational ride.

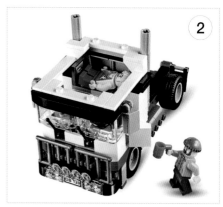

2

∧ **SLEEPER CAB** The cab roof of the white truck can be taken off to reveal a bed, TV, and seating for two minifigures.

∧ **PACKED AND STACKED** The ticket booth, dunk tank, high-striker, and juggler's stilts can be packed tidily onto the blue truck.

SHINKAI 6500 Submersible
• 2010 • LEGO® CUUSOO • #21100

Birds
• 2015 • LEGO® Ideas • #21301

"Here in Billund we are just a small group. Out there is a huge community capable of making a whole load of great stuff."

Lars Joe Hyldig, LEGO Design Manager

Micro World
• 2012 • LEGO CUUSOO – MINECRAFT • #21102

Hobby Train
• 2007 • LEGO Factory • #10183

Exo Suit
• 2014 • LEGO Ideas • #21109

Research Institute
• 2014 • LEGO Ideas • #21110

Market Street
• 2007 • LEGO Factory • #10190

Ghostbusters™ Ecto-1
• 2014 • LEGO Ideas • #21108

Hayabusa
• 2012 • LEGO CUUSOO • #21101

FROM DREAMS TO REALITY

Fan-designed LEGO® models through the years

Most LEGO® sets are created from start to finish by the company's professional model design team. But once in a while, there is the rare opportunity for a model designed by a fan to become a real LEGO set. It all started with 2002's online-exclusive Blacksmith Shop (3739), followed by the LEGO Factory program of 2005 to 2007. Today, the LEGO® Ideas (formerly LEGO CUUSOO) website lets fans upload and vote for their favorite custom creations… with the best-loved designs having a chance to become official LEGO sets!

The DeLorean Time Machine
• 2013 • LEGO CUUSOO • #21103

Blacksmith Shop
• 2002 • LEGO My Own Creation • #3739

4x4 Crawler
• 2013 • LEGO® Technic • #41999

NASA Mars Science Laboratory
Curiosity Rover
• 2014 • LEGO CUUSOO • #21104

Ghostbusters™ Ecto-1

2014 • LEGO® Ideas • #21108 • Pieces: 508 • Minifigures: 4

On the LEGO Ideas (formerly LEGO CUUSOO) website, fans submit their own custom model proposals, and other fans vote for their favorites. Creations that receive 10,000 votes are eligible to be produced as real LEGO sets. The sixth in the series, the Ghostbusters™ Ecto-1 set was released just in time for the classic film's 30th anniversary. It included the Ghostbusters team and their famous 1959 customized ambulance.

The biggest challenge in making a Ghostbusters model is in replicating the look of the movie's makeshift technology. Ecto-1's paranormal detection equipment is built out of lots of small and metallic LEGO elements, as are the team's proton packs and ghost-zapping neutrona wands. Pop off the car's roof and it has a tracking computer and seats inside.

"Every time a colleague would walk past my desk, they would stop and say, 'Are we really doing this?' Everyone was very excited!"

Marcos Bessa, LEGO Senior Designer

Winston Zeddemore wears a proton pack that clips on around the neck

The characters' initials feature on their suits—"R.S." for Raymond Stanz

Dr. Egon Spengler's minifigure holds a walkie-talkie

License plate is a printed tile

- Brent Waller, an Australian LEGO fan who works in the video game industry, submitted the original design to the LEGO CUUSOO website. LEGO Senior Designer Marcos Bessa created the official LEGO version, ensuring he kept the overall look the same, but that it had the proper stability and LEGO build experience.

- The set includes bricks with new printed designs featuring the iconic Ghostbusters logo and the Ecto-1 license plate.

- The minifigures can be lined up on a brick-built stand. Turn them around to see their first names printed on their backs.

- A barbell weight piece belonging to the LEGO Minifigures Weightlifter is used as a hub cap on the car. It is exclusive to this set in the silver color.

- The hose that connects to the proton pack is a whip element—seen here in black for the first time.

Guided Tour

KEY

Pneumatic hose provides decoration

Sloped red brick used for the tail fin creates the look of a 1950s Cadillac

Dr. Peter Venkman hunts ghosts with the ghost trap made from a bright-yellow grille piece

∧ **FRIGHTENED FACES** LEGO Senior Graphic Designer Adam Corbally gave the minifigures alternate, scared faces. They look so frightened, you would think they had just seen a ghost!

> **PROTON PACK** There was no time to create new elements in time for the film's 30th anniversary, so the proton pack is built with an existing round tile that was given a new print.

∧ **INSIDE THE CAR** The roof lifts off and three minifigures can sit inside. A fourth (and not-so-lucky) minifigure can recline behind the seat, too.

< **LADDER** A ladder on one side of the car allows the minifigures to reach the many antennas, lights, and gadgets on the roof.

Slave I®

2015 • LEGO® *Star Wars®* **Ultimate Collector's Series • #75060 •** Pieces: 1996 • Minifigures: 4

The most dreaded bounty hunter in the galaxy finally got a spacecraft befitting his reputation when Boba Fett's *Slave I* became a *Star Wars* Ultimate Collector's Series model in 2015. This latest incarnation of *Slave I* is made out of nearly 2,000 pieces, and precisely reproduces every sweeping curve, battle-worn scrape, and double blaster cannon seen in the screen version of Boba Fett's infamous vehicle from *The Empire Strikes Back*. It also includes a buildable flight display stand to show off the model in action.

Built in LEGO minifigure scale, the *Slave I* set has surprise flip-out weapons stowed inside its side panels, a cockpit with a pilot's chair that can be adjusted between landing and flight positions, rotating wings, and a compartment in the back to store the captive, carbonite-frozen hero Han Solo. Its Boba Fett figure is the most detailed version of the LEGO character yet.

> "I am a LEGO® *Star Wars*®
> set collector, so it is rather
> special if you can
> design the next
> addition to your
> collection yourself."

Hans Burkhard Schlömer, LEGO Designer

New removable trans-clear cockpit windshield is secured with three LEGO Technic pins

Boba's cockpit seat can be manually rotated 90 degrees to switch between flight and landing modes

Secret hatch opens to reveal concussion missile launcher

Rotating twin blasters move in unison with blasters on the other side

Hans Burkhard Schlömer | Designer

Hans worked as a music teacher for eight years, building LEGO models in his spare time, before joining the LEGO Group in 2008. He worked on LEGO Universe (a massively multiplayer online game), followed by LEGO Legends of Chima, which he worked on from its launch until its final year. Before officially moving to the LEGO *Star Wars* team, Hans was asked to help them out. He assumed he would be given a small set; instead, he was asked to design an Ultimate Collector Series model—*Slave I*. Hans is a huge fan of LEGO *Star Wars*, so becoming a LEGO *Star Wars* designer is a dream come true.

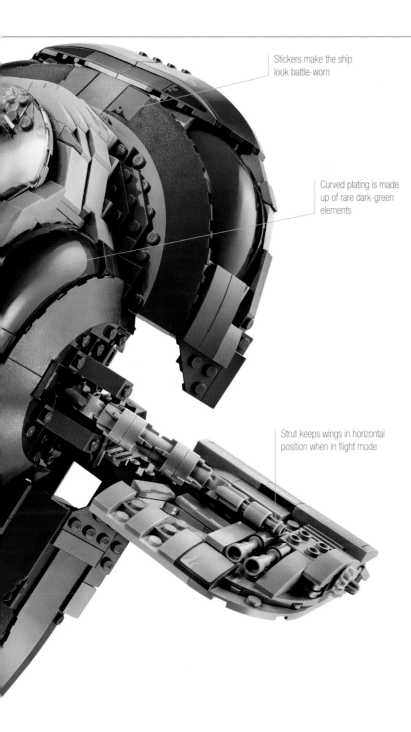

Stickers make the ship look battle-worn

Curved plating is made up of rare dark-green elements

Strut keeps wings in horizontal position when in flight mode

Guided Tour

KEY

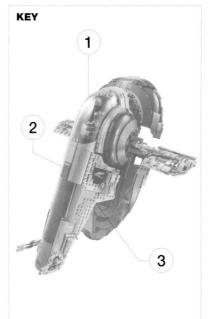

∧ **FLIGHT CONTROL** The cockpit has printed tiles and stickers for control panels. Boba's two blasters fit into clips on either side of his seat.

> **WEAPONS COMPARTMENT**
A hidden side hatch folds out to reveal a twin ion cannon. A concussion missile launcher is concealed in a compartment on the other side.

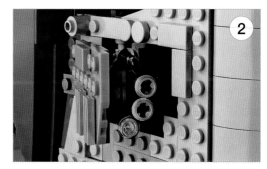

< **HAULING HAN**
A new variant of the Bespin Guard appears in this set. The carbonite block he carries (with Han inside!) can be clipped to the inside of the door while in flight.

• Existing pieces appear in this set for the first time in earth green, sand green, and dark red, such as the earth-green and dark-red arched bricks that make up the ship's curved plating.

• The instruction manual features 280+ pages of instructions, an introduction to the design team, facts and figures about *Slave I*, and an interview with the set designer, Hans Burkhard Schlömer.

• This carbonite block piece first appeared in LEGO *Star Wars Slave I* (8097) in 2010. A Han Solo minifigure fits into the back of this sculpted piece. Black printing details his shirt and pained expression.

• The new Boba Fett minifigure has intricate printing on his torso, shoulders, arms, and legs.

• Hans likes to include standard 2x4 bricks in his models whenever possible. *Slave I* includes this brick in black, brick-yellow, and different shades of gray.

• The first *Slave I* (7044) was released in 2000. Other sets have taken various forms and sizes, and it has even appeared as a pendant on a keychain.

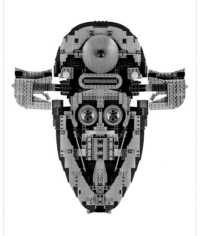

∧ **LANDING MODE** As the *Slave I* model is rotated into landing position, the ship's wings automatically turn through 90 degrees to lie flat.

∧ **UNDER *SLAVE I*** The large, round repulsorlift unit and trans-blue twin engines are clearly recognizable on the other side of the ship.

Detective's Office

2015 • LEGO® Creator Expert • #10246 • Pieces: 2262 • Minifigures: 6

The dawn of 2015 saw the release of the Detective's Office, an expert-level LEGO Creator set and the tenth entry in the Modular Buildings line. The detailed build recreated the look and feel of an early 20th century Prohibition-era private eye's home office—complete with messy desk and a safe full of evidence—built above a seedy pool hall, with a classic barbershop next door. And what's a detective's office without a good old-fashioned mystery to solve? Fortunately, the set has that too!

If builders investigate the model's nooks and crannies, they might uncover a secret cookie-smuggling operation that leads from the hidden rooftop kitchen down to the barbershop, where they can covertly slip a barrel full of freshly-baked treats under the stairs and through a sliding panel into the pool hall. Whether the detective will foil the plot or share in the tasty spoils is up to each builder!

"We've had a lot of fun with elements in this building."

Jamie Berard, LEGO Design Manager Specialist

Curved masonry element was originally developed as Unikitty's tail for THE LEGO MOVIE sets

Special brick-built lettering was new for this set

Hinged newspaper box, containing newspapers on printed tiles, can open up

Name of shop is rendered in bricks

Guided Tour

KEY

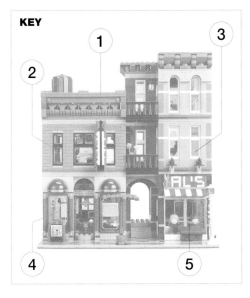

∧ ROOF TERRACE Detective Ace Brickman spots who is behind the cookie-smuggling enterprise! Standing beside the skylight of the detective's office, a mystery minifigure fills up a barrel with cookies—printed flat 1x1 round tiles.

∧ DETECTIVE'S OFFICE Above the pool hall is the detective's cluttered office. Printed newspaper, letter, and map tiles lie on his desk, and a "WANTED" poster hangs on the wall. The boat picture swings aside to reveal a secret safe.

> BLUE BATHROOM
There is a small bathroom at the foot of the stairs that lead up to the kitchen. This is the first time a brick-built, pull-chain toilet has featured in a LEGO set!

∧ POOL HALL The rotating ceiling fan can be moved aside to gain access to the brick-built pool table. The dartboard is a printed element—new for this set. Below the trophy, a black wall panel slides open for the barrel to roll in!

∧ BARBERSHOP Al's poky shop has room for one chair and a wall-mounted mirror—the first non-stickered mirror to feature in a LEGO set. The scissor element is also new. The cupboard behind Al can be swung open to smuggle in the barrel of treats.

• The details on the "WANTED" poster on the detective's office wall are the correct measurements of a minifigure.

• The designer, Jamie Berard, named the barbershop after his grandfather Al. The cookie smuggling storyline came from Jamie's love of cookies, too.

• A secret tunnel leads from the back of the barber's shop, under the alley, and into the pool hall. This allows the barrels to be moved around the building in secret.

• The water tower uses a sideways building technique for attaching the brown tiles that was first thought of when the tile element was created in the 1970s.

• There is space under the stairs for an extra barrel to be stashed. Another hidden barrel with cookies can be found in the promotional set Flower Cart (40140), also released in 2015.

BACK VIEW

Detective Ace Brickman searches for clues on the water tower

Kitchen, containing oven and other cookie-making equipment, on top floor

Black gate, hidden by foliage, opens to allow barrels to be smuggled into the barbershop

The Elves' Treetop Hideaway

2015 • LEGO® Elves • #41075 • Pieces: 442 • Mini-dolls: 3

In 2015, an ordinary girl named Emily took an unexpected journey to the magical world of the LEGO Elves. Filled with enchanting characters and creatures, as well as exciting new pieces and element colors, the imaginative theme featured the mini-doll figures premiered by LEGO Friends in 2012 in the framework of an epic fantasy story. The first stop on Emily's quest is the Treetop Hideaway, where she makes two Elf friends, Azari Firedancer and Farran Leafshade.

Stepping through the swirling portal, Emily emerges into a forest of trees covered with strangely-colored flowers and jewel-like fruit. A tour of Farran the Earth Elf's home reveals a magic ladder, a bucket lift with chain, a mini-waterfall and river, and a pot for cooking carrot soup to share with Azari the Fire Elf and her panther cub Enki.

Bucket has also appeared in two LEGO Friends sets

Recipe for carrot soup is a printed sticker on a tile

Three angled plates form steps that lead to the magic ladder

Shape of Azari the Fire Elf's skirt suggests flickering flames

BRICK BY BRICK

• The flower stem piece with six stems was new for the Elves theme.

• The magic portal with the swirling, glittery print was created for this set.

• Inside the treehouse is a sticker showing a picture of the four Elves together when they were younger.

• Enki the panther cub is made from an existing mold, in a new color and with new printing on the face.

• Each of the four Elves has magic powers to control one of the four elements—earth, wind, fire, and water. The Elves each carry a colored "power icon," made from a 1x1 round plate.

• Symbols of the Elves' elements are printed on their faces under their right eyes, on their left arms, and on their belts. Farran's leaf symbol, representing earth, also appears on the front of the treehouse.

Lavender-colored
branch-and-leaves element
made its debut in this theme

Emily Jones' bag
is new in gray

Goblets containing
juice sit on the table

Guided Tour

KEY

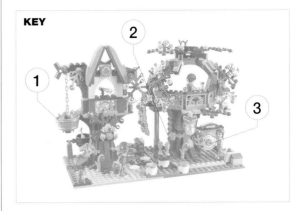

∧ **BUCKET LIFT** Up in the treehouse, Farran takes delivery of food items. The bucket with chain can be raised or lowered by turning the LEGO Technic connector above.

∧ **SECRET NOOK** There is a compartment inside one of the tree trunks. Farran discovers a letter—could it be from Aira the Wind Elf, who sends "tweets" (letters carried by birds) to her friends?

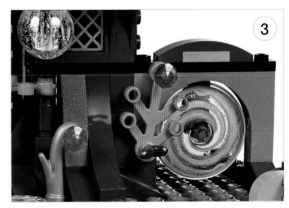

∧ **MAGIC PORTAL** At the base of the tree is the magic portal. The trans-cyan element can be spun from the center, and it can be hidden from prying eyes by sliding the pink leaf in front of it.

Tahu – Master of Fire

2015 • LEGO® BIONICLE® • #70787 • Pieces: 89

Following a five-year hibernation, the legendary "constraction" theme LEGO BIONICLE returned at last in 2015. Set on the island of Okoto in a whole new universe, the rebooted line re-introduced the original six element-powered Toa heroes and pitted them against a swarm of evil, mask-bodied Skull Spiders. Although inspired by his first set from 2001, the newest incarnation of Tahu was bigger, better armored, and more posable than ever before.

Tahu's twin fire blades can connect together and attach to his feet as a lava surfboard to let him navigate the molten rapids of Okoto's Region of Fire, while he uses his golden swords and gear-driven battle arms to fight the Skull Spider. If he succeeds, he'll win the Golden Mask of Fire. But if the spider strikes the right spot, Tahu's mask will pop off, leaving the hero defenseless.

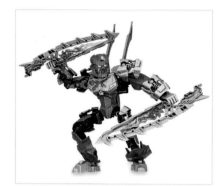

△ **FIRE BLADES** Tahu's lava board is made up of two fire blades that can be separated and attached to his hands. The pearl-gold-colored blades can be clipped to Tahu's back.

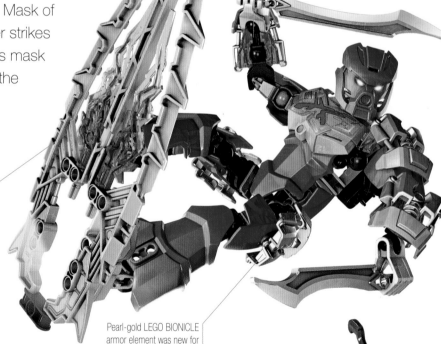

Bashing battle arms (operated by a gear on Tahu's back) swing up and down in opposite directions

Blade elements were new for 2015 and were first introduced in silver in this set

Pearl-gold LEGO BIONICLE armor element was new for the 2015 release

Skull spider can attach to Tahu's face in place of his mask

Guided Tour

KEY

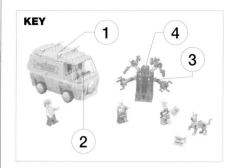

△ **MOBILE LAB** The sides of the van open out on hinges, and the roof can be lifted off. Inside, the van's kitchen is equipped with computers, a tape deck, and boards for pinning up clues.

△ **CHASING CLUES** The cabin has a steering wheel and space for two minifigures to sit. Scooby may ride along in the back, but his head pokes through into the cabin.

△ **HIDDEN CONTROLS**
Behind the tree is a mysterious green gem and a computer. Is someone using these to control the tree?

▷ **PERILOUS PINE**
The ball-jointed arms of the tree are posable, and its twiggy hands are just the right size to trap a minifigure—or a dog!

• The set also includes the Golden Mask of Fire, which can be worn instead of Tahu's regular mask.

• The masks have a "pop-off" mechanism. A tab on either side holds each mask in place. A trans-blue part underneath the mask rotates on an axle, and when the back is pushed down, the mask pops off.

• As part of the LEGO "constraction" system, Tahu's limbs are fully posable and he is capable of maintaining balance in a wide range of stances.

• Tahu can be upgraded by combining him with The Protector of Fire (70783).

• At New York Comic Con in 2014, 1,500 exclusive trans-clear Tahu masks were made available for fans to buy.

The Mystery Machine

2015 • LEGO® Scooby-Doo™ • #75902 • Pieces: 570 • Minifigures: 3, plus Scooby-Doo

Zoinks! 2015 saw the LEGO brick debut of a hauntingly hilarious new theme based on the classic Hanna-Barbera cartoon, *Scooby-Doo, Where Are You!* When danger threatened, the Mystery, Inc. crew are on the scene, including Shaggy, Fred, and cowardly canine sleuth Scooby-Doo himself, together with their famous Mystery Machine van. The rest of the gang could be found in other sets, along with plenty of snacks, clues, traps, and spooky foes for the team to foil.

This creepy forest is no place for the Mystery Machine to break down, especially when a scary zombie is on the loose. Fortunately, the back of the van is packed with mystery-solving gear that Scooby, Fred, and Shaggy can use to discover the zombie's true identity, and wrap up the case with a giant sandwich. Whew… and yum!

BRICK BY BRICK

• Each Scooby-Doo set features a clue for the gang to solve. This set has a newspaper (a 2x2 printed tile).

• The van is equipped with a camera, magnifying glass, computer, stove, tape recorder, and flashlight—everything the crew needs for a late night stakeout!

• Shaggy and Fred's minifigures have new hair elements and face prints. Their head pieces feature not-so-happy expressions on the other side.

• As usual in the Mystery, Inc. crew's world, all is not as it seems. The back of the "zombie" minifigure's head is printed with two buttons, revealing it to be a sneaky disguise.

• Different sets feature different versions of the Scooby figure. Altogether there are three Scooby heads and two bodies (sitting and standing), which can all be mixed and matched.

• In 2015, Scooby and the rest of the Mystery, Inc characters also appeared animated in LEGO form in a 22-minute LEGO special, produced in partnership with Warner Bros. Animation.

The Mystery Machine features elements that were created in medium azure and light green for the first time

New windshield element was created especially for this set

Silver-colored elements suggest this tree is perhaps less organic than it first appears

Scooby's head can move from side to side

Huge sandwich—it's over here, Scooby!

Index

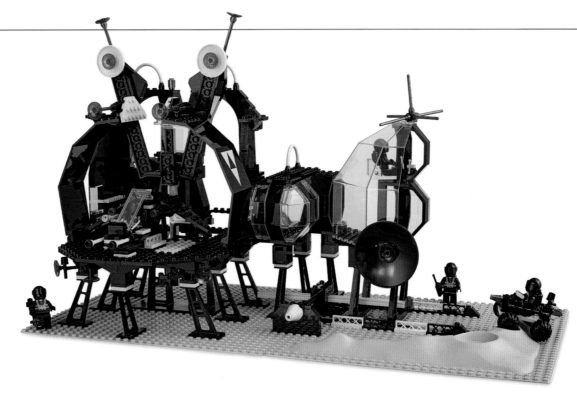

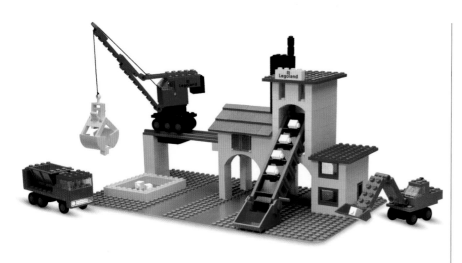

Acknowledgments

DK would like to thank the following people
for their help in producing this book:

Beth Davies, Clare Hibbert, Matt Jones, and Claire Sipi for editorial assistance • Toby Mann for additional text • Nick Edwards, Jon Hall, and Tina Vaughan for design assistance • Hilary Bird for the index • Randi Sørensen at the LEGO Group for all her help and patience • Jens Rasmussen at the LEGO Group for keeping us on track • Melody Caddick at the LEGO Group for designing the Mini Space Cruiser that comes with the trade edition of this book • Kristian Reimer Hauge and Jette Orduna at the LEGO Group for answering our queries about LEGO history, and Jette, for writing the foreword, too • Lisbeth Finnemann Skrumsager, Mette Jørgensen, and Vibeke List at the LEGO Group • Huw Millington and the brickset.com community for their help with selecting the sets to be included in the book • Jason Gross and Christopher at christophercooper.com for additional images on pp62–63, Joseph Olson at BrickTsar.com for additional images on pp72–73, Markos Chouris for additional images on pp94–95, and Brandon R. Gottschall for additional images on pp102–103 • Nick Barbrooke, Martin Boon at www.specialbricks.nl, Huw Millington, Duncan Reynolds, Martin Stiff, and Nicholas Taylor for lending us their LEGO models to be photographed • The wonderful LEGO designers and employees who took time out of their busy schedules to be interviewed for the book: Henrik Andersen, Matthew James Ashton, Jamie Berard, Marcos Bessa, Bas Brederode, Fenella Blaize Charity, Michael Thomas Fuller, Adam Siegmund Grabowski, Kristian Reimer Hauge, Lars Joe Hyldig, Chris Bonven Johansen, Elisabeth Kahl-Backes, Markus Kossmann, Bjarke Lykke Madsen, Cerim Manovi, Jette Orduna, Niels Milan Pedersen, Raphaël Pierre Roger Pretesacque, Hans Burkhard Schlömer, Mark John Stafford, Gitte Thorsen, Tara Wike; and Daniel August Krantz—who came out of retirement to share memories of his time working for the LEGO Group.

∧ **WHEN I GROW UP...** A five-year-old Matthew James Ashton plays with 1978's Yellow Castle (375). Now a Vice President at the LEGO Group, Matthew's childhood dream of becoming a toy designer came true.